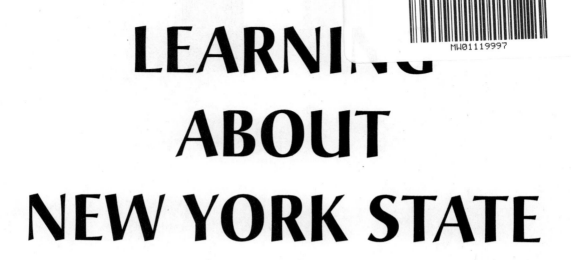

LEARNING ABOUT NEW YORK STATE

JAMES KILLORAN

STUART ZIMMER

MARK JARRETT

JARRETT PUBLISHING COMPANY

EAST COAST OFFICE
19 Cross Street
Lake Ronkonkoma, NY 11779

WEST COAST OFFICE
10 Folin Lane
Lafayette, CA 94549

631-981-4248 ❖ 1-800-859-7679
Fax: 631-588-4722
www.jarrettpub.com

ISBN 1-882422-55-4

Printed in the United States of America
First Edition

10 9 8 7 6 5 4 3 2 1 00 01 02 03 04

ABOUT THE AUTHORS

James Killoran is a retired New York City Assistant Principal. He has written *Government and You;* and *Economics and You.* Mr. Killoran has extensive experience in test writing for the New York State Board of Regents in Social Studies and has served on the Committee for Testing of the National Council of Social Studies. His article on Social Studies testing has been published in *Social Education,* the country's leading Social Studies journal. In addition, Mr. Killoran has won a number of awards for outstanding teaching and curriculum development, including, "Outstanding Social Studies Teacher" and "Outstanding Social Studies Supervisor" in New York City. In 1993, he was awarded an Advanced Certificate for Teachers of Social Studies by the N.C.S.S.

Stuart Zimmer is a retired New York City Social Studies teacher. He has written *Government and You* and *Economics and You.* He has served as a test writer for the New York State Board of Regents in Social Studies, and has written for the National Merit Scholarship Examination. In addition, he has published numerous articles on teaching and testing in Social Studies journals. He has presented many demonstrations and educational workshops at state and national teachers' conferences. In 1989, Mr. Zimmer's achievements were recognized by the New York State Legislature with a Special Legislative Resolution in his honor.

Mark Jarrett is a former Social Studies teacher and a practicing attorney at the San Francisco office of Baker and McKenzie, the world's largest law firm. Mr. Jarrett has served as a test writer for the New York State Board of Regents, and has taught at Hofstra University. He was educated at Columbia University, the London School of Economics, the Law School of the University of California at Berkeley, and Stanford University, where he is a doctoral candidate in history. Mr. Jarrett has won several academic awards, including Order of the Coif at Berkeley, and the David and Christina Phelps Harris Fellowship at Stanford.

ALSO BY KILLORAN, ZIMMER, AND JARRETT

The Key To Understanding Global History
The Key To Understanding U.S. History and Government
Mastering Global History
Mastering U.S. History
North Carolina: The Tar Heel State
Mastering Ohio's 9th Grade Citizenship Test
Mastering Ohio's 12th Grade Citizenship Test
Michigan: Its Land and Its People
Ohio: Its Land and Its People
Ohio: Its Neighbors, Near and Far
Mastering The Social Studies MEAP Test: Grade 5
Texas: Its Land and Its People
Historia y gobierno de los estados unidos
Principios de economía

ACKNOWLEDGMENTS

The authors wish to acknowledge the help of **Dr. Joel Fischer,** who provided some ideas for the activities. The authors also wish to thank **Lloyd Bromberg,** former Director of Social Studies, New York City Board of Education, for his many suggestions and advice regarding the needs of New York educators. In addition, several New York teachers reviewed this book. Their comments, suggestions and recommendations proved invaluable. These teachers are:

- **Christine Antonio:** P.S. 26, Albany City School District.
- **Doreen Dell:** Dodge Elementary School, Williamsville School District.
- **Mary Duffin:** Moses DeWitt School, Jamesville DeWitt School District.
- **Deanna Washinsky:** P.S. 212, N.Y.C. Community School District 21.
- **Susan Wasserman:** Shaw Avenue School, Valley Stream School District.

We would also like to thank the following school administrators for their insights and suggestions:

- **Ann R. Flanagan:** Principal of Lynwood Avenue School, Sachem School District.
- **Dr. Michael Romano:** District Chairperson of Social Studies, Northport-East Northport U.F.S.D.

Finally, the authors would like to thank Julie Fleck and Hanna Kisiel for their many suggestions and insightful comments on the manuscript.

Cover design by Burmar Technical Corporation, Albertson, N.Y.
Maps and graphics by C.F. Enterprises and Burmar Technical Corporation.
Layout, maps/graphics and typesetting: Burmar Technical Corporation, Albertson, N.Y.

This book is dedicated to...

my wife Donna, and my children Christian, Carrie, and Jesse .... *James Killoran*

my wife Joan, and my children Todd and Ronald,
and my grandchildren Katie and Jared .... *Stuart Zimmer*

my wife Gośka, and my children Alexander and Julia .... *Mark Jarrett*

TABLE OF CONTENTS

OPENING ACTIVITY — THE IMAGE I HAVE OF NEW YORK IS ... ?

This school year you will learn about the state you live in: New York. You will also make connections between your community, your state, your country and the world. This book will involve you in many new and interesting activities, and the authors hope you enjoy your journey through its pages.

IMPORTANT NOTE

This is an interactive textbook. It asks you to participate in exciting activities as you learn new information. Even though there are empty spaces on many pages, please **do not write in this book** without asking your teacher. Your teacher may want you to do all of your writing on a separate piece of paper or in a notebook.

Introduction — WHAT DOES "NEW YORK" MEAN TO YOU?

Before we start our journey together, let's find out what images or thoughts you have about New York. Millions of people around the world have an image of New York as a place with tall skyscrapers and crowded streets. When other people hear the words "New York" they may think of Niagara Falls. Still others think of New York as the Empire State—big and bold. But what does New York mean to **YOU?**

Niagara Falls

THINK ABOUT IT

List or draw the images and thoughts that "New York" brings to your mind.
When I think of New York, I think of ...
Next, compare your thoughts about New York with those of your classmates.

Now you are ready to begin your journey. The first unit of this book will give you some handy tools for studying and learning—making your trip a more enjoyable and rewarding one. Later units will introduce you to the geography, history, culture, economy and government of New York State and its communities.

UNIT 1

KEYS TO LEARNING WITH SUCCESS

Social Studies is exciting and fun because it teaches you about people and how they relate to one another. You also learn about the past and how we came to be the way we are today. In this book, you will learn about New York State and its connections to the United States and the world. There will be many facts and ideas for you to learn and understand. You will need to participate actively by reading, doing activities and studying. This unit focuses on the keys to becoming a successful student.

🗝️ 1: VISUALIZING IMPORTANT INFORMATION

Social Studies involves knowing about many important terms and ideas. To help you learn and remember them, you will be asked to complete two Vocabulary Cards at the end of each activity in this book.

Vocabulary Cards are index cards with information on them. They will help you remember important terms and ideas. As you go through the activities in this book, you should develop your own set of cards to use for studying. Each Vocabulary Card has two parts:

❖ **Front of the card.** This is for writing about the term or idea.

❖ **Back of the card.** This is used to create a "picture" of the term or idea.

THE FRONT OF THE CARD: WRITTEN INFORMATION

On the front of each card, you will be asked to describe or define a term or idea. Here are two examples:

When you have to learn a specific term, like the Declaration of Independence, you should describe it and explain why it is important. The vocabulary cards at the end of each activity will have questions about the term for you to answer.

Example #1

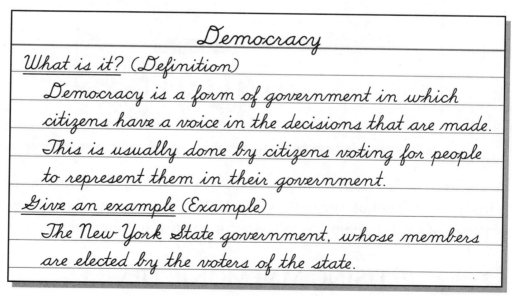

Declaration of Independence

What is it? (Description)

A document written mainly by Thomas Jefferson in 1776. It announced to the world that America wanted to be independent from Great Britain.

Why is it important? (Explanation)

The document established the basic idea that governments are created to protect people's rights. It serves as a basis for our government.

When you learn about a new idea, like **democracy,** you will usually be asked to define the idea and to give an example of it.

Example #2

Democracy

What is it? (Definition)

Democracy is a form of government in which citizens have a voice in the decisions that are made. This is usually done by citizens voting for people to represent them in their government.

Give an example (Example)

The New York State government, whose members are elected by the voters of the state.

THE BACK OF THE CARD: VISUAL INFORMATION

Pictures are often easier to remember than words. On the back of each card, you will be asked to draw a picture about the information on the front. Making your ideas into pictures will help your understanding and your memory. Let's see what the information on these two vocabulary cards might look like when put into picture form.

At the end of each activity in this book, you will find two terms or ideas to use for creating your own set of Vocabulary Cards. By the end of the book, you will have a complete set of cards to help you prepare for any test in fourth grade Social Studies.

2: USING MNEMONIC DEVICES

Another way to learn and remember factual information is to use mnemonic (*ne-mon-ik*) devices. **Mnemonic devices** are rhymes and other verbal "tricks" that help you to remember. They are especially useful when you have to learn a list of items—such as planets, continents, cities, rivers or important historical events.

THE PICTURE METHOD

With this method, you think of a picture for each name or word you must learn. For example, three cities in New York State that receive large amounts of snowfall are Buffalo, Rochester and Syracuse.

1. Think of a word that rhymes with or reminds you of the name of each city:

❖ **Buffalo**–<u>b</u>uffalo (both words start with "b")

❖ **Rochester**–<u>r</u>uns (both words start with "r")

❖ **Syracuse**–<u>s</u>now (both words start with "s")

2. Now visualize these words together as a picture that will help you to remember them. For instance:

Buffalo ➞ runs in the snow.

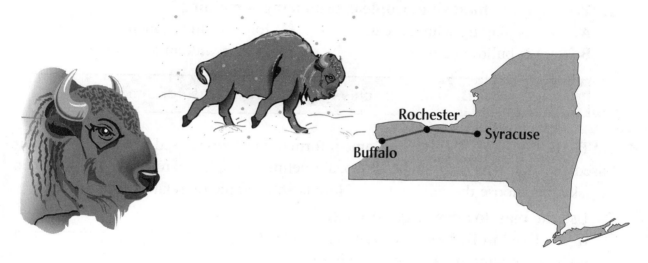

THE KEY SENTENCE METHOD

A third mnemonic technique is to take the first letter of each item you have to learn and to make a sentence or word with all the first letters.

States Bordering New York State

❖ <u>V</u>ermont   ❖ <u>N</u>ew Jersey   ❖ <u>P</u>ennsylvania

❖ <u>C</u>onnecticut   ❖ <u>M</u>assachusetts

Creating a key sentence, such as "<u>V</u>ery <u>n</u>ice <u>p</u>eople <u>c</u>limb <u>m</u>ountains," helps you remember the five states that border New York.

Another helpful mnemonic is to form a word by using the first letter of each word on a list. For example, the word H-O-M-E-S might help you to remember the names of the five Great Lakes: <u>H</u>uron, <u>O</u>ntario, <u>M</u>ichigan, <u>E</u>rie and <u>S</u>uperior.

3: ANSWERING MULTIPLE-CHOICE QUESTIONS

Taking tests is something that all students must do. Many tests will have multiple-choice questions. Here are some hints that will help you to answer them.

WHAT THE QUESTION WILL LOOK LIKE

Multiple-choice questions are usually followed by a list of four possible answers. Only one of the answers will be correct. The others are wrong. You must choose the correct answer. There are two kinds of multiple-choice questions: general questions and data-based questions.

❖ **GENERAL QUESTIONS.** These questions test your knowledge of specific information. Here is an example:

1. **Which of the following people is producing something?**
   A. Joan is playing with her cat.   **C.** John is eating lunch.
   B. Sam is building a house.   **D.** Fran is watching a movie.

> The answer is **B.** Sam is the only one producing (*making*) something.

❖ **DATA-BASED QUESTIONS.** Some information (*data*) is used to introduce a data-based question. The data can be a map, a timeline, a graph or a reading. You will then be asked to choose the right answer. Here is an example of a data-based question.

2. **Use the map to answer question 2.**
   If you lived in Buffalo and wanted to visit your aunt in Albany in which direction would you need to travel?
   A. north   **C.** east
   B. south   **D.** west

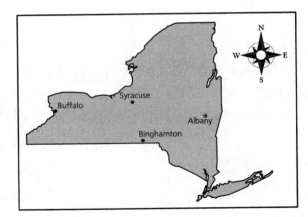

> The answer is **C.** To travel from Buffalo to Albany, you must go east.

MAIN SUBJECTS OF MULTIPLE-CHOICE QUESTIONS

Most multiple-choice questions will be about the following:

❖ **RECOGNIZING TERMS, IDEAS AND PEOPLE.** This type of question tests your knowledge of a term, idea or person. The following is an example:

3. One of the main powers of the Governor of New York State is to
    A. make national laws   **C.** interpret city laws
    B. enforce state laws   **D.** make state laws

> The answer is **B.** The main power of the Governor of New York State is to enforce the laws of the state.

To help you recognize main terms, ideas and people, these are presented in **bold print** throughout the book. Key words in each activity appear in a `grey` box.

❖ **RECOGNIZING CAUSES AND EFFECTS.** Cause-and-effect questions test your understanding of how two or more events are related. The *cause* is the event that happened first. The *effect* is what happened as a result of the first event. In other words, the cause is the reason for the *effect.* Here is an example of this type of question:

4. Buffalo is one of the most important economic centers in New York. A major reason why Buffalo has become an economic center is that it
    A. is located near Lake Erie   **C.** has tall buildings
    B. is the capital of New York   **D.** is the oldest city in New York

> The answer is **A.** Buffalo is located near Lake Erie. Being close to a large body of water and at the end of the Erie Canal brought trade and business to Buffalo. This helped make Buffalo an important economic center.

To help you answer cause-and-effect questions, important causes and effects are identified in each unit of the book. **Activity 3F** also examines cause-and-effect relationships in greater detail. Here are some key words or phrases to look for when answering cause-and-effect questions:

CAUSES	*EFFECTS*
❖ Because of …	❖ This resulted in …
❖ A main reason for …	❖ This led to …
❖ On account of …	❖ This affected …

4: THE WRITING PROCESS

To do well you also need to know how to organize your thoughts and write them down.

STEPS IN THE WRITING PROCESS

The writing process is not one step, but several. It takes practice and skill to be a good writer. Let's take a look at each of the steps in the writing process:

❖ **Step 1: Prewriting.** In this first step, ask yourself, "Why am I writing this?" Your answer will determine *what* and *how* you write. Decide whether the purpose of the writing is to *inform, persuade, describe* or to *tell about* an event.

❖ **Step 2: Drafting.** Putting ideas on paper is similar to an architect following a blueprint when building a house. Your "blueprint" is your first draft or preliminary writing. Imagine your first draft resembles a "cheeseburger," with a top bun, patties of meat, and a bottom bun. The top bun is your beginning, the meat is the middle, and the bottom bun is the conclusion of your essay. These may be separate sentences in a single paragraph or separate paragraphs in a longer essay.

❖ **Step 3: Revising and Proofreading.** This is the most important part of the writing process. You need to read over your work to see if you have included all your main ideas. Some writers like to read their work aloud to see how it "sounds." Re-reading also allows you to edit your essay for grammar, punctuation and spelling.

APPLYING THE STEPS IN THE WRITING PROCESS

Let's use what you have just learned for the following writing assignment.

> Write a short essay explaining the importance of getting a good education.

STEP 1: PREWRITING

> **Your Purpose:** To explain why it is important to get a good education.
>
> ### Main Ideas:
>
> I. A good education makes us more aware of ourselves and the world.
>
> II. A good education will help us to get a job when we get older.
>
> III. A good education helps us to become good citizens.
>
> **Conclusion:** Society's future depends on the education of its young people.

STEP 2: DRAFTING

Let's use the information from your outline to create a first draft, using the "cheeseburger" method.

In society today, it is very important to have a good education. There are several reasons why this is so.

One of the most important reasons for a good education is that it makes us more aware of ourselves and the world around us. In social studies we learn how people lived in the past. In science, we learn how nature and our bodies work.

A good education prepares us for getting a job. We improve our reading skills for future work. Another reason for a good education is to become a good citizen. This prepares us to face the important responsibilities of voting, holding office and serving on a jury.

Therefore, we can see that it is important to have a good education. The future of our society depends on the quality of the education it provides.

Top Bun (*Introduction*). At the beginning of your essay, write your *thesis statement.* It should state the assignment's topic. Notice how your thesis statement lets your reader know precisely what you are going to write about. The next sentence should connect your thesis statement to the main body of the writing. For example, you might write: *"This essay will show why this is true."* or *"There are several reasons why this is so."* Notice how this connecting sentence introduces the next section you are going to write.

Patties of Meat (*Main Body*). In the "patties of meat" section, you give specific examples and facts that support your opening statement. It is the main part of your essay. Notice how these sentences give facts that support the main idea or topic sentence.

Bottom Bun (*Ending Sentence*). Your last sentence should be similar to your opening topic sentence, except that it is now expressed as a conclusion. The conclusion is used to remind the reader of what you have just explained in your essay. There are several concluding sentences that you can choose from: *"Therefore, we can see that …"* or *"Thus, we can see that …"* Again, notice how this sentence ends the essay by reminding the reader of the purpose of the essay.

STEP 3: REVISING AND PROOFREADING

After you have finished your draft, you should re-read it. You may want to share your essay with other members of your class. Sharing your written work with your classmates allows you to get suggestions about what and how you wrote. **Peer editing** (*editing by other students*) provides important feedback in helping you improve your essay. Then correct it for errors in grammar, punctuation and spelling. You are now ready for the last reading. Be sure to re-read your essay one last time before you hand it in.

PRE-READING HINTS

You have now learned some practical ways of remembering information, answering test questions and writing down your ideas. In the following units, you will learn a great deal about New York and the United States. To help you through these units, each section will be introduced by an icon. An **icon** is a symbol—something that stands for something else. Think of each icon as your personal guide, telling you what to expect in each section of the activity. The following list identifies each icon used in the book.

Each activity usually begins with an introduction. Here you will learn what is required of you in order to carry out the activity.

These sections provide information for doing the activity. For example, you will be given information about New York's geography to create a map of what New York State "looks" like.

These sections will introduce you to a new word or idea. For example, you will learn the definitions of the words "concept" and "generalization."

In these sections you will be asked to complete a task. For example, you might be asked to fill in a chart, write a paragraph or locate places on a map of New York State.

These sections will teach you a new skill. For example, you might learn how to read a map, interpret a line or bar graph, write a business letter or create an outline of a reading selection.

In these sections you will be asked to carry out research outside of the classroom. For example, you might be asked to read a book from the library, interview an adult or conduct a survey.

In these sections the activity comes to a close. When this occurs, you will often be asked to think about what you have done and to re-examine the focus question that began the activity.

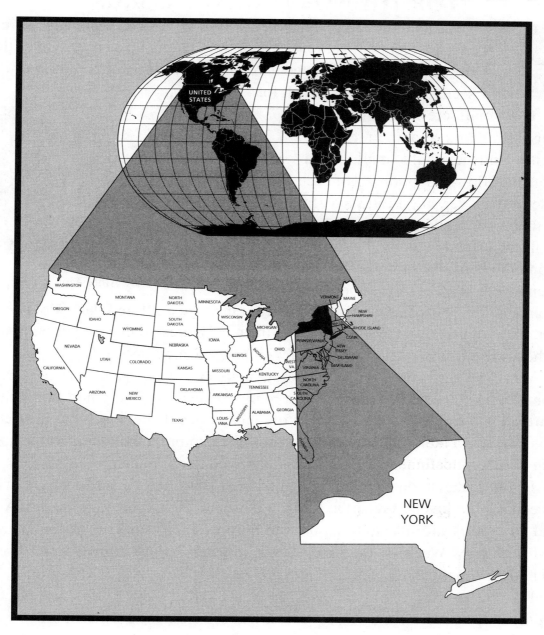

W_here_ we live often determines _how_ we live. The study of geography developed from the need to know "where." It tells us where different places are and what they are like. This information is important because we come into contact with people and products from many places.

HENRY HUDSON SEARCHES FOR THE NORTHWEST PASSAGE

t was a hot day in early September 1609. A small wooden ship, not much larger than your classroom, was sailing up a river. Wind filled the ship's six sails. Painted in bright colors, its name could clearly be seen: *Halve Maen*—Dutch for "Half Moon."

Hudson's *Half Moon* sails up the Hudson River as Native Americans look on.

The small crew of Dutch and English sailors and their captain, Henry Hudson, could smell the fragrance of flower blossoms. On each side of the river stood forests as far as their eyes could see. Some of the men saw brightly colored butterflies along the banks. Adding to the rich scene were several canoes bobbing alongside the ship. Native Americans from the forest offered the sailors corn, pumpkins, tobacco and oysters. Some of them were dressed in deerskins and furs. Others wore feathers and were armed with bows, arrows and clubs.

What was the little sailing ship doing on this river, thousands of miles from home? The story begins more than a hundred years earlier, when Europeans started exploring the oceans. At that time many people believed that the Earth was flat, like a tabletop. However, most of the explorers thought it was shaped like a ball, with all the world's oceans connected to each other.

In 1492, Christopher Columbus sailed west from Europe across the Atlantic Ocean. Columbus believed the Earth was round. He expected to land in Asia and buy spices and silks to bring back to Europe. To his surprise, he found himself in a "New World"—the Americas. Europeans hadn't known about North and South America.

Five years later, explorer Vasco da Gama sailed from Europe around the southern tip of Africa, and east to Asia. In 1519, Ferdinand Magellan sailed west from Europe and around the southern tip of South America. His crew continued across the Pacific Ocean and back to Europe, proving the world was round. At that point, the race was on to discover the best route from Europe to the riches of the "Indies"—as India and East Asia were called at the time.

After studying maps and talking to the wisest geographers of his day, Henry Hudson became convinced that the shortest route to India and East Asia was over the North Pole. Other explorers feared sailing northward through ice and snow, but not Henry Hudson. He had twice tried to sail north of Norway. The wealthy merchants of the Dutch East India Company soon heard of this brave Englishman. In 1609, they invited him to Holland. Soon after, they hired him and supplied him with a ship and small crew. In late March, Hudson and his crew left the Dutch capital of Amsterdam in search of a route northwards.

First, Hudson tried again to sail north of Norway, but was stopped by snow and ice. Then he turned westward, hoping for a passage through the icy waters to the Indies. After crossing the Atlantic to Canada, Hudson turned south, staying near the coast in search of a passage. After sailing past the settlement of Jamestown, Virginia, Hudson turned his ship north again.

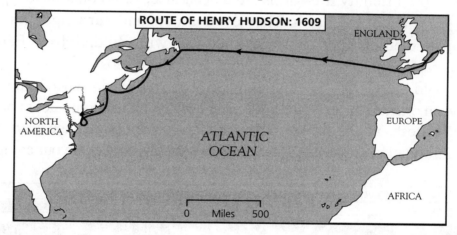

On September 3rd, Hudson and his men rounded the southern tip of Brooklyn. Many Native Americans came to stare at these unusual men and their ship. Some boarded the *Half Moon* to trade corn and tobacco for beads and knives.

Hudson admired the beauty of the land around him. Its forests could provide plenty of lumber to make ships and houses. The Native Americans had copper pipes for their tobacco. Hudson thought these copper pipes might mean there were copper mines in the area. After going ashore briefly, Hudson returned to the ship. He wrote in his log, "The land is the finest for planting that I have ever in my life set foot upon, and it is rich in trees of every description."

From Staten Island, the ship entered New York Harbor. Hudson began the journey up the river that would later be named after him—the Hudson River. Would this river lead north to the Indies? Would he discover new lands and fame as Columbus had done? What else would he find on his journey?

In this unit you will learn the answers to some of the questions that Hudson and his crew asked themselves as they sailed up the river on that sunny day.

CAN YOU PLEASE GIVE ME SOME DIRECTIONS?

2A

In this activity, you will learn some of the ways that geographers locate places on the Earth. Look for the following important words:

▶ North and South Poles ▶ Equator ▶ Region

▶ Continent ▶ Prime Meridian ▶ Country

To help you, the ▶ symbol appears in the margin where the **term** is first explained.

It is the year 2100. Friendly life-forms have been discovered on a far-off planet. They are eager to learn about the Earth. They even understand our languages. These life-forms encourage their children to become pen-pals with children from Earth. Imagine that you have been communicating with your pen-pal, Wedosh, for almost a year.

Wedosh would like to visit you this summer. However, Wedosh needs to know exactly where you live in order to locate your house. You decide to use a computer to help you write directions for Wedosh. You hit the keys of your computer to bring up the instructions for the "Geography-Information" Program. Here is the first thing you see on your computer screen:

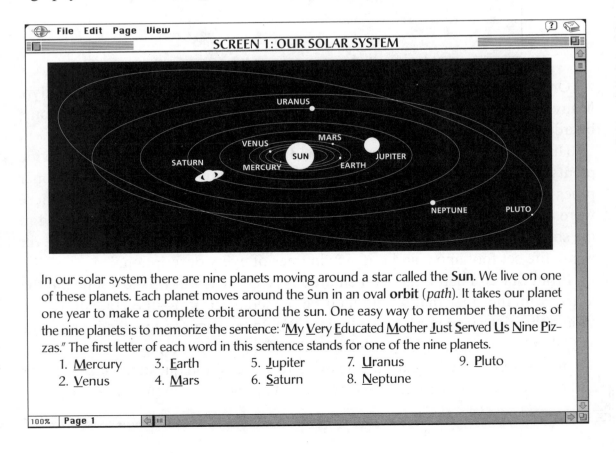

File Edit Page View

SCREEN 1: OUR SOLAR SYSTEM

In our solar system there are nine planets moving around a star called the **Sun**. We live on one of these planets. Each planet moves around the Sun in an oval **orbit** (*path*). It takes our planet one year to make a complete orbit around the sun. One easy way to remember the names of the nine planets is to memorize the sentence: "<u>M</u>y <u>V</u>ery <u>E</u>ducated <u>M</u>other <u>J</u>ust <u>S</u>erved <u>U</u>s <u>N</u>ine <u>P</u>iz–zas." The first letter of each word in this sentence stands for one of the nine planets.

1. <u>M</u>ercury   3. <u>E</u>arth   5. <u>J</u>upiter   7. <u>U</u>ranus   9. <u>P</u>luto
2. <u>V</u>enus   4. <u>M</u>ars   6. <u>S</u>aturn   8. <u>N</u>eptune

100% Page 1

Why don't you take notes after viewing each screen? You can use these notes to help you in writing directions to your pen-pal, Wedosh.

NOTES FOR MY LETTER:
The name of the planet that I live on is called ___?___ .

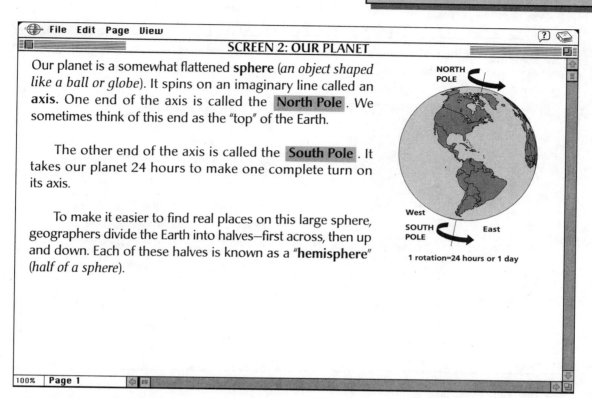

SCREEN 2: OUR PLANET

Our planet is a somewhat flattened **sphere** (*an object shaped like a ball or globe*). It spins on an imaginary line called an **axis**. One end of the axis is called the North Pole . We sometimes think of this end as the "top" of the Earth.

The other end of the axis is called the South Pole . It takes our planet 24 hours to make one complete turn on its axis.

To make it easier to find real places on this large sphere, geographers divide the Earth into halves—first across, then up and down. Each of these halves is known as a "**hemisphere**" (*half of a sphere*).

NORTH POLE

West

SOUTH POLE   East

1 rotation=24 hours or 1 day

100%   Page 1

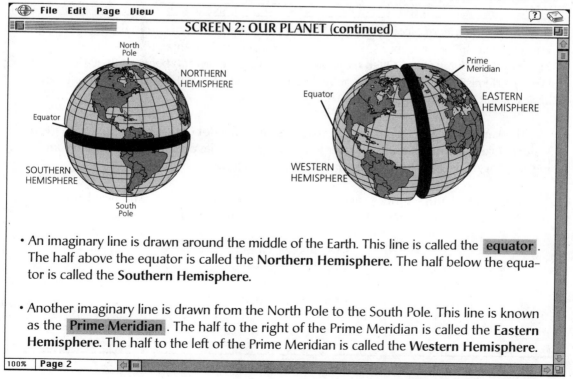

SCREEN 2: OUR PLANET (continued)

North Pole

NORTHERN HEMISPHERE

Equator

SOUTHERN HEMISPHERE

South Pole

Prime Meridian

Equator

EASTERN HEMISPHERE

WESTERN HEMISPHERE

- An imaginary line is drawn around the middle of the Earth. This line is called the equator . The half above the equator is called the **Northern Hemisphere**. The half below the equator is called the **Southern Hemisphere**.

- Another imaginary line is drawn from the North Pole to the South Pole. This line is known as the Prime Meridian . The half to the right of the Prime Meridian is called the **Eastern Hemisphere**. The half to the left of the Prime Meridian is called the **Western Hemisphere**.

100%   Page 2

NOTES FOR MY LETTER:

I live in both the ___?___ Hemisphere and the ___?___ Hemisphere.

File   Edit   Page   View

SCREEN 3: CONTINENTS AND OCEANS

Continents are the major land masses of the world. Geographers have divided these land masses into seven continents. In order of size, they are: **Asia, Africa, North America, South America, Antarctica, Europe** and **Australia.**

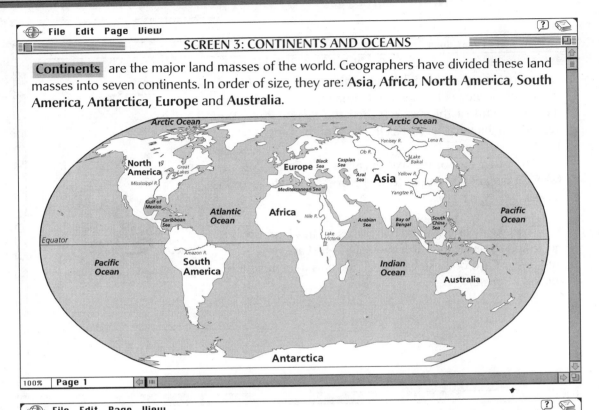

100%   Page 1

File   Edit   Page   View

SCREEN 3: CONTINENTS AND OCEANS (continued)

The continents of North America, South America and part of Antarctica make up the Western Hemisphere. Europe, Africa, Asia, Australia and part of Antarctica are the continents of the Eastern Hemisphere. Often mapmakers will draw the division between the Eastern and Western Hemispheres slightly west of the Prime Meridian. This is done to show all of Europe and Africa in the same hemisphere.

The Earth is the only planet in our solar system with a lot of water. The Earth has fresh water in lakes and rivers, and salt water in oceans. Human life depends on water—for drinking, farming, fishing, manufacturing and for transportation.

Most of the Earth's surface is covered by oceans. An **ocean** is an extremely large body of salt water. Minerals in the water give it a salty taste. There are four main oceans:

- the Atlantic Ocean
- the Pacific Ocean
- the Arctic Ocean
- the Indian Ocean

100%   Page 2

NOTES FOR MY LETTER:

I live on the continent of ___?___ , located between the ___?___ Ocean and the ___?___ Ocean.

✔ **CHECKING YOUR UNDERSTANDING** ✔

Use the map in screen 3 to answer the following questions:

1. Which continents are located completely in the Southern Hemisphere?
2. Which continents are located completely in the Western Hemisphere?

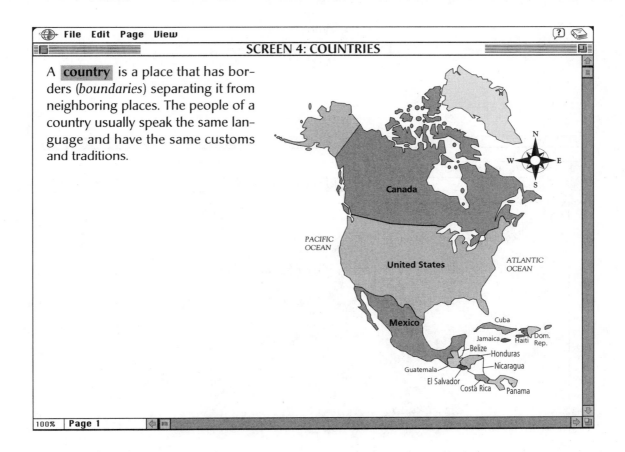

File   Edit   Page   View

SCREEN 4: COUNTRIES

A **country** is a place that has borders (*boundaries*) separating it from neighboring places. The people of a country usually speak the same language and have the same customs and traditions.

Canada

PACIFIC OCEAN

United States

ATLANTIC OCEAN

Mexico

Cuba

Jamaica   Haiti   Dom. Rep.

Belize

Guatemala   Honduras

El Salvador   Nicaragua

Costa Rica   Panama

100%   Page 1

NOTES FOR MY LETTER:

The country in which I live is called ___?___ . It is located directly north of a country called ___?___ . It is located south of a country called ___?___ .

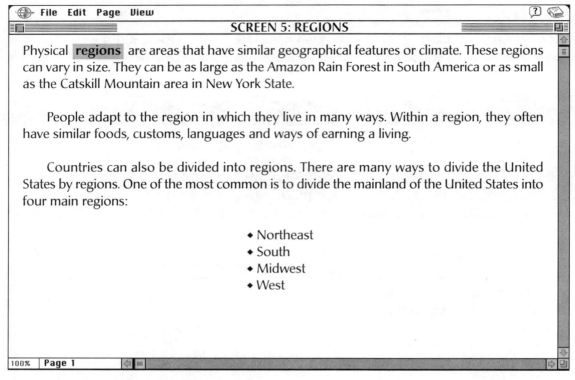

File   Edit   Page   View

SCREEN 5: REGIONS

Physical **regions** are areas that have similar geographical features or climate. These regions can vary in size. They can be as large as the Amazon Rain Forest in South America or as small as the Catskill Mountain area in New York State.

People adapt to the region in which they live in many ways. Within a region, they often have similar foods, customs, languages and ways of earning a living.

Countries can also be divided into regions. There are many ways to divide the United States by regions. One of the most common is to divide the mainland of the United States into four main regions:

- Northeast
- South
- Midwest
- West

100%   Page 1

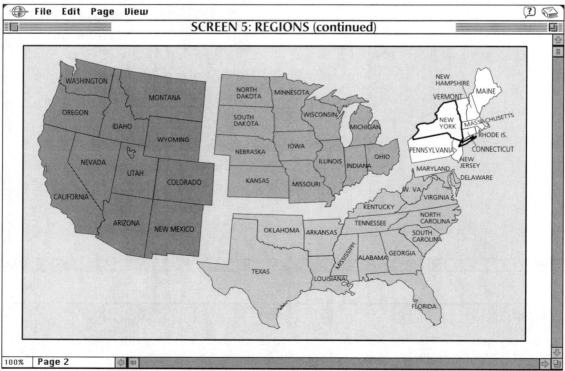

File   Edit   Page   View

SCREEN 5: REGIONS (continued)

100%   Page 2

NOTES FOR MY LETTER:

The region I live in is known as the ___?___ . The number of states in the region in which I live is ___?___ . The names of these states are ___?___ .

File   Edit   Page   View

SCREEN 6: STATES AND COUNTIES

Most countries are divided into smaller political units known as states or provinces. The United States is divided into 50 **states**. Can you locate the state in which you live?

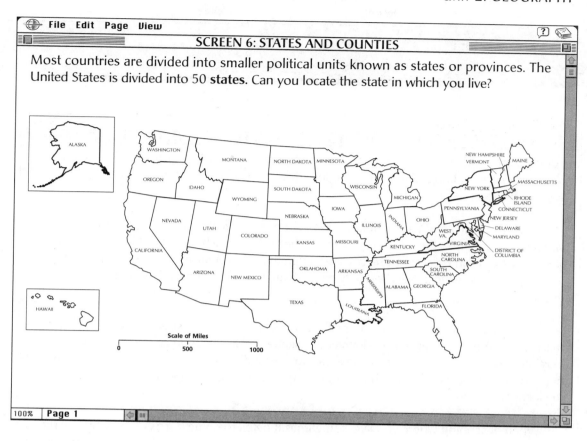

100%   Page 1

File   Edit   Page   View

SCREEN 6: STATES AND COUNTIES (continued)

Each of the 50 states is further divided into smaller units called counties . New York State is divided into 62 counties. What is the name of your county?

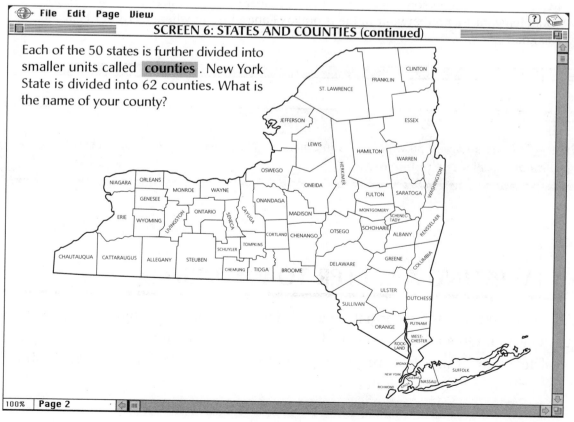

100%   Page 2

NOTES FOR MY LETTER:

I live in the state of ___?___ and the county of ___?___.

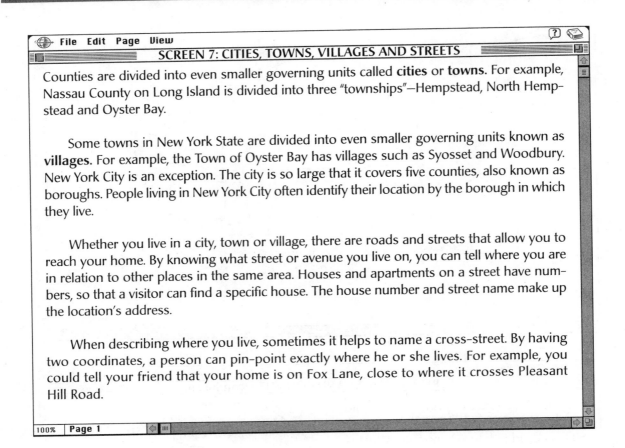

File   Edit   Page   View

SCREEN 7: CITIES, TOWNS, VILLAGES AND STREETS

Counties are divided into even smaller governing units called **cities** or **towns**. For example, Nassau County on Long Island is divided into three "townships"—Hempstead, North Hempstead and Oyster Bay.

Some towns in New York State are divided into even smaller governing units known as **villages.** For example, the Town of Oyster Bay has villages such as Syosset and Woodbury. New York City is an exception. The city is so large that it covers five counties, also known as boroughs. People living in New York City often identify their location by the borough in which they live.

Whether you live in a city, town or village, there are roads and streets that allow you to reach your home. By knowing what street or avenue you live on, you can tell where you are in relation to other places in the same area. Houses and apartments on a street have numbers, so that a visitor can find a specific house. The house number and street name make up the location's address.

When describing where you live, sometimes it helps to name a cross-street. By having two coordinates, a person can pin-point exactly where he or she lives. For example, you could tell your friend that your home is on Fox Lane, close to where it crosses Pleasant Hill Road.

100%   Page 1

NOTES

I live in ___?___. The street on which I live is called ___?___. The nearest cross street is ___?___. My house or apartment number is ___?___.

Closing

WRITING A LETTER TO WEDOSH

You now have enough information about where you live for anyone to identify your unique location. On a separate sheet of paper, write instructions to Wedosh explaining how to find your home. Before you start your letter to Wedosh, read the following hints for writing a **"how to"** letter.

Skill Builder

THE "HOW TO" FORM OF WRITING

A "how to" writing gives step-by-step directions to the reader about how to do something. "How to" writings can be about almost anything. For example, they can explain how to make a cake, assemble a toy or ride a bicycle. Here are some helpful hints on creating a "how to" writing.

HELPFUL HINTS

1. **Start with a thesis statement.** This statement should explain what the reader will be doing. For example:

    Here are the directions for finding my house at 75 Fox Lane.

2. **Use a "bridge" sentence.** Sometimes you will need a connecting sentence to introduce the reader to the details of what you are writing about. For example:

    If you follow my directions carefully, it should take you about an hour to reach my house.

3. **Write a step-by-step list of what to do.** Starting with the first step, explain to the reader how each step should follow another until the task is completed. Some useful words that show the reader you are moving from one step to another are: "first," "next," "then," "later," "afterwards" and "finally." For example:

    First, take Route 680 going east. Then, get off Route 680 at the exit sign for Pleasant Hill Road. Next, drive up the hill past two traffic lights. Finally, make a right turn at Fox Lane. Ours is the second house on the right.

4. **Point out what may go wrong.** Tell the reader about any problems that might occur and how to avoid them. For example:

    Sometimes people have trouble seeing the street sign for Fox Lane, since it is partly hidden by a large tree. You can easily recognize Fox Lane by the gas station on the corner.

5. **Write a conclusion.** Provide a closing sentence. For example:

    If you follow these directions carefully, I'm sure you will have no trouble finding my house. I look forward to seeing you soon.

Now that you better understand the "how to" form of writing, let us put your new skill to use. Review the notes that you made at the end of each computer screen. Use the information in your notes to write a letter to Wedosh, your pen-pal from outer space.

INTER-GALACTIC COMMUNICATION

Dear Wedosh: [Greeting]

[Thesis Statement]: _____ ？
_____

[Bridge Sentence]: _____ ？
_____
_____

B
O
D
Y

[Step-by-Step]: _____
_____
_____ ？
_____
_____
_____

[Conclusion]: _____ ？
_____

Your Pen-Pal, [Closing]

_____(sign your name)_____
[Signature]

REVIEWING YOUR UNDERSTANDING

Creating Vocabulary Cards

Equator
What is the equator?
What two hemispheres does it separate?

Prime Meridian
What is the Prime Meridian?
What two hemispheres does it separate?

You will find brief exercises following the Vocabulary Cards in each activity in this book. Completing these exercises will help you sharpen your Social Studies skills.

Locating Places on Maps

Directions: Place the number of each of the following items in its correct location on the map of the United States: (1) Great Lakes; (2) Mississippi River; (3) Gulf of Mexico; (4) Rocky Mountains; (5) Appalachian Mountains; (6) Great Plains; (7) Atlantic Ocean; (8) Pacific Ocean. Consult an atlas or encyclopedia for help in locating these features.

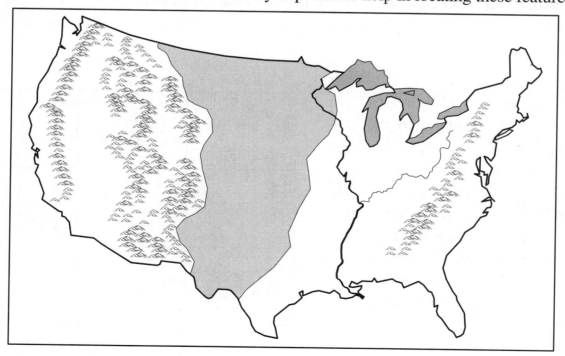

HOW WOULD YOU MAP
YOUR COMMUNITY?

2B

In this activity, you will learn how maps help us to locate places. Look for the following important words:

▶ Map   ▶ Legend (Key)   ▶ Latitude
▶ Symbol   ▶ Scale   ▶ Longitude

Your friend in California has sent you a map of an imaginary community that he made as a school project. You look at his map, and say to yourself: "This seems like an interesting project for me to do. I'm going to make a map too."

Definition

WHAT ARE MAPS?

▶ You ask your teacher for advice on how to begin. Your teacher explains that a **map** is really a small picture, diagram or model of a larger place. It shows where things are located. Your teacher says the easiest way to understand maps is by mapping things in a small area. She suggests you start by making a map of your desktop.

You draw a picture of a box representing your desktop. Your teacher then puts three objects in different locations on the top of your desk. She says, "Now pretend you are a bird, flying over the desk. Can you describe *exactly* where the objects on your desk are located?"

You find this hard to do. Your teacher agrees that it is not easy. Your teacher tells you that **cartographers** (*people who make maps*) have the same problem. To help them locate places on a map, cartographers make a grid like the one on the "desk map" to the right. A **grid** uses straight lines that cross each other. The crossing lines create boxes. The rows along the top and side are given letters and numbers.

	A	B	C
1		(coins)	
2			(pen)
3	(candy)		

LEARNING TO INTERPRET A MAP

Maps are drawings, models or diagrams of a part of the Earth. They come in different sizes and shapes. Some maps show countries, states or cities. These maps will indicate political boundaries. Other maps show geographic features such as mountains, oceans and rivers. Still others show airports, parks and schools. A **globe** is a special kind of map. It is a three-dimensional sphere that represents the entire Earth.

THE TITLE

To understand a map, first look at its title. The title tells you what information is found on the map.

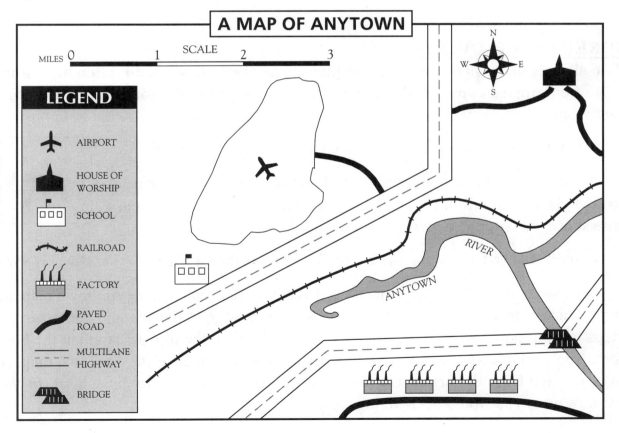

A MAP OF ANYTOWN

THE LEGEND

The secret to using any map is to understand its symbols. Instead of writing the word "highway," "railroad," "airport" or "school" each time it appears on the map, map-
► makers use symbols to represent these things. A map **symbol** is a drawing that stands for an actual place or a real thing.

►   Mapmakers provide a **legend** to explain each symbol in words. The legend unlocks the meaning of the symbols. It is sometimes called the "key." Symbols may appear as shapes, lines, dots, dashes, or drawings. Each map will have its own set of symbols. For example, the symbol for an airport on one map may be different on another map. Each symbol is explained in the legend, so you can tell what it means.

✔ CHECKING YOUR UNDERSTANDING ✔

There are 8 symbols on the map of Anytown. On a separate sheet of paper, draw the symbol used for:

- a factory   • a school   • a bridge   • an airport

DIRECTION INDICATOR

To make it easier to find directions on a map, mapmakers provide a **direction indicator**. It is often called a **compass rose.** The compass rose shows the four **cardinal** (*basic*) directions:

- **north** (N)   • **south** (S)   • **east** (E)   • **west** (W)

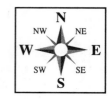

A compass rose can also show other directions. Sometimes we need to find places that fall in between the four basic directions. A compass rose shows the intermediate (*in-between*) directions:

- **northeast** (NE)   • **northwest** (NW)   • **southeast** (SE)   • **southwest** (SW)

Let's see how well you understand what you have just read. On the Anytown map, in which direction would you travel to go from the bridge to the school? Here are the steps to figure out the answer. Most maps show north at the top and south at the bottom. Look at the compass rose in the upper right hand corner of the Anytown map. If you traveled from the bridge (*in the eastern part of Anytown*) to the school (*in the western part*) you would be traveling west.

✔ **CHECKING YOUR UNDERSTANDING** ✔

In which direction would you be traveling if you went from:

- the house of worship to the bridge?
- the airport to the bridge?

- the factories to the river?
- the school to the airport?

SCALE

Just as a model airplane is a small version of a large, real airplane, a map is a small diagram of a large, real place. If a map were the same size as the area it shows, it would be too big to use. Imagine a map the actual size of your school! The larger the area represented, the less detail the map can have. For example, a map of the United States can only show outlines of the states and some cities. A map of your school can show much more detail, such as each classroom.

Mapmakers use a **scale** to show what distances on a map stand for in real life. The ◀ scale can be used to figure out the distance between any two places on a map. Scales tell us the real distance in miles or kilometers. Map scales are usually shown as a line marked: "Scale of Miles." Mapmakers may use one inch to represent (*stand for*) one mile. On a map of a large area, one inch may represent 100 miles.

Let's see how we can find the distance from Rochester to Syracuse. First, look at the map to the right. Put a ruler under the scale on the map. One inch on the scale of miles represents a real distance of 100 miles.

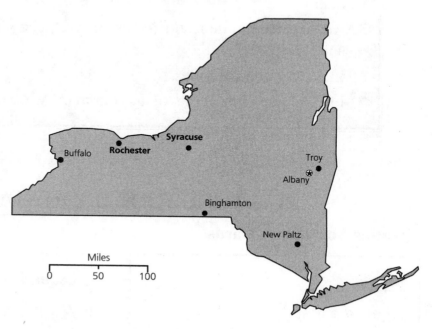

On the map, line up the edge of a piece of paper with Rochester. Then move the paper to the left until it touches Syracuse. Mark both spots with a pencil or pen. Now use a ruler to measure this distance. It measures about three-fourths of an inch. Therefore, the distance from Rochester to Syracuse is about 75 miles $\left(\frac{3}{4}\text{ths of }100=75\right)$.

✔ **CHECKING YOUR UNDERSTANDING** ✔

Let's practice your new skill. What would be the distance from:

- ◆ Albany to Syracuse?
- ◆ Buffalo to Albany?

- ◆ Troy to Binghamton?
- ◆ New Paltz to Albany?

Closing

MAPPING AN IMAGINARY TOWN

Now you have enough information to draw a map as good as the one your friend from California has drawn. You decide to map an imaginary town named after you. For example, if your name is Brian, you'll call the town <u>Brian</u>ville. If your name is Maria, the town will be called <u>Maria</u>ville. To help you, use the following steps to create your map:

1. Decide how many different features you want to show on your map.
2. Think of where on the map you will draw each feature.
3. Draw each feature on your map.
4. Create symbols for a legend or "key" to explain the features on your map.
5. Add a direction indicator (*compass rose*) showing north, south, east and west.
6. Include a scale of miles.
7. Finally, put a title at the top of your map: MY MAP OF __?__ VILLE

REVIEWING YOUR UNDERSTANDING

Creating Vocabulary Cards

Maps
What is a map?
Name four items used on a map
to help locate places:

Legend
What is a legend?
What is a legend used for?

Creating a Map of your Community

Think of a map as a picture, taken from high in the air. In the past, people could only make maps by observing carefully what they saw while sailing along a coast or traveling on horseback and on foot. For example, Henry Hudson drew maps as he sailed up and down the Atlantic coast. Today, many maps are based on photographs of areas actually taken by satellites in outer space.

What would it be like to make a map of part of your own community? In this section, you will be asked to create such a map. First, find a central point around which to organize your map—like your house or school. Then, draw a map extending approximately one or two blocks in each direction from that central location.

On your map, create at least three different symbols to show where things are located, such as parks, stores, schools and highways. For example, you might draw a square with dollar signs $$$ inside it to symbolize a bank.

Then compare and contrast the symbols that you have created with those of your classmates. See if the class can arrive at some symbols that most students think are best.

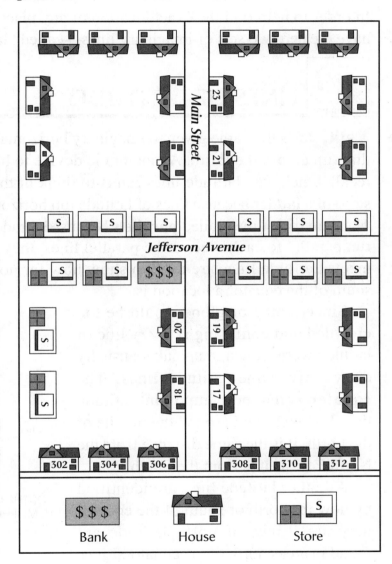

EXPLORING BEYOND
New York State

LEARNING ABOUT LATITUDE AND LONGITUDE

In order to help find the exact location of any place on a map or globe, geographers have created two sets of imaginary lines—called "latitude" and "longitude" lines.

LINES OF LATITUDE

Latitude is the name given to imaginary horizontal lines that run across the Earth. A mnemonic device to help us recall which way latitude lines run is to think of them as steps of a **lad**der because lines of latitude run horizontally. They are sometimes called **parallels** because latitude lines run parallel to each other. Like parallel lines, they never meet. Latitude lines are used to show how far north or south of the equator a location is.

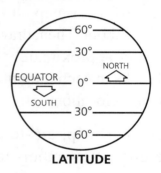

LATITUDE

Since a map or globe would be too crowded and confusing if *every* line of latitude were shown, mapmakers usually draw only some latitude lines. The **equator** is the most important latitude line. It stretches all around the middle of the Earth. It is the same distance from the North Pole as it is from the South Pole.

All other latitude lines are identified by how far north or south of the equator they are. Lines of north latitude are found in areas north of the equator. Lines of south latitude are found in areas south of the equator.

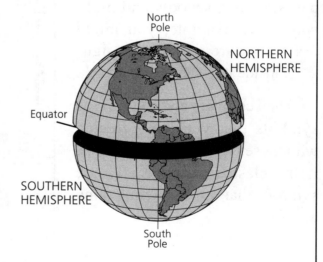

Each latitude line is assigned a number in degrees to show its distance from the equator. The symbol for **degrees** is °. Going in either direction from the equator, we mark latitude lines from 1° to 90°. An "**N**" or "**S**" is added after the number of degrees to show if the line is north or south of the equator. For example,

❖ CONTINUED

a latitude line 87 degrees north of the equator would be written as 87° N. Lines south of the equator have an "S" after the number of degrees.

At the equator, 0° degrees latitude, the weather is generally hot. The sphere of the Earth curves away from the Sun as you go towards the North and South Poles. As a result, the higher the latitude number, generally the colder the climate will be. The angle of the Earth's tilt as it revolves around the Sun makes the seasons change. When it is winter north of the equator, it is summer south of the equator. At the equator, there are no seasonal changes.

LINES OF LONGITUDE

Longitudes are a set of imaginary lines that run up and down a map or globe. They are drawn as lines connecting the North Pole to the South Pole. They are sometimes called **meridians.** Unlike latitude lines, they are not parallel. All the longitude lines meet at both the North and South Poles. Longitudes are used to show location east and west of the Prime Meridian.

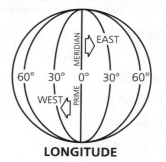

LONGITUDE

The **Prime Meridian** is the most important longitude line. Geographers use it to divide the Earth into two hemispheres (*east and west*) and to mark the starting line of longitudes. The half of the Earth west of the Prime Meridian is known as the Western Hemisphere, while the half to the east is known as the Eastern Hemisphere. As you learned earlier, mapmakers often draw the division between the hemispheres slightly west of the Prime Meridian to show all of Europe and Africa in the Eastern Hemisphere.

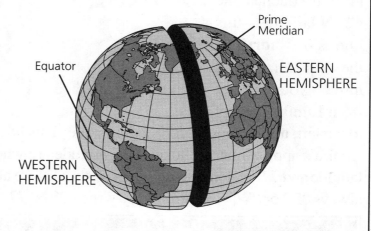

Like the equator, the Prime Meridian is identified as zero degrees (0°). Going in either direction from the Prime Meridian, we mark longitude lines from 1° to 180°, adding "**E**" or "**W**" to indicate if the line is east or west of the Prime Meridian.

Because longitude lines are not parallel, they are not always the same distance from one another. At the equator, each degree of longitude is about 69 miles apart.

◆ CONTINUED

However, as one moves closer to the North or South Pole, each degree of longitude measures fewer and fewer miles. Finally, all longitude lines meet at both the North and South Poles.

When latitude and longitude lines both appear on a map or globe, they form a grid pattern. By knowing the points at which latitude and longitude lines intersect (*meet*), you can locate any place on the surface of the Earth.

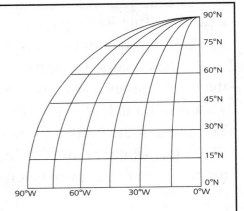

USING LATITUDE AND LONGITUDE

Your Task

Look at the map to the right. What is the approximate latitude and longitude of Elmira? To find out, put your finger on the small dot representing Elmira. Move your finger down until it touches the 42° N latitude—this line is 42° **north** of the equator. Next, move your finger from Elmira slightly

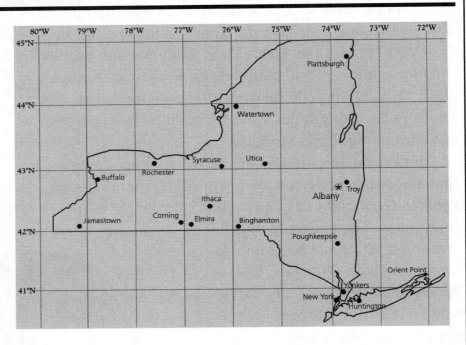

to the left, until it touches 77° W longitude. This line is 77° **west** of the Prime Meridian. Elmira's approximate latitude and longitude are where these two lines cross—at 42° N latitude and 77° W longitude. Because latitudes are always "N" or "S" and longitudes are always "E" or "W," we can simply write 42° N, 77° W.

✔ CHECKING YOUR UNDERSTANDING ✔

Figure out the approximate latitudes and longitudes of:

1. Syracuse	**4.** Poughkeepsie	**7.** Jamestown
2. Watertown	**5.** Buffalo	**8.** Yonkers
3. Orient Point	**6.** Albany	**9.** Rochester

◆ CONTINUED

WHAT DOES NEW YORK STATE "LOOK" LIKE?

2C

In this activity, you will learn about some of the important physical features of New York State. Look for the following important words:

▶ Mohawk River   ▶ Great Lakes   ▶ Weather

▶ Hudson River   ▶ Finger Lakes   ▶ Climate

One day you get a letter from your friend in California. She writes that she will be visiting you this summer. Before arriving, she would like to learn about the physical features of New York State. New York State is so large that you don't know what to write.

Definition

TWO WAYS TO DESCRIBE NEW YORK

You decide to ask your teacher what to write. Your teacher says, "Please try this first. Draw what an apple looks like. Then, write a description of what an apple looks like." That seems simple enough, you think to yourself.

MY APPLE DRAWING	MY APPLE DESCRIPTION
?	?

After you have completed the task, your teacher asks:

❖ Which was easier—drawing an apple or describing it?

❖ Which provides more information, the drawing or the description?

❖ Do they both provide the same kind of information? Explain your answer.

Ah! Now you understand what your teacher meant. To give someone accurate information about a place, it is sometimes best to provide both a picture **and** a description. You decide to send your friend a written description and a "picture" of New York State.

You start by getting a book about New York from the library. However, there is a problem. The book has no pictures, only written descriptions of New York State. You again ask your teacher for help. She says that written descriptions give you an opportunity to play the role of an "amateur cartographer."

"A cartographer? What's that?" She tells you that **cartographers** are people who make maps. Modern cartographers often begin with a photo of the region they intend to map, taken from an airplane or satellite. Then they review other maps and conduct research about the region to fill in the details. Your teacher hands you an outline map of New York. She says this map should help you to "picture" New York. With the descriptions in your book, fill in the details on your outline map.

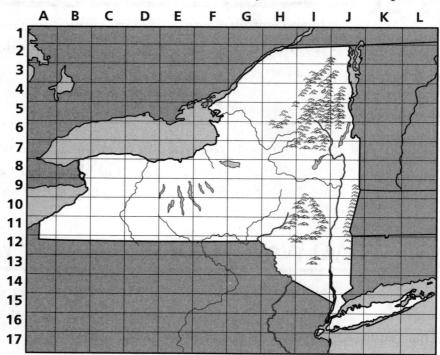

When you turn to your library book on New York, here is what you find:

THE GEOGRAPHY OF NEW YORK: THE EMPIRE STATE

SIZE

New York State is shaped something like a giant triangle. It has a total area of over 54,000 square miles, including its bodies of water. In size, it ranks 27th out of the 50 states in the United States.

THE BOUNDARIES (BORDERS) OF NEW YORK

New York is one of the most important states in the nation. Its location helps to explain why: a large portion of New York's borders consists of bodies of water. In fact, New York is the only state that touches both the Atlantic Ocean and the Great Lakes.

In the far north, New York State shares a land boundary with **Canada.** (*To help you find places on the map above, grid letters and numbers are supplied for the general location. For example, the location of Canada is generally around E3*). To the northwest, **Lake Erie** (around A10), **Lake Ontario** (around D6), the **Niagara River** (around B8) and the **St. Lawrence River** (around G3) make up the rest of the border with Canada.

Along its eastern side, New York shares a border with three New England states: **Vermont** (K4), **Massachusetts** (K10) and **Connecticut** (K13). To the south, New York borders **New Jersey** (I16) and **Pennsylvania** (D14). The southeastern end of the state—New York City and Long Island (K15)—touches the **Atlantic Ocean** (K17). There are hundreds of miles of Atlantic Ocean shoreline on Long Island. This provides New York with some of the best beaches in the nation.

> **THE AMATEUR CARTOGRAPHER**
> On your map, label the states that border New York State.

RIVERS AND LAKES

Rivers are long, narrow bodies of fresh water that flow into other rivers or the ocean. There are 70,000 miles of rivers and streams in New York State. In addition, there are thousands of lakes and ponds. These bodies of water make up one of New York's most important resources. Among New York's major rivers are the **Hudson, Mohawk, St. Lawrence, Genesee, Niagara, Oswego, Delaware, Susquehanna, Allegheny** and **Chenango.**

The two largest rivers entirely within the state are the Hudson and Mohawk. Beginning in the center of the state, the **Mohawk River** (H8) winds for 148 miles before joining the Hudson River just north of Troy. The **Hudson River** (I6) starts high in the Adirondack Mountains and flows south to empty into the Atlantic Ocean.

The St. Lawrence River as seen from the Canadian side
What other major rivers are there in New York State?

Together, these two rivers form one of the nation's greatest waterways. Barges can travel from New York City north on the Hudson River. They can connect, through the Mohawk River and a system of canals, to the **Great Lakes** : Lake Huron, Lake Ontario, Lake Michigan, Lake Erie and Lake Superior. A mnemonic device to help you remember the names of the Great Lakes is **H-O-M-E-S** .

Lakes are bodies of water surrounded by land. There are 8,000 lakes in New York—some small and others quite large. The two largest are **Lake Erie** (A10) and **Lake Ontario** (D6), both part of the Great Lakes. Lake Erie lies along the southwestern corner of New York State. Lake Ontario, to the northeast of Lake Erie, is the smallest of the Great Lakes.

Northeast of Syracuse is **Oneida Lake** (G8), the largest lake found entirely within New York State. **Lake Champlain** (J3) is a long, narrow lake that separates New York and Vermont. In western New York are the six **Finger Lakes** (E10), named by Native

Americans for their long narrow shape, resembling fingers.

In addition to its many rivers and lakes, New York has one of the world's most spectacular waterfalls—**Niagara Falls** (B9). Located near Buffalo, Niagara Falls is made up of two waterfalls, separated by a small island. The "American Falls" is in New York while the "Horseshoe Falls" is in Canada. Other New York waterfalls include Taughannock Falls near Cayuga Lake (*northwest of Ithaca*) and the 18 waterfalls in Watkins Glen State Park.

Niagara Falls, also the site of the city of Niagara Falls

THE AMATEUR CARTOGRAPHER

On your map, draw the major rivers and lakes of New York State. Also show the location of Niagara Falls.

TOPOGRAPHY

Cartographers also study the land forms or **topography** of the Earth. These land forms were created by different processes that occurred throughout the history of our planet. New York's mountain areas were created by pressures on the Earth's crust, causing it to rise up and fold. Less than two million years ago, the **Ice Age** began. The Earth's climate grew colder. Continuous snow created huge sheets of ice known as **glaciers.** These glaciers extended downward from the North Pole. They eventually covered most of New York State. As the glaciers moved, they cut into mountains and created valleys. When they finally melted, they created rivers and lakes.

As a result of these forces, we can think of New York State today as a large triangle with three highland areas. The southwest part of New York contains a high plateau known as the **Appalachian Plateau,** with its highest part in the Catskill Mountains. Along the eastern side of the Hudson River, from Poughkeepsie to Albany, are the **Taconic Mountains.** To the north is a third highland area called the **Adirondack Mountains** (I5).

On each side of the highland areas, and running through the middle of them, are New York's lowlands. The lowland area in the southeast is part of the **Atlantic Coastal Plain.** Long Island and Staten Island are located here. A second lowland area begins north of the Adirondacks, and follows along the northwest border with Canada. The St. Lawrence River, Lake Ontario and Lake Erie are located in this lowland area, known as the **St. Lawrence Lowlands.**

The other lowland areas are actually two corridors (*narrow passageways*) carved through the highlands. One corridor runs from the Great Lakes Plain east to the Hudson River, and is known as the **Mohawk Valley.** A **valley** is an area of lowlands between mountains and hills. The second corridor is a long valley running along the eastern side of New York State. It begins with the coastal plain in the southeastern part of the state and runs northward through the **Hudson Valley**

The Hudson River
What is New York State's other major river?

into Lake Champlain. This narrow valley was formed in part by the movement of glaciers. The Mohawk Valley connects with the Hudson-Champlain Valley near Albany, forming the shape of a giant "T" resting on its side. [——┤]

THE AMATEUR CARTOGRAPHER

On your map, label:

- Appalachian Plateau
- Catskill Mountains
- Taconic Mountains
- Adirondack Mountains
- Atlantic Coastal Plain
- Great Lakes Plain
- St. Lawrence Lowlands
- Mohawk Valley
- Hudson Valley

CLIMATE

We often hear people talk about the weather. **Weather** is a description of an area's day-to-day temperature, wind and amount of sunshine. A key factor that plays a role in an area's weather is its temperatures—how hot or cold it is. Weather also involves the amount of **precipitation**—the moisture that falls to Earth as rain, snow, hail and sleet. New York averages 32 to 54 inches of precipitation each year.

Climate is different from weather. **Climate** is the average of all of these weather conditions over a long period of years. Climate is affected by location, landforms and nearness to bodies of water.

New York State is located midway between the North Pole and the equator. Its climate varies from region to region. In general, most upstate areas have cold winters. Cities located in the "snowbelt"—Buffalo, Rochester and Syracuse—often receive heavy amounts of snowfall.

A sailboat gently floats along in the Erie Basin Marina with Buffalo City Hall in the background. *How might this Buffalo summer scene be different in winter?*

With an average of 108 inches of snow a year, Syracuse receives more snow than any other city in the state.

During the summer, temperatures are pleasant in the Catskills and Adirondack Mountains. On the other hand, summers in New York City and Long Island sometimes become unpleasantly hot, and people travel to the beaches. Moisture from the ocean makes the air humid (*wet*) as well as warm. In winter, the same warm ocean currents usually prevent New York City from having heavy snow and extreme cold.

Temperatures vary in the state from north to south. In the north, at Lake Placid, the average winter temperature is about 15°F (–9°C). In summer it is 65°F (18°C). In the Albany area, in the central part of the state, the average winter temperature is about 23°F (–5°C), with an average summer temperature of about 72°F (22°C). In Setauket, on Long Island, the average winter temperature is 33°F (0.5° C). In summer, the average temperature is about 74°F (23°C).

THE AMATEUR CARTOGRAPHER

On your map, locate the cities in the snow belt. In addition, label the winter and summer temperatures for Lake Placid, Albany and Setauket.

HOW GOOD A CARTOGRAPHER ARE YOU?

How well did you do as an amateur cartographer? Compare your map with the one found on page 238. Then:

❖ Describe any similarities or differences you find.

❖ Write a brief description of each item on your map. Include these descriptions when you send your map to the friend who asked you about New York's geography.

REVIEWING YOUR UNDERSTANDING

Creating Vocabulary Cards

Weather
What does weather mean?
Give an example of weather:

Climate
What does climate mean?
What is the climate of your area?

WHAT DO NEW YORK'S REGIONS "LOOK" LIKE?

2D

In this activity, you will learn to identify the seven major regions of New York State. Look for the following important words:

▶ Upstate/Downstate ▶ Plateau

Your friend was very happy with the map and written description you sent her to describe New York State. But she still wants more information. What are the main regions of the state? Where are the state's most important cities?

GEOGRAPHIC REGIONS OF NEW YORK STATE

In this activity, you will read about the different regions in New York State — including their landforms and major cities. You will then be asked to use these descriptions to make a map of the region. To help you keep track of differences among the regions, make a copy of the following chart:

Geographic Region	Describe Its Approximate Location	Describe Its Main Physical Features	Identify Its Major Cities
St. Lawrence Lowlands	?	?	?
Adirondack Mountains	?	?	?
Great Lakes Plain	?	?	?
Hudson and Mohawk Valleys	?	?	?
Appalachian Plateau	?	?	?
New England Upland	?	?	?
Atlantic Coastal Plain	?	?	?

WHAT ARE REGIONS?

A **region** is an area with similar geographic features. Places within a region are more like one another than they are like areas outside the region. New York is so large that it has several regions. Geographers sometimes disagree, however, about the best way to divide the state into regions.

The simplest way to divide New York State is into two regions—"upstate" and "downstate." But what do these terms mean? There is no single answer. Some people draw an imaginary line from Binghamton to Albany. They consider everything south ► and east of this line as **downstate**; land north and west is considered **upstate**.

Other people mark the dividing line at the northern border of Westchester County. They think of land north of this line as "upstate," while land south of it is "downstate." Throughout this book we will use this second definition of upstate/downstate.

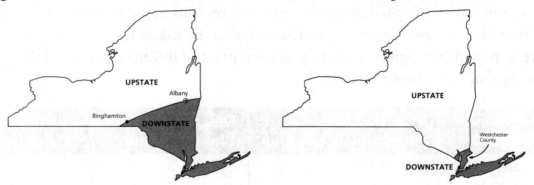

Most professional geographers divide New York State into more than two regions. Once again, there is no single list of regions that all geographers accept. In this book, you will learn about the major land regions of New York that most geographers agree to.

Think of New York as having seven major land regions. Moving from north to south and from west to east, the regions are: the St. Lawrence Lowlands, the Adirondack Mountain Region, the Great Lakes Plain, the Hudson and Mohawk Valleys, the Appalachian Plateau, the New England Upland and the Atlantic Coastal Plain.

THE AMATEUR CARTOGRAPHER

In the next few pages, you will read about the seven regions of New York. You will find a blank outline map for each region. Photocopy or trace the outline to make your own map. You will be asked to label cities, land forms and major bodies of water in each region. At the end of this activity, you will be asked to put all of these regional maps together to form a larger map of New York State.

ST. LAWRENCE LOWLANDS

The St. Lawrence Lowlands consist of the St. Lawrence River, Lake Champlain and the narrow plains extending from these bodies of water. The area is separated from the Adirondack Mountains by a hilly region known as the **Tughill Plateau.** Most of the St. Lawrence Lowlands is flat. It is also narrow, less than 20 miles wide. The region is known for its dairy farms and fruit orchards.

Many dairy farms and fruit orchards are located throughout the St. Lawrence Lowlands.

The **Thousand Islands** are a group of more than 1,000 islands that stretch for 50 miles along the St. Lawrence River. Wellesley Island, twenty miles long, is the largest. Some of the smaller islands are no bigger than your classroom. One of the main attractions in the region is **Boldt Castle,** located on Heart Island.

FAMOUS NEW YORKERS

George Boldt (1851–1916) made a fortune as the owner of the elegant Waldorf-Astoria hotel in New York City and the Bellevue-Stratford hotel in Philadelphia. Soon after marrying, he decided to build a castle as a gift for his wife Louise. He selected Heart Island—one of the Thousand Islands. To show how much he loved his wife, he had the island reshaped in the form of a heart. In 1900, construction began on the $2.5 million, 120-room castle. Sadly, his wife died suddenly in 1904. A grieving George Boldt ordered all construction to stop immediately—even though only one more year was needed to complete the project. Soon the castle fell into disrepair. In 1977, the Thousand Islands Bridge Authority bought the property and began to restore the castle.

Boldt Castle, Thousand Islands
For whom was Boldt Castle originally built?

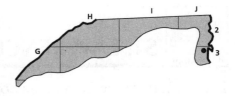

The largest city in the region is **Plattsburgh** (G3), located on Lake Champlain. The city is named after the owner of a large tract of land—Zephaniah Platt of Dutchess County. One of the major attractions in the city is the State University of New York at Plattsburgh.

THE AMATEUR CARTOGRAPHER

On your map, give a title to the region and its major rivers. Also label the city of Plattsburgh and the Thousand Islands area.

ADIRONDACK MOUNTAIN REGION

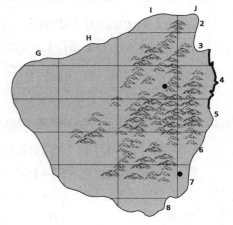

Just south of the St. Lawrence Lowlands are the Adirondack Mountains. The Adirondack region covers almost 5,000 square miles and is circular in shape. Its landscape includes mountain peaks, forests, lakes, rushing streams and waterfalls. The region is favored by tourists who enjoy hiking or canoeing on many of its 2,000 lakes. Because of its cold winters, few people live in the Adirondacks all year round. **Mount Marcy** in the Adirondacks, rising 5,344 feet, is New York's highest mountain.

Poor soil makes the Adirondacks unsuitable for farming. The many forests in the region have led to the growth of a local lumber industry. Lead, iron and zinc mining are other industries in the area. Since 1892, development has been limited because most of the Adirondacks has been preserved as one of the nation's largest parks.

Lake Placid (I4) is one of the Adirondack's most beautiful lakes. It was the site of the 1932 and 1980 Winter Olympic Games. **Lake George** (J7) is a popular summer destination for tourists. **Fort Ticonderoga,** also in the area, was built by the French in 1755 to control the area where Lake George drains into Lake Champlain. Today, the fort is a major tourist attraction. Another popular tourist site is **Ausable Chasm,** a gorge (*narrow canyon*) carved out by the Ausable River.

Lake Placid is one of the Adirondacks' most popular tourist attractions.

THE AMATEUR CARTOGRAPHER

On your map, give a title to the region and label its major rivers and lakes. Also label the city of Lake Placid. Use your own symbol to mark the location of the Adirondack Mountains. See if you can find and label Mount Marcy.

GREAT LAKES PLAIN

The **Great Lakes Plain** is a lowland area located in the northwestern part of the state. This region runs along the shores of Lake Erie and Lake Ontario. Apples, cherries, peaches and grapes grow well in the region's fertile soil. However, the growing season is short and the plains receive heavy snows in winter.

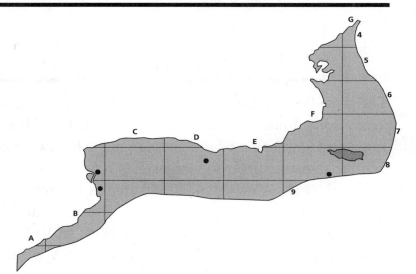

Many industries are located in this region because of its excellent transportation system. After 1825, farmers from the Midwest could ship their goods on the Great Lakes and through Buffalo to the Erie Canal. In addition, Niagara Falls provides electricity at a low price. Three of New York State's largest urban areas are located on the Great Lakes Plain—Buffalo, Rochester and Syracuse.

Buffalo (B9), located on the eastern shore of Lake Erie, is the state's second largest city. The city has become an important center for professional sports. Visitors can also enjoy nearby **Niagara Falls** (B8). The Albright-Knox Gallery, Buffalo Zoological Gardens, Beaver Island State Park and the Peace Bridge are some of its other attractions.

Rochester (D8), the state's third largest city, is located south of Lake Ontario. Many people link the city with it biggest company, Eastman Kodak. This company makes cameras, film and other photographic equipment. The city's cultural institutions include the University of Rochester, the Rochester Institute of Technology, the Eastman School of Music and the Museum of Arts and Sciences.

The Rochester skyline
Rochester has many important businesses. Can you name one?

Just at the southern border of this region is **Syracuse** (F10), located near a salt spring. Syracuse first became an important city after the building of the Erie Canal. Today, Syracuse is the fifth largest city in New York State. It boasts the Everson Museum of Art, the Salt Museum and Syracuse University.

THE AMATEUR CARTOGRAPHER

On your map, give a title to the region and label the cities of Buffalo, Niagara Falls, Rochester and Syracuse.

 # APPALACHIAN PLATEAU

The Appalachian (or Allegheny) Plateau region occupies most of southwestern New York. Sometimes it is called the "Southern Tier." It is located south of the Great Lakes Plain and southwest of the Hudson and Mohawk Valleys. Of all of New York's geographic regions, this is the largest.

► A plateau is an area of land that is higher than the regions around it. In fact, the Appalachian Plateau has many different land features, including the **Catskill Mountains** (H10) and the **Finger Lakes.** (E 9+10). The Catskills are located in the eastern part of the region. They are part of the Appalachian Mountain chain. Some of the Catskill Mountains reach heights of 4,000 feet. The Finger Lakes are located northwest of the Catskills. West of the Finger Lakes are rolling hills.

Farming is important in the Appalachian Plateau. The best farm land in the region is in the Finger Lakes area. Because of its fertile soil, this area is known for its vineyards (*where grapes are grown*) and nurseries.

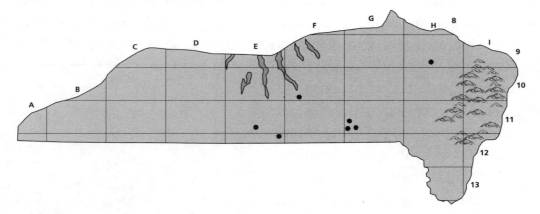

Located in the Appalachian Plateau is the tri-city region of **Binghamton** (G11), **Endicott** and **Johnson City.** These cities have the Roberson Memorial Center, Chenango Valley State Park and one of the nation's oldest zoos, Ross Park Zoo. The State

University of New York at Binghamton is also located in this area. **Corning** (E11) has given its name to one of the world's most famous brands of glassware. Today, Corning has a museum highlighting the long history of glass-making in the world. Visitors can watch glass-blowers and glass-cutters at work in the Corning glass factory.

The Baseball Hall of Fame at Cooperstown.

Ithaca (F10) is on the southern shore of Lake Cayuga, in the scenic area of the Finger Lakes. Cornell University and the Rensselaer Art Gallery are located near Ithaca. One of America's greatest writers, Mark Twain, is buried at the Woodlawn Cemetery in **Elmira** (E12). Twain wrote the well-known adventure tale *Tom Sawyer* while living in Elmira. On the eastern end of the Appalachian plateau lies **Cooperstown** (H9), one of the state's most popular tourist attractions. The town is home to the Farmer's Museum and the Baseball Hall of Fame.

THE AMATEUR CARTOGRAPHER

On your map, give a title to the region and label the Finger Lakes and the Catskill Mountains. Also label the cities of Binghamton, Endicott, Johnson City, Corning, Ithaca, Elmira and Cooperstown.

Information

THE HUDSON AND MOHAWK VALLEYS

The Hudson and Mohawk Valleys provide one of the best passages through the great Appalachian Mountain range running from New England to Georgia. This gave early New Yorkers easy access to the Great Lakes and the interior of the United States. Starting in the 1820s, the Erie Canal allowed New Yorkers to ship goods by water through the Mohawk and Hudson Valleys. Later, the New York Central Railroad and the New York Thruway were built along the same route.

Some people enjoy a leisurely boat ride on a canal.

The fertile soil on the banks of the Mohawk and Hudson Rivers makes these areas ideal for fruit orchards, dairy farms and other farms. Some of America's best apples and grapes come from this region. Waterfalls on the Mohawk and Hudson rivers provide a source of energy. These falls once powered early factory machines. Today, they provide power for making electricity.

Schenectady along the Mohawk River in 1830
What other major cities in New York are located along the Mohawk River?

THE HUDSON VALLEY

The Hudson River was named after the Dutch explorer Henry Hudson. The valley along the banks of the Hudson is only about 30 miles wide. It cuts through ridges sometimes over a thousand feet high. Many important cities developed in the valley, including Albany, Schenectady, Kingston and Poughkeepsie. In the south, the Hudson River meets the Atlantic Ocean at New York City.

Albany (J9) is one of the oldest cities in the United States and the state's sixth most populated city. In 1789, Albany became the capital of New York State. This means it is where the state's government is located. Albany's neighbor to the northwest is **Schenectady** (I9). The city is home to the General Electric Company. The Schenectady Museum, Jackson Botanical Garden and Union College are also located in Schenectady.

The 11 marble and glass buildings of the Empire State Plaza dominate the Albany skyline.

Another important city in the Hudson River valley is **Kingston** (I12). Kingston can be thought of as a city of firsts. It was the first capital of New York State. The first meeting of the New York State Senate also took place in Kingston. **Poughkeepsie** (J13) has many beautiful areas made up of lakes and small villages. It is the location of Vassar College, one of the best-known women's colleges in the nation. **Hyde Park** (J12) near Poughkeepsie, was once home to President Franklin D. Roosevelt. Today, it is a public park where visitors can see mementoes of Roosevelt's life and times.

THE MOHAWK VALLEY

The Mohawk River is an important **tributary** (*river branch*) flowing into the Hudson River. The river was named after an Iroquois tribe that lived in the area. Starting in upstate New York, the Mohawk Valley runs eastward. Because of its geographical location between the Appalachian and Adirondack Mountains, early pioneers used this valley as a route through to the interior of the American continent. In addition, the Mohawk Valley was an ideal location in which to build a canal that would connect the

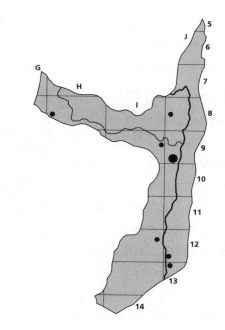

Great Lakes to the Hudson River. New York's first factories opened along the banks of the Mohawk in the early 1800s. Many factories once made carpets and fabric for clothes here. During the 1970s and 1980s, many industries in this region closed down. Despite this, the Mohawk Valley continues to be a major center of population in New York State.

Utica (H8) is located in the Mohawk Valley, at a spot where several Native American trails once met. The city was built on the site of Fort Schuyler. Many industries around Utica contribute to the economic health of the city. The Children's Museum, with its many "hands-on" displays, and the Italian Cultural Center are some of the city's attractions.

The city of **Saratoga Springs** (J8) was the scene of a famous battle during the American Revolution. Today, it is famous as a health spa and for its horse racing. Saratoga became a gathering place for wealthy New Yorkers in the early 1800s. They went to improve their health by bathing in Saratoga's spring waters. In 1863, the racetrack was built to entertain those who came to use the springs.

The racetrack attracts thousands of visitors to Saratoga each summer.

THE AMATEUR CARTOGRAPHER

On your map, give a title to the region and its major rivers. Also label the cities of Utica, Saratoga Springs, Albany, Schenectady, Kingston, Poughkeepsie and Hyde Park.

NEW ENGLAND UPLAND

This is an area of low mountains and rolling hills, found along New York's eastern border. It runs from the northern border of New York City to about halfway up the state. The New England Upland includes the Taconic Mountains and the southern part of the Hudson River Valley. Some of New York City's northern suburbs, such as Westchester, are considered to be a part of this region.

Close to where the Hudson River meets the New England Upland lies **West Point** (I14), the home of the United States Military Academy, where many U.S. Army officers receive their training.

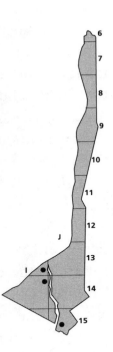

Yonkers (J15) is the fourth largest city in New York. It lies just north of New York City. One of its most noted attractions is the Hudson River Museum of Westchester. This museum focuses on the area's natural, social

Generals Grant, Lee, Pershing, MacArthur and Eisenhower all graduated from West Point.

and cultural history. During part of the American Revolution, **Newburgh** (I13) was the site of George Washington's headquarters. Now a museum, the building that served as his headquarters was the very first historic house ever bought by a state.

THE AMATEUR CARTOGRAPHER

On your map, give a title to the region and label the Hudson River. Also label West Point and the cities of Yonkers and Newburgh.

ATLANTIC COASTAL PLAIN

This region is part of a wide, flat plain that runs along the eastern coast of the United States from Massachusetts to the southern tip of Florida. In New York State, the Atlantic Coastal Plain includes Long Island and Staten Island (*a part of New York City*). Some geographers place Manhattan and the Bronx in the New England Upland. However, in this book, all of New York City will be considered part of the Atlantic Coastal Plain.

LONG ISLAND

Islands are pieces of land surrounded by water on all sides. Long Island is located at the southern end of New York State. It extends 120 miles out into the Atlantic Ocean. Some people think the island is shaped like a giant fish. The fish's head is near New York City and its two fins are at its eastern end.

There are also special types of islands. One type is known as a **barrier island.** It is an island created by waves pushing sand up to form pieces of land that rise above the ocean surface. Barrier islands protect coastlines from erosion by ocean waves. **Fire Island,** (K16) off the coast of Long Island, is an example of a barrier island.

Long Island was one of the first parts of the state to be settled by Europeans. The western end of the island (*now part of New York City*) was settled by the Dutch in the early 1600s. English colonists from Connecticut rowed across Long Island Sound and established the first towns on eastern Long Island. Long Island has some of the world's best beaches, making it a favorite summer vacation spot. Fishing and farming have been important ways of earning a living on the island since the 1600s.

Montauk Lighthouse on Long Island marks the easternmost point of New York State. Commissioned by President George Washington in 1795, it was completed the following year.

A NOTE ABOUT LONG ISLAND

Although Brooklyn and Queens are geographically part of Long Island, these two areas joined Staten Island, the Bronx and Manhattan to form New York City. Ever since, when people speak of "Long Island" they are usually referring to only the two eastern counties—Nassau and Suffolk. These two counties are **not** part of New York City. With over two and a half million people living in Nassau and Suffolk, their population is greater than that of 16 states.

After World War II, **Nassau County's** (J15 + 16) population grew a great deal. Many new housing developments were built and people moved from New York City to the county's many towns and villages. There are many popular vacation and recreation spots in Nassau County. **Jones Beach** is one of the area's most beautiful beaches. Nassau's scenery, landmarks and museums attract millions of visitors each year. Some attractions that visitors particularly enjoy

President Theodore Roosevelt delivers a speech at his home at Sagamore Hill on Long Island.

are Sagamore Hill, which was once President Theodore Roosevelt's home in Oyster Bay, and Old Westbury Gardens.

Suffolk County (K15 + L15) gets more sunshine than any other county in the state. Many New England farmers and fishermen first settled in Suffolk in the mid-1600s. Towns such as Huntington and Montauk still have homes dating back to this period. The pirate Captain Kidd came to Suffolk in 1690. Some believe that Kidd buried his treasure somewhere on Long Island, but the treasure has never been found. The Hamptons, on the eastern end of Long Island, attract many tourists during the summer. Suffolk County grows more food, in dollar amounts, than any other county in the state.

NEW YORK CITY

New York City is the nation's largest city. Many consider it to be the greatest city in the world. New York City is an entertainment, financial and cultural center. People from all over the world go to visit and live there. The city itself is made up of five "boroughs" (**areas**): the Bronx, Brooklyn, Manhattan, Queens and Staten Island.

Young children enjoy an animal ride at the Bronx Zoo.
What zoos have you visited?

The **Bronx** (J15) is New York City's most northern borough. Fordham University and Lehman College are located here. It contains the Bronx Zoo, home to more than 3,600 different kinds of animals. The New York Yankees are also based in the Bronx, playing at Yankee Stadium.

Brooklyn (J16) is the westernmost point of Long Island. It is the most heavily populated of the boroughs. Many of its neighborhoods are closely identified with particular ethnic groups. Visitors to Brooklyn enjoy seeing the Brooklyn Bridge, Brooklyn Museum, Prospect Park and the Brooklyn Botanical Gardens. At the southern tip of Brooklyn is Coney Island, known for its beaches, amusement rides and boardwalk.

The Brooklyn Bridge connected Brooklyn with Manhattan. The drawing on the left shows the bridge when it opened. The photo on the right was taken 100 years later.
What differences do you notice between these pictures?

Manhattan (I16) is the oldest part of New York City and still the center of city life. Manhattan contains the city's major businesses and places of entertainment. Millions of people visit Manhattan to see Radio City Music Hall, the New York Stock Exchange, the Empire State Building, Madison Square Garden and the United Nations. Central Park is located in Manhattan, as well as world-class museums like the Metropolitan Museum of Art and the American Museum of Natural History.

Radio City Music Hall

New York Stock Exchange

Queens (J16) is the largest borough in terms of area. It is the home of many different ethnic groups. A visitor to Queens today can see New York's two great airports, La Guardia and Kennedy International. Shea Stadium, where the New York Mets play baseball, was built in Queens for the 1964 World's Fair.

In many ways **Staten Island** (I16) is different from the other four boroughs. It has fewer people than any other borough. Many people think of Staten Island as a group of small towns rather than as part of a large city. Before the Verrazano-Narrows Bridge was built in 1964, the only direct way to get from Staten Island to any of the other boroughs was by ferry.

THE AMATEUR CARTOGRAPHER

On your map, give a title to the region and label its major rivers. Also label the two counties of Long Island and the five boroughs of New York City.

Closing

YOUR FINAL TASK

When you read about each region in New York, you completed a map for that region. Now cut out and combine all seven maps. Fit your seven regions together to form a single map of New York State. Compare your map to the map of New York State that appears on page 238. Are these two maps similar? If not, make corrections on your map.

REVIEWING YOUR UNDERSTANDING

Creating Vocabulary Cards

Plateau
Define the term:
The Appalachian Plateau
occupies most of which portion
of New York State?

Upstate/Downstate
Describe the area most often referred
to as "upstate" New York:
Describe the area often referred
to as "downstate" New York:

Finding Out More About New York State

There are many interesting places in New York State besides those listed in this activity. Look up the following places in a travel guide, encyclopedia or atlas. Then add them to your map. Provide a brief description on a separate sheet of paper.

❖ Fort Ticonderoga
❖ Oyster Bay
❖ New Paltz
❖ Monticello
❖ Cold Spring Harbor

❖ Stony Brook
❖ Lake George
❖ Howe Caverns
❖ Seneca Falls
❖ James Town

People wait to take a boat ride in Howe Caverns, a geological wonder 160–200 feet below ground.

Looking at Your Town or City

The town that you live in is part of one of the regions that you just read about. Let's learn more about your town or city:

❖ Name a region that your town or city is a part of.
❖ On a map, highlight this region.
❖ On that map, mark the location of your town or city.
❖ Name some of the other cities, towns or communities located in your county.

WHERE WOULD YOU LOCATE YOUR BASKETBALL TEAM?

2E

In this activity, you will apply your knowledge of geography to a specific purpose: choosing the best city for a new women's basketball team. Look for the following important words:

▶ Population Density
▶ Per Capita Income

▶ Almanac
▶ Table

Wow! It is hard to believe your good fortune over the last two weeks. First, your rich uncle left you over $100 million. Then you successfully bid on buying a new women's basketball team. All your life you have been a basketball fan, and at last your dream has come true. You are now the owner of a team. There is just one problem! You must find a city in New York to locate your new team.

─── THINK ABOUT IT

1. In which city would you locate your basketball team?
2. Why would you want to locate the team in that city?

CHOOSING A CITY FOR A BASKETBALL TEAM

You hire a panel of experts to help you with this decision. They tell you the location of your team requires a lot of thought. The final decision depends on many factors. For one thing, you cannot choose New York City or Albany, since they have already been selected by someone else. Your experts have narrowed the list of cities in New York State that you can choose from:

❖ Buffalo   ❖ Rochester   ❖ Yonkers

Make a copy of the map above. Then, using an atlas, mark the location of each of these cities. This will allow you to see where each city is located and help in your decision.

LOOKING AT SOME DEMOGRAPHIC FACTORS

As the owner of a women's basketball team, you will need fans to attend games to help make a profit. Your experts now tell you there are **demographic** (*having to do with population*), economic and cultural factors to think about. These include:

❖ **Population.** The city should have a population large enough to support a team.

▶ ❖ **Population Density** is the average number of people living in an area. To find the population density of a city, divide the number of people living in it by the size of the city's land area. For example, assume a city has a population of 6,000 people. The area of the city is 30 square miles. To find the city's population density, use a calculator to divide the population by the number of square miles:

$$\frac{6,000}{30} = 200 \qquad \left\{ \begin{array}{l} \text{The city has a population density} \\ \text{of about 200 people per square mile.} \end{array} \right.$$

❖ **Unemployment.** The city should have a low unemployment rate. This means that most people are working and can afford to attend some games or to buy products from advertisers who sponsor the games.

▶ ❖ **Per Capita Income** is the average amount of money each person earns. The city should have many people who earn a reasonable income to spend on advertisers' products or on activities like attending a basketball game.

❖ **Tourist Attractions.** The city should have interesting tourist attractions. This will encourage people in surrounding areas to visit the city. While they are visiting, they may want to attend a basketball game.

You ask your experts, "Where can I find that kind of information about each city?" They tell you that this information is available in most almanacs. An

▶ **almanac** is an important reference book.

Eastman House is a popular tourist attraction in Rochester. The founder of Eastman Kodak once lived here. Today, it is a museum.

ALMANAC

An almanac is a book of facts. A new edition is published every year, so it is always up to date. An almanac covers a wide range of subjects—such as art, astronomy, business, countries of the world, education, entertainment, farming, geography, history and religion. Almanacs also contain lists of movie stars, explorers, musicians, writers, Nobel prize winners and athletes.

A variety of information can be found in an almanac. For example, you can find out which team won the football Super Bowl last year, or which city in New York State has the largest population. Although there are many different almanacs, two of the best known are:

- *The World Almanac and Book of Facts*   - *The Information Please Almanac*

HOW TO FIND INFORMATION IN AN ALMANAC

Almanacs are easy to use. The key is knowing where to look. To locate the information you need, use the following steps:

❖ Get a copy of *The World Almanac and Book of Facts*.

❖ Open to the **index** in the almanac. The index of a book is a way for a reader to find specific information. While a table of contents gives a reader a general idea of what is in the book, an index helps a reader to find specific things, by giving the page number where the information is located.

❖ Look for the listing "Cities, U.S." by turning to the page shown in your almanac.

❖ CONTINUED

Much of the information found in almanacs is presented in table form. If you are unsure about how to read or use a table, the following will help you.

INTERPRETING INFORMATION IN A TABLE

A **table** is an arrangement of words or numbers in columns. It is used for organizing large amounts of information so facts can be easily located and compared. The table shows different categories of information. These categories are named in the headings found across the top of the chart. The table below shows the population of New York State compared to the U.S. population from 1850 to 1990. The dates are listed down the left-hand side. You can find a year's population by looking down the column and then across the row.

New York's Population in Comparison to the U.S. Population			
Years	N.Y. Population	U.S. Population	NY's Population*
1850	3,097,394	23,191,876	13%
1870	4,382,759	39,818,449	11%
1890	6,003,194	62,947,714	9.5%
1910	9,113,614	91,972,266	10%
1930	12,588,066	122,775,045	10%
1950	14,830,192	150,697,361	10%
1970	18,241,391	203,302,031	9%
1990	17,990,455	248,709,873	7%

*As a percentage of the U.S. Population

✔ CHECKING YOUR UNDERSTANDING ✔

❖ In what year did New York first show a population of more than 10,000,000?

❖ In what year did the U.S. population exceed 200 million?

❖ In which 20-year period did New York's population increase the most?

There are other sources of information besides almanacs. Some of the information you need may also be found by looking in:

❖ an encyclopedia. Look under New York State.

❖ *I Love New York Travel Guide*. The New York State Department of Economic Development, Bureau of Media Services, provides this free travel guide. The guides are available at tourist information centers and libraries.

❖ the tourism agencies of many cities in New York State. You can find their addresses and telephone numbers by looking in your local phone book.

USING AN ALMANAC

While gathering your information, you should fill in the following table to keep track of the data you find.

	BUFFALO	ROCHESTER	YONKERS
Population	?	?	?
Population Density	?	?	?
Rate of Unemployment	?	?	?
Per Capita Income	?	?	?
Major Tourist Attractions	?	?	?

MAKING A DECISION

YOUR DECISION

After you have done your research and completed the table, you should **compare and contrast** the information you have recorded. To do this, you need to weigh one piece of information against another. There is no single correct answer. Each city will have its own advantages and disadvantages. After you have considered all the information:

❖ In which city would you locate your women's basketball team?

❖ Explain some of the factors that helped you reach your decision.

❖ Is this city different from the city you chose at the start of this activity? If so, what factors made you change your mind?

❖ In addition to a name, each team needs its own **logo**—a team symbol that will appear on its members' shirts. For example, Buffalo's football team uses a charging buffalo as its team's symbol. Make a copy of the basketball shirt to the right. On your copy, design your team's new logo. Explain why you chose your particular design. In addition, what two colors would you choose to be your team colors?

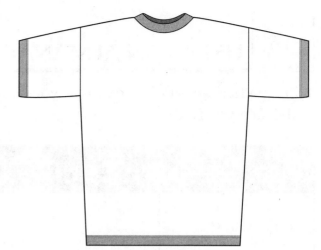

CLASS DECISION

After you have made your decision, compare it to the choices of your classmates. Students who have chosen the same city should organize themselves into a group. Then students in that group should make an oral presentation to the class. The presentation should focus on their reasons for selecting that city. Each group should have an opportunity to defend its choice. Finally, the class should vote which city it thinks is best for locating the basketball team.

FAMOUS NEW YORKERS

Jackie Robinson (1919–1972) was the first African American to play major league baseball. Before Robinson, there was an unwritten rule that excluded African Americans from playing in the major leagues. Robinson's success with the Brooklyn Dodgers from 1947 to 1956 encouraged the end of color barriers in baseball and other sports. In his early years, Robinson faced much abuse—beanballs aimed at his head, jeers, insults, hate mail and even death threats. Despite this, he kept calm and refused to fight back. His courage soon won admiration from other players, sportswriters and fans around the nation. At his funeral, the Reverend Jesse Jackson's comments summed up the feelings of many Americans: "When Jackie took the field, something reminded us of our birthright to be free."

Jackie Robinson
Why did his playing baseball for the Brooklyn Dodgers make news?

REVIEWING YOUR UNDERSTANDING

Creating Vocabulary Cards

Population Density
Define population density:
Why might a city's population density be important to a business?

Per Capita Income
Define per capita income:
Why might a city's per capita income be important to a business?

Separating Relevant from Irrelevant Information

An important Social Studies skill is the ability to tell the difference between relevant and irrelevant information.

❖ **Relevant information** is information connected to your topic. Relevant information is useful and appropriate and has some connection with what you are looking for.

❖ **Irrelevant information** is information not related or connected to your topic. It is either not useful for solving the problem you are working on, or it has no connection with what you want to know.

How well do you understand the difference between relevant and irrelevant information? Imagine you wanted to identify the name of a state from the following information. You will need to decide which clues would be relevant and which would be irrelevant.

A. **This state borders New York State.** This information is relevant. It narrows your search from 50 states to the five states that border New York— (1) Vermont, (2) Massachusetts, (3) Connecticut, (4) New Jersey and (5) Pennsylvania.

B. **This state has a governor.** This information is true, but irrelevant. Since every U.S. state has a governor, the information is not helpful.

❖ CONTINUED

LEARNING ABOUT NEW YORK STATE

C. This state has a major league baseball team. This information is relevant. Only two of the five states bordering New York State have major league baseball teams—the Pittsburgh Pirates and the Philadelphia Phillies in Pennsylvania and the Boston Red Sox in Massachusetts. This piece of information further narrows your search to Pennsylvania and Massachusetts.

D. This state has a state flag. This information is also true, but irrelevant. Every state has its own flag. This clue does not help you identify the state in question.

E. This state borders Lake Erie. This final clue is relevant. It eliminates Massachusetts, which does not border Lake Erie. Pennsylvania, however, does border Lake Erie. Therefore, the answer is Pennsylvania.

Now that you understand the difference between relevant and irrelevant information, let's put your knowledge to the test. Use the information in the following box to identify the mystery city referred to by the clues.

IDENTIFY THE MYSTERY CITY:
1. This city is located in New York State.
2. This city is located in the Hudson and Mohawk Valleys.
3. This city is part of upstate New York
4. This city is home to a well-known university.
5. People in this city often celebrate weddings with large parties.
6. The Erie Canal once passed through this city.
7. The area's salt deposits first made this city economically successful.

✔ CHECKING YOUR UNDERSTANDING ✔

1. Was clue #1 relevant? If so, why?
2. Was clue #2 relevant? If so, why?
3. Was clue #3 relevant? If so, why?
4. Was clue #4 relevant? If so, why?
5. Was clue #5 relevant? If so, why?
6. Was clue #6 relevant? If so, why?
7. Was clue #7 relevant? If so, why?
8. What is the name of the mystery city?

AMERICAN HERITAGE

View of Buffalo in 1825

Immigrant children selling bread on the
streets of New York City

Construction of locks on the Erie Canal

The term "American Heritage" refers to what we have gained from the past—
our ideas, laws, type of government and customs. We enjoy the life-styles we
lead today because of the struggles and accomplishments of those who lived
before us. In this unit, you will learn about the history of your state.

NEW YORK CELEBRATES THE ERIE CANAL

n October 26, 1825, New Yorkers celebrated the completion of the Erie Canal. Governor DeWitt Clinton, the main sponsor of the canal, began the celebration by leading a parade through the streets of Buffalo to a group of waiting barges. Stretching for hundreds of miles along the length of the canal, cannons stood ready to sound their thunder. At exactly 10:00 a.m., the cannons in Buffalo began firing. As soon as the blast was heard in the next town, those cannons fired also. The roar of cannons echoed the entire length of the canal and down the Hudson River all the way to New York City. The chain of cannon fire took an hour and half to travel the route, after which it reversed itself, and the cannons fired all the way back from New York City to Buffalo. When the cannons fell silent, Clinton and other officials got onto the barges.

ERIE, OSWEGO and CHAMPLAIN CANALS

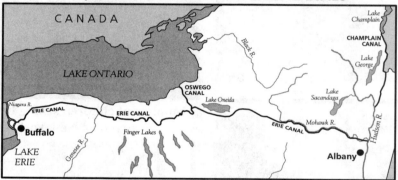

During the next week, the barges moved slowly along the canal from town to town. They carried goods from the West—barrels of flour, apples, butter, whitefish, special woods and newly-made brooms and pails. At Lockport, the barges had to be lowered through a system of five locks. At Waterford, the barges passed through another 16 locks. These locks were spaces that could be closed off. They acted like giant bathtubs in which boats could be raised or lowered with the water, in order to pass over the mountains and come down gradually to the level of the Hudson River.

Governor DeWitt Clinton was the main sponsor of the Canal.

As the barges reached each new location, the townspeople greeted Governor Clinton and the other officials with cheers, church bells, music and fireworks. At Albany, it seemed as if the whole city had come out to greet them. From Albany the barges turned south, down the Hudson River.

They entered New York harbor on November 4, to be greeted by ships from all nations, spread out as far as the eye could see. Governor Clinton poured a barrel of water from Lake Erie into the Hudson. Then he went on land to meet President John Q. Adams and four former Presidents—John Adams, Thomas Jefferson, James Madison and James Monroe.

New Yorkers had been inspired by the success of canals in Great Britain and nearby Massachusetts. The Erie Canal was the most ambitious canal ever constructed up to that time. In 1817, Clinton had convinced the New York legislature to build it. A path 50 feet wide was to be cut through forests, swamps and hillsides. Then a ditch 40 feet wide and 4 feet deep had to be dug, with a towpath on one side for mules to pull barges along the canal.

Without the equipment we have today, thousands of workers were needed to cut trees, pull out tree stumps and blast through rock. One out of every four workers was Irish. Other workers included local farmhands, African Americans, and immigrants from England and Germany. In summer, workers fought off mosquitoes and disease. In winter, they suffered from the freezing temperatures—all to earn a dollar a day.

A lock along the Erie Canal

The first sections of the canal opened in 1819. Six years later the entire canal was completed. Completion of the canal was cause enough for a gala celebration. But many New Yorkers wondered whether the canal was worth all the expense and hardship it had cost to build. What effect would the canal have on the future of New York and the nation?

In this unit you will learn the answers to these and other important questions about New York's past.

3A HOW WOULD YOU EDIT THIS ARTICLE?

In this activity, you will learn about the Native American groups that once lived in New York. Look for the following important words:

- ► Fact
- ► Opinion
- ► Native American
- ► Algonquian
- ► Iroquois
- ► Wigwams
- ► Longhouses
- ► Sachem
- ► Iroquois Constitution

To help you, the ► symbol appears in the margin where the **term** is first explained.

Imagine that your school will soon print its annual student magazine. This year's edition will focus on the Native American Indians who once lived in New York. You have been given your first assignment by the Editor-in-Chief—the person who puts the magazine together. "Here is an article to read," the editor says. "It was written by one of your classmates. I need you to make sure it contains only facts. I don't want any opinions in this article. Read it and report back to me when you have finished. However, before you begin, you should read this comparison of facts and opinions."

THE DIFFERENCE BETWEEN FACT AND OPINION

► A statement of **fact** (*factual statement*) is something that can be checked for accuracy. You check something for **accuracy** by looking at other sources to see if they agree that the statement is correct.

Correct	*Incorrect*
Albany is the capital of New York.	Syracuse is the capital of New York.

► An **opinion** is a statement of personal beliefs. It is not a statement that is true or false. An opinion *cannot* be checked for accuracy. There are two main types of opinion statements:

Opinions of personal taste express a person's feelings. For example, "New York is the best state to live in."

Opinions about the future make a prediction. For example, "When I grow up, I will go to college."

"Telling the difference between fact and opinion is only one part of your assignment," the editor continues. "I also need you to check facts and to look for errors in punctuation, spelling and grammar. Lastly, I would like to know what you thought was the most interesting thing about the Native Americans of New York." Here is the article you are asked to read.

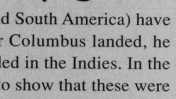

EDITOR'S INSTRUCTIONS:
Read the following paragraphs and identify all opinion statements. In addition, identify one factual statement.

Information

THE FIRST NEW YORKERS: THE NATIVE AMERICANS

～   A NOTE OF NAMES   ～

The first settlers in the Western Hemisphere (North and South America) have been identified by various names. When Christopher Columbus landed, he called them "Indians" because he thought he had landed in the Indies. In the 1960s, the term **Native American** began to be used, to show that these were the first people to live in the Americas. More recently, some people have called them Indigenous Peoples. Indigenous means native to a particular area.

(**1**) Hundreds of thousands of years ago the land that is now New York was covered by thick forests. (**2**) At least 20,000 years ago, people from Asia crossed the narrow plain that once connected Asia to Alaska. (**3**) The new arrivals were hunters, moving from place to place in search of food. (**4**) From Alaska, these people spread southwards throughout North and South America.

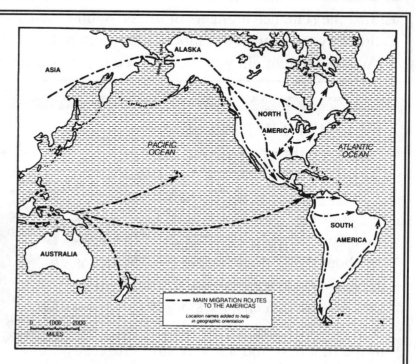

MAIN MIGRATION ROUTES TO THE AMERICAS
Location names added to help in geographic orientation

❖ CONTINUED

THE ALGONQUIANS AND IROQUOIS ENTER NEW YORK

(5) About five thousand years ago, the first Native Americans entered New York. ► (6) The first group belonged to the **Algonquian** (al-gong-kwee-en) tribe. (7) A second group of Native Americans arrived in New York as recently as 1,000 years ago. (8) They occupied the northwest of New York. (9) They became known ► as the **Iroquois** (ir-e-kwoi).

   (10) Both the Algonquian and Iroquois were made up of several tribes of people who shared similar customs and beliefs. (11) These tribes were divided into smaller groups known as **clans**—groups of related families. (12) To many Native Americans, their clan was more important than their tribe.

THE ALGONQUIANS AND IROQUOIS INFLUENCE NEW YORK

(13) The Native Americans were the most important people ever to live in New York. (14) Although small in number, their influence survives in the words we use, the foods we eat and the stories we tell. (15) For example, many Algonquian words have entered the English language, such as *moose, squash, moccasin* and *tomahawk.* (16) It is important for us to learn more about these peoples.

✎ YOUR NOTES ✐

1. List the sentence numbers of **all** the opinion statements.
2. Identify the sentence number of **one** factual statement.
3. What source might you check to see if your factual statement is accurate?

FAMOUS NEW YORKERS

James Fenimore Cooper (1789–1851) was born in New Jersey. In 1790 Cooper's family moved to Cooperstown, New York, a frontier settlement founded by his father. Cooper became one of America's's most popular writers. His most famous work was a series of five novels about the frontier and Native Americans in New York. One of these novels was *The Last of the Mohicans,* the story of Uncas, an Algonquian. Cooper's novels contain some of the first descriptions of frontier life read by many Americans.

An illustration from one of
Cooper's novels

ALGONQUIAN AND IROQUOIS HOMES

Information

EDITOR'S INSTRUCTIONS: Continue to identify all opinion statements and find one factual statement. Also, find answers to certain questions.

(1) The Native Americans of New York lived in villages. (2) The Algonquian peoples made round houses, or **wigwams**. (3) The men took branches that could be easily bent and drove them into the ground in a circle. (4) Then they tied the branches together at the top with vines, roots or strips of bark. (5) Women covered the frame with tree bark or mats of grass. (6) An animal skin was used for a door. (7) The family slept on animal skins. (8) A fire stood at the center of the wigwam for cooking and heating. (9) A hole at the top of the wigwam let the smoke from the fire escape.

(10) The Iroquois made their houses in a different shape. (11) From five to ten families shared a **longhouse**, which was 50 to 100 feet long, and about 20 feet wide. (12) Like a wigwam, it was made of branches covered with bark. (13) Holes in the roof allowed smoke to escape. (14) Benches along the sides of the longhouse were used by families for sitting, eating and sleeping. (15) Life in the longhouse was smoky, crowded and noisy, especially in winter when people spent most of their time inside. (16) We are much better off today in the kinds of houses we live in.

Interior of an Iroquois longhouse

(17) Some Algonquian tribes built longhouses for tribal meetings or religious ceremonies. (18) Each village had a leader, known as a **sachem**. (19) Both Iroquois and Algonquians often surrounded their villages with high walls. (20) Logs were pushed into the ground next to each other. The tops of the logs were sharpened to a point. (21) The wall of logs protected villagers from wild animals or enemy tribes. (22) Life was a great deal safer a thousand years ago than it is today.

✎ YOUR NOTES ✎

1. List the sentence numbers of **all** opinion statements, and **one** factual statement.
2. How was life in the wigwam similar to life in the longhouse?
3. Why did the Iroquois and Algonquians surround their villages with walls?

EDITOR'S INSTRUCTIONS: *Continue to identify all opinion statements and one factual statement. You will also need to check some punctuation, especially the use of periods and question marks.*
  • *Periods (.) are used when you wish to end a sentence.*
  • *Question marks (?) are used at the end of a question.*
In addition, continue finding answers to certain questions.

Information

ALGONQUIAN AND IROQUOIS LIFESTYLES

GATHERING FOOD

(1) Generally, Algonquian and Iroquois men hunted and fished. (2) They used stone, wood and bone to make tools, weapons and other objects. (3) Spears, hooks and nets of plant fibers were used for fishing. (4) Bows and arrows, spears and clubs were used to kill deer, rabbits, moose, squirrels, beavers, ducks and turkeys. (5) Meat and fish were preserved by drying and then stored for winter. (6) If a village did not store enough food, its members could starve [./?]

An Iroquois out hunting
What kinds of animals did they usually hunt?

(7) Algonquian and Iroquois men built canoes for fishing and trading with other villages. (8) The Algonquians sewed pieces of bark together to cover the frame. (9) Then they used sticky tree sap to cover where the bark was sewn together, to make the canoe waterproof.

A Native American fishing from a canoe
What were canoes made of?

(10) Algonquian canoes were similar but lighter than Iroquois canoes and could easily be carried from one stream to another. (11) Algonquian canoes were probably much better than Iroquois ones.

❖ CONTINUED

PLANTING CROPS

(**12**) How were these tribes able to produce enough food to live on [./?] (**13**) Women gathered berries, nuts and other wild plants to eat. (**14**) They were also in charge of growing corn, squash and beans. (**15**) To plant crops, men cleared the land by burning the trees. (**16**) The ashes were then mixed with the soil. (**17**) Women used sticks to loosen the soil and plant seeds. (**18**) After 15 to 20 years, the village moved to a new place and cleared the lands for new fields [./?]

APPEARANCE

(**19**) The first residents of New York made skirts, moccasins, leggings and clothes from the skins of deer and other animals. (**20**) They used sharp porcupine needles to scratch designs in the leather. (**21**) They sometimes tattooed their faces and decorated themselves with paint, feathers and shells. (**22**) Most men wore their hair long, but some shaved the sides of their heads and left a short strip of hair on top. (**23**) I think that the Native Americans had a better sense of fashion than most of us do today [./?]

A village of longhouses
What activities took place in the longhouse?

THE ROLE OF WOMEN

(**24**) What was the role of women in Native American societies [./?] (**25**) Women had a special role in both Algonquian and Iroquois societies. (**26**) They grew and prepared the food, while men were often away hunting or trading. (**27**) Women were widely respected and helped to make many community decisions, such as choosing the sachems. (**28**) In Iroquois society, one's name and residence depended on the woman's side of the family. (**29**) For exam-

A Native American village
What roles did the women play?

ple, when an Iroquois man married, he left his family's home and lived in the longhouse of his wife's family. (**30**) Iroquois children took their names from their mother's family, not their father's.

❖ CONTINUED

RELIGIOUS BELIEFS

(31) The Algonquian and Iroquois tribes had similar religious beliefs. (32) They worshipped a "Great Spirit," believed to exist in all things. (33) Tribal medicine men or women helped communicate with the spirit world. (34) Animals identified with each clan were also considered special spirits [./?] (35) To please the Great Spirit, the tribes celebrated several special holidays of thanksgiving.

✎ YOUR NOTES ✎

1. List the sentence numbers of **all** the opinion statements.
2. Identify the sentence number of **one** factual statement.
3. Which is the correct punctuation for sentence:
   - ▶ **6:** (period / question mark)   ▶ **23:** (period / question mark)
   - ▶ **12:** (period / question mark)   ▶ **24:** (period / question mark)
   - ▶ **18:** (period / question mark)   ▶ **34:** (period / question mark)
4. What types of foods did the Algonquian and Iroquois eat?
5. What role did religion play in Algonquian and Iroquois society?

EDITOR'S INSTRUCTIONS:
List all opinion statements and one factual statement. Editors also need to check a writer's spelling. In this section, use a dictionary to find the correct spelling for the words highlighted in brackets ([ ]).

THE ALGONQUIAN TRIBES OF NEW YORK

Information

The main Algonquian tribes in upstate New York were the Mohican, Wappinger and Delaware (*or Lenape*). A large number of Algonquian-speaking tribes lived on Long Island, including the Montauk, Shinnecock and Massapequa. Members of the Algonquian tribes were the first people to live on Long Island.

A trading post in upstate New York where Native Americans traded furs for beads and silver ornaments

❖ CONTINUED

THE ALGONQUIAN TRIBES OF UPSTATE NEW YORK

Members of the Delaware tribe were located in New Jersey, [**Pennsylvania/ Pensylvannia**] and Delaware, as well as New York. The tribes of the **Wappinger Confederacy** (*alliance or league*) lived along the Hudson between Manhattan and Poughkeepsie. Their traditional enemies were the Mohawk (*an Iroquois tribe*). The Mohicans lived in the northern Hudson Valley. Their largest village, Schodac, was near present-day Albany. Like the Wappinger, their traditional [**enemies/enemeis**] were the Mohawk.

NATIVE AMERICAN PEOPLES OF NEW YORK

THE ALGONQUIAN TRIBES OF LONG ISLAND

Long Island was home to a number of Algonquian tribes. Many places on Long Island today are named after these tribes, such as Canarsie, Rockaway, Jamaica and Montauk. The Algonquians of Long Island were famous for their **wampum.** These were beads made from shells and strung together. Wampum was used in ceremonies or for money or gifts. Tribes also had ceremonial pipes of clay or stone. These were used to smoke tobacco leaves on special [**occasions/ocassions**], and were greatly prized.

In central Long Island, Tackapausha, the sachem of the Massapequa tribe, signed treaties giving lands to English settlers. In eastern Long Island, the Montauk became

❖ CONTINUED

the most powerful tribe. They hunted whales and fished in the ocean in large canoes made from logs. They must have been very brave to risk these ocean adventures!

The wisest sachem in all Long Island history was **Wyandanch** of the Montauk. In 1637, Wyandanch crossed Long Island Sound to meet the commander of the local English fort, **Lion Gardiner.** As a present, Wyandanch gave the commander an island at the eastern end of Long Island, now known as Gardiner's Island. This event made Gardiner the first English landowner in New York.

In 1653, hostile Connecticut tribes raided the main Montauk village and kidnapped Wyandanch's daughter. Wyandach went to Gardiner and received help from the English in getting his daughter back. As a reward, Wyandanch gave Gardiner a large area of land near present-day Smithtown. The English made Wyandanch the "Great Sachem" of all Long Island, in charge of all the other tribes. However, the other sachems never **[accepted/acceppted]** his title.

The introduction of guns by the Europeans made conflicts with other tribes bloodier. As the number of settlers in colonial New York increased, the Algonquians were pushed out of their traditional homelands. The Iroquois destroyed many of the Algonquian villages in the Hudson Valley. Large numbers also died from exposure to European diseases like smallpox. The tribes had no **[resistance/ resistence]** to these illnesses.

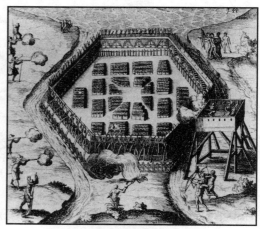

Today, only a few thousand Algonquians remain on **[reservations/resarvations]** in New York. For example, the Shinnecocks have a reservation in Southampton, on Long Island. Most of the surviving Algonquians, however, intermarried with other peoples. They are found throughout the country today.

A French and Algonquian force attacks an Iroquois village

✎ YOUR NOTES ✐

1. List the sentence numbers of **all** the opinion statements.
2. Identify the sentence number of **one** factual statement.
3. Which word is spelled correctly?
   - ▶ [Pennsylvania / Pensylvannia]   ▶ [accepted / acceppted]
   - ▶ [enemies / enemeis]   ▶ [resistance / resistence]
   - ▶ [occasions / ocassions]   ▶ [reservations / resarvations]

EDITOR'S INSTRUCTIONS: Identify all opinion statements. Editors also check a writer's grammar. One frequent error is using the wrong verb forms: "He (singular) do (should be _does_) what he wants." A similar mistake is to use a plural noun with a singular verb: "They (plural) eats (should be _eat_) their dinner early." In this section look for problems in the use of nouns with verbs and answer certain questions.

Information

THE IROQUOIS CONFEDERACY

Five Iroquois tribes occupied most of western New York. The Seneca (sen-i-ka) lived near the Genesee River. The **Cayuga** (ka-yu-ga) lived east of the Seneca in the Finger Lakes area. The **Mohawk** occupied the Mohawk River Valley, while the **Onondaga** (on-an-da-ga) lived in the valley south of Lake Ontario. The **Oneida** (o-nye-da) settled in the lands between the Mohawk and the Onondaga.

The Iroquois thought of their territory as one giant longhouse, stretching from Lake Ontario almost to the Hudson River. The Mohawks **[were/was]** called the keepers of the "Eastern Door," while the Seneca were the keepers of the "Western Door." Trails connected the tribes. The most important trail ran from Lake Erie to the Hudson River. This later proved to be the best route for roads and canals.

THE LEAGUE OF FIVE NATIONS

Around 1570, these five tribes formed the Iroquois Confederacy or **League of Five Nations.** According to legend, the Great Spirit visited Deganawida, the "peace-maker," in a dream. To end the constant fighting between the tribes, Deganawida was told to unite them. He persuaded **Hiawatha,** a Mohawk, to preach peace and unity throughout the lands of the five tribes. The tribes promised not to fight each other again.

The capital of the Confederacy was located in the village of Onondaga, where the Great Council met once a year. At the Great Council, the leading sachems of the Iroquois met to deal with important matters facing the whole Confederacy—such as whether to go to war. Such decisions required the approval of all five tribes before the Confederacy could act.

The Iroquois' method of government was one of the most advanced among all the Native Americans. Thomas Jefferson and the other founders of our country **[was/were]** influenced by the **Iroquois Constitution** in planning the structure of the government of the United States.

◀

❖ CONTINUED

Historic Documents: *The Iroquois Constitution*

The Iroquois Constitution

The Onondaga lords shall open each council by expressing their gratitude to their cousin lords, and greeting them, and they shall offer thanks to the Earth where men dwell, to the streams of water, the pool, the springs, the lakes, to the corn and the fruits, to the medicinal herbs and the trees, to the forest trees for their usefulness, to the animals that serve as food and who offer their furs as clothing, to the great winds and the lesser winds, to the Thunderers, and the Sun, the mighty warrior, to the moon, to the messengers of the Great Spirit who dwells in the skies above, who gives all things useful to men, who is the source and the ruler of health and life. Then shall the Onondaga lords declare the council open.

Not all Iroquoian-speaking people joined the League. The Susquehanna to the south, the Erie and Neutral to the west, and the Huron to the north were all Iroquoian peoples who never became members. One Iroquoian tribe several hundred miles away, however, **[joins/joined]** the League in about 1715. This was the **Tuscarora** (tus-ka-ror-uh) tribe. They were officially admitted into the Confederacy, making it the League of Six Nations.

Hendrick, Great Sachem or Chief of the Mohawks, in colonial clothing.

THE IMPACT OF THE EUROPEANS

The Iroquois were greatly respected for their bravery in battle. They were great warriors. Young boys were trained to be warriors from an early age. By the time they were teenagers, they began raiding other tribes or European settlements. When they captured prisoners, they either **[kills/killed]** them through torture or adopted them as members of their tribe.

Most people would agree that the arrival of Europeans doomed the Iroquois. In the 1700s, the Iroquois became deeply involved in the struggle between the English and the French for control of North America. The Iroquois generally helped the English and fought against the French. When the American Revolution broke out, most of the Iroquois nations sided with the British. The Oneida and Tuscarora, however, took the side of the colonists. This destroyed the unity of the Confederacy. The council fire, symbol of Iroquois unity, was allowed to burn out.

❖ CONTINUED

Led by **Joseph Brant,** Mohawk warriors raided a settlement near Albany in 1778. More than 30 Americans were killed. General George Washington sent 4,000 soldiers into Iroquois territory in 1779 to burn their villages and crops. The Iroquois tribes never fully recovered from these blows. After the Revolution, Brant led the Mohawk to Canada. The Oneida sold most of their lands and moved west. The Seneca recognized the new country as the United States and obtained some reserved lands. The Cayuga **[went/goes]** with the Mohawk to Canada. The Onondaga moved to western New York.

Today, the Iroquois **[is/are]** found on seven reservations in Canada and five in New York. Most Iroquois have mixed with other peoples and live in big cities like Buffalo, New York City or Toronto. Every year on Labor Day, members of the Six Nations meet for the Six Nations Festival at Cobbleskill, New York.

Joseph Brant, also known as Joseph Thayendanegea, was a Mohawk Chief.

From our studies of the Algonquians and Iroquois, we can see how these people used nature to their benefit. We can also see how they were affected by war and exposure to new cultures. We can learn a great deal from their experiences.

✎ YOUR NOTES ✐

1. List the sentence numbers of **all** the opinion statements.
2. Which is the correct word to be used?
   ▶ **[were / was]**
   ▶ **[was / were]**
   ▶ **[joins / joined]**
   ▶ **[kills / killed]**
   ▶ **[went / goes]**
   ▶ **[is / are]**
3. What was the Iroquois Confederation?
4. What famous United States document borrowed ideas from the Iroquois?

Closing

REVIEWING AND CHECKING THE ARTICLE

Now that you have finished reviewing the article, it's time to write to your Editor-in-Chief. You must tell her whether the article was completely factual or contained opinions. You should also discuss any errors that the article contained.

Dear Editor-in-Chief,

   I have reviewed the article. I found that the article contained (some/many) opinions. I found (some/many) sentences with errors. In addition, the most interesting thing that I learned about the Native Americans living in New York was ...

Sincerely,

_____
(sign your name)

Two days later you meet the editor again. She thanks you and asks you to do one more thing—to check the **accuracy** of the article. Remember, a factual statement is accurate if you can show that it is true and error-free. Since it would take too long to check every fact in the article, she suggests you choose any two factual statements. You can refer to either a textbook, encyclopedia or almanac to check the accuracy of these two factual statements.

Statements You Selected to Check	Source Used	The Statement is:
(1) ?	?	☐ Accurate ☐ Not Accurate
(2) ?	?	☐ Accurate ☐ Not Accurate

REVIEWING YOUR UNDERSTANDING

Creating Vocabulary Cards

Factual Statement
What is a "factual statement"?
Give an example of a factual statement:

Opinion Statement
What is an "opinion statement"?
Give an example of an opinion statement:

Learning to Use an Encyclopedia

One place to find information about Native Americans is in a **reference book.** One very useful reference book is an **encyclopedia.** The term comes from the ancient Greek for a "general education." Encyclopedias give their readers access to current knowledge on a wide variety of subjects.

ENCYCLOPEDIA

Encyclopedias contain articles with information on many topics. You can find facts about history, science, music and current events. Encyclopedias also have articles about countries, states and famous people. Subjects are arranged in alphabetical order. Encyclopedias often consist of many volumes. The first volume starts with the letter "A" and the last volume ends with the letter "Z." Each volume has guide words or letters on the spine to help you find particular subjects more easily.

Your Task

USING A VENN DIAGRAM

A **Venn diagram** uses circles to compare two or more items and show how they are related. Each item is represented by a circle. The area where the circles overlap shows how the items are similar. The outer part of each circle shows how the items are different. Let's use your knowledge of Native Americans to compare and contrast the Algonquians with the Iroquois. The Venn diagram below has been started for you. Make a copy of the diagram and then add **two** other points in each part of the diagram to compare and contrast these two groups.

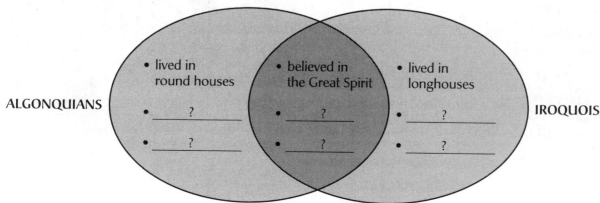

ARE YOU A GOOD HISTORIAN OF COLONIAL TIMES?

3B

In this activity, you will read about some exciting events in the days when New York was a colony. Look for the following words:

▶ New Netherland

▶ Patroons

▶ American Revolution

▶ Declaration of Independence

Historians are people who study the past. They often try to understand what it was like to live in another time. As you read the following pages, you will be asked to play the role of an amateur historian. Try to imagine what it would have been like to live in the past.

THE EUROPEANS COME TO NEW YORK

Five hundred years ago, trade between Europe and East Asia was very profitable. Most European traders used land routes that were long and dangerous. They wanted to find an easier and safer way. European nations sent out explorers to find an all-water route to the "Indies"—the islands of East Asia.

～ A Note on the Countries of Western Europe ～

Portugal, Spain, France, Great Britain and Holland were all active in early overseas exploration. Spain and France were kingdoms in Western Europe. Great Britain, an island west of Europe, was made up of three kingdoms: England, Scotland and Wales. After 1603, the King of England ruled over all three kingdoms. People from Great Britain are often referred to as British, but can also be called English, Scottish or Welsh (depending on where they come from). Holland, sometimes referred to as the Netherlands, became independent in the 1580s. The people of Holland are known as the Dutch.

THE EUROPEANS EXPLORE NEW YORK

As you read, look for answers to the following questions:

1. Who were some of the early explorers of New York?
2. What was Henry Hudson trying to find?

In 1492, **Christopher Columbus** sailed west across the Atlantic Ocean to find a shorter route to the Indies. Instead, he found a new continent, the "Americas." When he returned to Europe, he spoke of great riches in what became known as the "New World." Later, explorers from other European countries sailed in search of gold and other riches. In 1524, **Giovanni Da Verrazano,** an Italian explorer sailing for France, became the first European to enter New York harbor.

Giovanni da Verrazano

It was another 85 years before Europeans again entered the waterways of New York. **Henry Hudson,** an English sea captain, was hired by Dutch merchants who were also looking for a faster route to Asia. In September 1609, Hudson reached New York harbor and began sailing up the river that bears his name today. Hudson and his crew sailed as far north as present-day Albany. By that time he decided that the Hudson River was not the Northwest Passage to Asia that he was seeking, and turned around. In that same year, the King of France sent another explorer, **Samuel de Champlain,** on a journey through the lakes and forests of upstate New York. Lake Champlain in the northeastern part of the state is named after him.

French explorer Samuel Champlain explored Canada and upstate New York.

THE DUTCH COLONY OF NEW NETHERLAND

As you read, look for answers to the following questions:

1. Where did the early settlers of New York establish a colony?
2. What kinds of goods did the Native Americans and the Dutch trade?

Based on Hudson's explorations, the Dutch set up a successful fur trade with the native peoples of the Hudson River Valley. They were the first Europeans to settle in New ▶ York. The Dutch called their colony New Netherland . The Dutch government gave control of the colony to the Dutch West India Company.

In 1624, thirty families came to settle **Fort Orange,** known today as Albany. More settlers arrived the next year and established a second fort at the tip of Manhattan island. The Dutch governor, **Peter Minuit,** gave beads and other trinkets to the Algonquians of Manhattan to buy the island. The settlement was called **New Amsterdam,** after the Dutch city of Amsterdam.

The New Netherland colony was a trading post for furs. Beaver skins and other furs were highly valued in Europe at that time. The city of New Amsterdam, with its fine natural harbor, soon became a leading center for trade. In order to provide protection against attacks from Native Americans or other European countries, the settlers built a long wall along the north side of New Amsterdam. Later, this wall became where Wall Street is currently located.

Peter Minuit is said to have "purchased" Manhattan Island for $24 in beads and trinkets from the Algonquians.

At first, the Dutch got along quite well with most of the Native Americans. Their friendship was important to the Dutch, because the tribes showed them how to fish, hunt and grow new crops. In return, the Native Americans received goods such as guns, sugar, metal tools and woven cloth. Unfortunately, relations between the Dutch and the tribes soon became less friendly. War broke out in the 1640s and almost led to the destruction of the colony of New Netherland.

Dutch settlers sign a treaty with Native Americans at Fort Amsterdam

THE DUTCH COLONY GROWS LARGER

> ### As you read, look for answers to the following questions:
>
> **1.** What was a patroon?
>
> **2.** How did New Netherland become a British colony?
>
> **3.** Why were the English interested in gaining control of New Netherland?

In the following years, Dutch colonists set up new farming communities at Haarlem (*Harlem*), the Broncks (*Bronx*), Schenectady, Breukelen (*Brooklyn*), Wiltwyck (*Kingston*) and Rensselaerwyck (*Rensselaer*). Growth of the colony of New Netherland was slow. Few Dutch people wanted to leave the comfort and safety of the Netherlands for the dangers of the "New World."

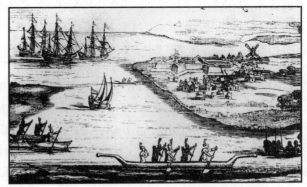

The earliest known view of New Amsterdam (1651)
In what ways has New York City changed in the last 350 years? ◀

To encourage more people to settle in New Netherland, the Dutch West India Company came up with a plan. Sixteen square miles of land were given to wealthy landowners called **patroons**. In exchange for the land, each patroon agreed to bring in 50 new settlers. The patroon offered settlers land, seed and animals in exchange for payments of rent. However, most of the patroons were unsuccessful.

Despite the failure of the patroon system, the number of settlers in New Netherland slowly began to grow. The Dutch welcomed people from other countries in Europe. Walking around New Amsterdam in 1660, a visitor might see Irish, British, German, French, Native American and African people in the streets. Most Africans in New Netherland were brought there as enslaved peoples.

One thing that made the Dutch colony unusual was its acceptance of diverse religions. Many religious groups, including Quakers and Jews, were allowed to practice their religion in New Netherland. The Dutch governor, **Peter Stuyvesant,** sometimes complained about this religious freedom. He thought all the settlers should belong to the Dutch Reformed Church. But the merchants in Holland who owned the colony told Stuyvesant that religious freedom should be protected.

Peter Stuyvesant became Governor in 1647. Many of those living in New Netherland complained about his arrogance and bad temper.

As the years went by, more and more English people settled in New Netherland. English colonists from Connecticut crossed the waters of Long Island Sound to start their own towns on Long Island. In 1650, the Dutch agreed to give the Connecticut Valley and western Long Island to England.

The government in England, however, had its eyes on the whole Dutch colony. New Netherland was viewed as a valuable trading center, with an excellent port and an important river leading into the interior. Most important of all, the Dutch settlement physically separated the English colonies along the Atlantic coast. When England and Holland went to war for control of world trade in 1664, four English ships sailed into the harbor of New Amsterdam. Governor Stuyvesant wanted to fight, but the townspeople refused. Without soldiers, Peter Stuyvesant had no choice but to surrender.

THE AMATEUR HISTORIAN: RECREATING THE PAST

1. **Creating Models.** What did Fort Orange or the walled city of New Amsterdam look like? Build a small model of Fort Orange or New Amsterdam out of cardboard, clay, paper maché or other materials. Label as many buildings as you can and tell the role each building played in the life of the settlement.

2. **Locating Historical Places.** On a map of New York State, locate some of the original Dutch settlements: Fort Orange (*Albany*), Haarlem (*Harlem*), the Broncks (*Bronx*), Schenectady, Breukelen (*Brooklyn*), Wiltwyck (*Kingston*) and Rensselaerwyck (*Rensselaer*).

THE ENGLISH TAKE OVER THE NEW YORK COLONY

NEW NETHERLAND BECOMES NEW YORK

The colony of New Netherland lasted less than 60 years. The King of England, Charles II, gave the conquered colony to his brother James, the Duke of York. In the Duke's honor, New Netherland was renamed **New York.** New Amsterdam became **New York City.** Fort Orange was renamed **Albany.**

The English agreed to let the Dutch settlers keep their lands and businesses. The Dutch influence left an important mark on New York State. Many of the names of cities were originally Dutch words. Many of the earliest churches and other buildings in New York date back to the days of Dutch rule.

Under English rule, New York continued to prosper. New York City became an important port. Other parts of the colony developed rapidly. **Fort Stanwix** (*now Rome*), and Oswego became centers for the fur trade. On Long Island, coastal ports like Cold Spring Harbor and farm villages like Smithtown developed.

LIFE IN COLONIAL NEW YORK

> ### As you read, look for answers to the following questions:
> 1. How did the jobs of men and women on farms differ in colonial New York?
> 2. Explain why churches were an important part of life in colonial New York.

Outside New York City, most colonists were farmers, living in the valleys of the Hudson or Mohawk Rivers or on Long Island. Many of them owned their own small farms and grew food to meet their own needs. Others rented land from wealthy landowners. A large number of these farmers sold lumber and wheat to the merchants of New York City.

Life in colonial New York was hard.
One of the most difficult jobs for settlers was clearing the land to plant crops.

Families in these days were often large, with five or more children. Everyone on the farm had a special job. The men cleared land, farmed, fished, hunted and built houses and farm buildings. The women cooked, cleaned, sewed, and helped with the farm work. During leisure time, people would sing, dance and enjoy a meal with their friends and families.

New York City was dominated by a small group of wealthy merchants, landowners and lawyers. They financed overseas trade or owned large pieces of land in the Hudson Valley. The city also had a large middle class made up of shopkeepers and craftsmen. The craftsmen made the ships, sails, bricks, furniture and other things needed by colonial society. Finally, there were many workers, servants and slaves. They owned no property. They did many of the hardest jobs and often lived in the worst conditions.

New York under British rule continued the Dutch policy of religious freedom. The church was the center of life and the main meeting place in many New York towns. It was a place of learning and a place to go with family to meet friends. New homes were often constructed near the church. In many places, the minister was the most important person in the community.

NEW YORKERS ENJOY BASIC RIGHTS

> ### As you read, look for answers to the following questions:
> 1. Describe the government of the New York colony.
> 2. Describe the charter that the Governor gave to the citizens of New York.

At first, New Yorkers had little say in their government. The king appointed a **Governor** to lead the colony, who chose his own advisers, known as the **Council.** In 1665, the towns of Long Island won some powers of local self-government. Then in 1682 the Governor of New York gave all citizens a charter. This charter guaranteed freedom of religion and trial by jury. It also created a law-making body called the **Assembly.** Its members were elected by the colonists. Membership in the Assembly was limited. Women, enslaved peoples and workers without land were not allowed to vote.

George III was the King of England at the time of the American Revolution.

By the late 1700s, it seemed to many New Yorkers that Great Britain was controlling more and more of what they could do. Disagreements arose between the Assembly representing the colonists and the Parliament (*law-making body*) in Great Britain. The colonists felt that many of the laws passed by Parliament benefited the people living in Great Britain more than the colonists. Many people in other American colonies felt the same. Eventually, these feelings
▶ would lead to the   **American Revolution** .

THE AMATEUR HISTORIAN: RECREATING THE PAST

1. **Writing Letters.** Pretend you are a person living in the colony of New York in the early 1700s. Write a letter to your friends in Europe. In your letter describe what life was like in colonial New York in those days.

2. **Writing An Editorial.** An editorial is an article written in a newspaper. It provides opinions about important issues. Pretend it is the 1700s. Write a five-sentence editorial giving your opinion about whether women, slaves, Native Americans and workers without land should be allowed to vote for members of the Assembly.

Information

NEW YORK'S ROLE IN THE AMERICAN REVOLUTION

Between 1754 and 1763, Great Britain and France fought a war for control of Canada and the lands west of the Appalachian Mountains. The Iroquois sided with the British, while other Native American tribes helped the French. The war became known as the **French and Indian War.** By 1763, Great Britain had conquered Canada and won the war.

THE ROAD TO THE AMERICAN REVOLUTION

> ### *As you read, look for answers to the following questions:*
>
> 1. How did the British need for money after the French and Indian War lead to disagreements with the American colonists?
> 2. Who were the patriots and the loyalists?

Great Britain wanted the Americans to help pay some of the costs of fighting the war. The British placed many new taxes on the colonists, without first discussing this with them. The cry of "no taxation without representation" quickly spread throughout the British colonies. Many colonists began to feel they would be better off without Great Britain as a Mother Country. Finally, fighting broke out between colonists and British soldiers in 1775. This was the start of the American Revolution. A **revolution** is a change of government by force.

Some colonists, to protest English taxes on tea, disguised themselves as Native Americans and dumped tea into Boston Harbor.

The idea of breaking away from Great Britain divided the American colonists. Many colonists believed that they should become independent from England. They called themselves **patriots.** Among the patriots were farmers and settlers who had come to New York from countries other than England. A large number of African Americans, both free and enslaved, also supported the patriots. Those who were enslaved hoped to gain their freedom if the colonists became independent. Two of the six Iroquois nations also supported the patriots.

Other colonists opposed the idea of independence from Great Britain. They were known as **loyalists** or **Tories.** New York had more active loyalists than any other colony. While these people opposed many of the new taxes, they still believed New York was better off under British rule. Among the loyalists were wealthy business people, rich farmers and large landowners. The British offered freedom to any slaves who fought on their side. This convinced many enslaved Africans to fight on the side of the British. In addition, four of the six Iroquois nations supported the British.

THE IDEA OF INDEPENDENCE GROWS

Protests turned to warfare when shots were fired between British soldiers and colonists at Concord, Massachusetts in 1775. Fighting quickly spread to the other colonies. Leaders from all 13 colonies called a meeting of the **Continental Congress** in Philadelphia. After much debate, they decided to declare their independence from Great Britain.

Fighting broke out between American colonists and English soldiers in Massachusetts in 1775.

▶   A committee was chosen to write a **Declaration of Independence**. Thomas Jefferson was the main author. This document explained to the world why the colonists sought independence from Great Britain.

Historic Documents: *The Declaration of Independence*

The Declaration of Independence laid the foundation for the United States to become the first democratic nation in modern times. It also served as an inspiration to later generations. The first paragraph of the Declaration, issued on **July 4, 1776,** stated:

The Declaration of Independence

We hold these truths to be self-evident [obvious], that all men are created equal, that they are endowed [given] by their Creator [God] with certain unalienable [cannot be taken away] rights, that among these are life, liberty and the pursuit of happiness. That to secure [protect] these rights, governments are instituted [created] among Men, deriving [getting] their just powers from the consent of the governed; that whenever any form of government becomes destructive [harmful] of these ends, it is the right of the people to alter [change] or abolish [end] it, and to institute new government …

Sometimes, words written over 200 years ago are hard to understand. Let's see how well you understand this document by answering the following questions:

1. What do you think the writers meant by the following words or phrases?

   ❖ "All men are created equal"   ❖ "Unalienable rights"
   ❖ "Liberty"   ❖ "Pursuit of happiness"

2. The second sentence of the Declaration explains why governments are created.

   ❖ Can you explain the writers' position in your own words? Do you agree?

NEW YORK'S ROLE IN THE AMERICAN REVOLUTION

As you read, look for answers to the following questions:

1. Why did the British and the colonists believe that New York was an important place to control at the time of the American Revolution?

2. Why has the Battle of Saratoga been called the "turning point" of the American Revolution?

Some of the earliest battles of the Revolution were fought in upstate New York. The colonists hoped to attack British Canada from New York. **Fort Ticonderoga,** located at the southern end of Lake Champlain, controlled travel between Quebec and the American colonies. In May 1775, a group of colonists from Vermont, known as the Green Mountain Boys, entered northern New York. Led by **Ethan Allen,** they captured the fort. Later, the fort was recaptured by the British and held by them until 1777.

The capture of Fort Ticonderoga

British troops left New York City in 1775. In April 1776, General **George Washington** led the colonial army into the city. Washington built fortifications in various sections of the city. In August, British troops attacked Washington's forces at Brooklyn Heights in the **Battle of Long Island.** Washington soon had to retreat. He moved his army across the East River from Brooklyn to Manhattan.

During the next two months, Washington faced the British again at Harlem Heights and White Plains. Washington lost these battles and was forced to retreat up the Hudson and southward into New Jersey. The British took over New York City, which became their American headquarters for the rest of the Revolution.

George Washington commanded the colonial army against the British.

The location of New York, between New England and the Southern Colonies, made it important to control. The British thought they could divide the colonies in two if they could capture the rest of New York. They drew up a plan to send three armies through different parts of New York. The three armies were to meet near Albany.

THE BRITISH PLAN FOR TAKING NEW YORK, 1777

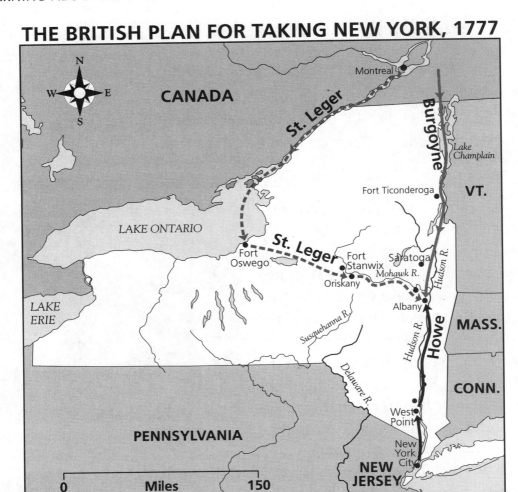

THE BRITISH PLAN	WHAT HAPPENED
One army was to be sent from Canada to Lake Ontario, under the command of **Colonel Barry St. Leger**. His army was to march east along the Mohawk River to Albany.	At the **Battle of Oriskany**, American troops under the leadership of **General Nicholas Herkimer** fought the British to a draw. Finally, additional American soldiers arrived and drove the British away.
A second army, under the command of **General William Howe**, was to march north along the Hudson River from New York City to Albany.	Instead of moving up the Hudson, General Howe decided to turn south to attack Philadelphia. Later, British troops began marching up the Hudson, but it was too late.
The largest army, commanded by **General John Burgoyne**, was to march south from Canada along Lake Champlain. Its mission was to capture first Fort Ticonderoga and then Albany.	At the **Battle of Saratoga**, American soldiers under the command of **General Horatio Gates** defeated the British. They captured five thousand British soldiers.

The Battle of Saratoga in 1777 was the turning point of the Revolutionary War. This victory prevented the British from dividing the colonies. It also convinced the French to enter the war to help the Americans. The French had been waiting for a chance to strike back at the British for their own defeat in the French and Indian War. With French help, the colonists won the war. In 1783, Great Britain recognized American independence.

British General John Burgoyne surrendered to General Horatio Gates after the Battle of Saratoga.
Why was this battle considered the turning point in the Revolutionary War?

During the American Revolution, more fighting took place in New York than in any other state. After the war, large numbers of New York loyalists fled to Canada. Other New Yorkers took over their lands. Another important effect of the war was the destruction of many Native American settlements along the Mohawk River and in the Finger Lakes region.

THE AMATEUR HISTORIAN: RECREATING THE PAST

1. **Creating A Picture Gallery.** Many of our national heroes come from the days of the American Revolution. What did these people look like and what roles did they play? Create a picture gallery of some of the key people identified with the American Revolution. To help you get started, make a copy of the following diagram.

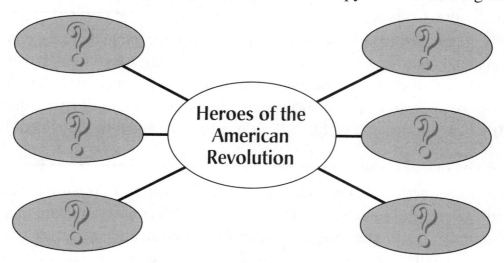

In each circle, paste a picture of a person active during the American Revolution. Be sure to include women and people of diverse backgrounds. Under each picture, write **one** sentence describing that person's role in the war.

❖ CONTINUED

2. **Mapping Battles.** Make a map showing the sites where major battles of the American Revolution were fought throughout New York State. You can draw pictures of soldiers from both sides fighting at various places. Use different colors for each side. Be sure to include the dates of the battles. Find out if any battles were fought near where you live, and be sure to include these battles on your map.

3. **Considering Other Points of View.** Imagine you are a British soldier sent to colonial New York during the American Revolution. Write a letter to a local colonial newspaper explaining the British viewpoint on the war.

REVIEWING YOUR UNDERSTANDING

Creating Vocabulary Cards

American Revolution
What was the American Revolution?
Why did it begin?

Declaration of Independence
What is the Declaration of Independence?
Why was it issued?

Making a History Collage

A **collage** is an artwork of several different pictures on the same topic. In this activity, you learned about New York's history during colonial times. Make a collage of some of the events that you read about. You can draw pictures or photocopy illustrations from history books or encyclopedias. For example, you might want to illustrate daily life in colonial America. For this, use pictures of different people and how they lived.

Creating a Historical Cape

You have probably watched television and seen Superman or Batman wearing a cape. Some people make "fashion statements" with capes. Select an event from this activity. Create different ways of showing the event. For example, use a picture of a person closely related to the event, or a date cut from paper to show when it took place. Create several items that tell a story about the event. Cut an old bed sheet into the shape of a cape. Spread out the fabric and decide how you will cover it with your items. Arrange the items on the fabric, then paste or glue these items onto the cape. To wear the historical cape, simply tie the top two corners around your neck.

ARE YOU A GOOD HISTORIAN OF EARLY NEW YORK STATE?

3C

In this activity, you will read about New York State from the time of independence (1776) to just before the Civil War (1860). Look for the following words:

▶ Articles of Confederation

▶ Age of Homespun

▶ War of 1812

▶ Erie Canal

In the previous activity, you learned how historians often try to understand what it was like to live in the past. In this activity, you will read about New York's early years as a state while you continue to play the role of an amateur historian.

A NEW STATE AND NATION ARE BORN

At the end of the American Revolution, many New Yorkers celebrated their victory over the British. However, becoming a new state in an independent country soon led to unexpected problems.

ADOPTING A NEW CONSTITUTION

As you read, look for answers to the following questions:

1. List two problems Americans faced in setting up a new government.

2. Why did Americans create a weak central government after the Revolution?

After the Revolutionary War, each of the former colonies became a separate, independent state. New York and the other new states each wrote its own state **constitution**—a written plan explaining how the government would work. New Yorkers adopted their first state constitution at Kingston in 1777. **John Jay** was the major author. That same year, **George Clinton** was elected as the state's first Governor.

The thirteen states also created a weak national government under an agreement called the **Articles of Confederation**. The new nation was called the **United States of ◀ America.** After their experiences with Great Britain, the former colonists did not want the central government to be too strong. Therefore, the states kept the most important powers for themselves—such as coining money, collecting taxes and raising an army.

Unfortunately, the new nation had so many problems in its first few years that Americans began to demand a change. In 1787, a convention met in Philadelphia and wrote a new constitution. This constitution proposed a stronger national government. There was to be a President, a Congress and a Supreme Court. In addition, the new national government would have the power to collect taxes, issue money and raise its own army.

In New York, there were heated debates about whether to approve the new Constitution. Some people feared the new national government would impose harsh taxes and would not respect people's rights. Other New Yorkers, like **John Jay** and **Alexander Hamilton,** argued that the United States would not last very long unless the new Constitution was adopted.

Eventually, New York and the other states all agreed to accept the new Constitution. **George Washington** was elected as the nation's first President. For a short time, New York City served as the nation's capital. Washington was sworn in as President at Federal Hall in New York City on April 30, 1789. John Jay became the first Chief Justice of the U.S. Supreme Court. Alexander Hamilton became the first Secretary of the Treasury.

Washington and his advisors:
[left to right]
Secretary of War Knox,
Secretary of State Jefferson,
Attorney General Randolph,
Secretary of the Treasury
Hamilton, and
President Washington

THE AGE OF HOMESPUN

> ### As you read, look for answers to the following questions:
> 1. What is meant by the Age of Homespun?
> 2. What caused the War of 1812 between the British and the Americans?

In the first years after independence, New York State grew rapidly. Many of the soldiers who had fought in the Revolution were paid with farmland in upstate and western New York. Many people from New England also moved to New York. Soon new townships sprang up with names like Rome, Ithaca, Syracuse, Buffalo, Rochester and Utica. By 1820, New York was the state with the largest population (*most people*). Almost one and a half million people called themselves New Yorkers.

▶ These years (1800–1850) are sometimes called the **Age of Homespun** . Pioneer farmers in western New York made by hand most of the things they needed for survival. They cleared forests, built their own homes and obtained their food by hunting and farming.

In the early 1800s, New York City benefited from a new war between Britain and France. Both countries bought goods and supplies shipped out of New York. However, as the war went on, the British began stopping American ships. This violated America's right to freedom of the seas. In 1812, war broke out between the British and the Americans. The conflict became known as the War of 1812 because it started in that year. ◀

   Much of the fighting during the War of 1812 took place in upstate New York. In 1813, British troops from Canada burned the settlement at Buffalo. Other major battles took place at Fort Niagara, Sacket's Harbor and Plattsburgh. New Yorkers rejoiced when the war ended in December 1814. American independence had been preserved.

THE AMATEUR HISTORIAN: RECREATING THE PAST

1. **Drawing a Poster.** Imagine that you are a supporter of the new U.S. Constitution. Draw a poster that you think would convince others to support it.

2. **Illustrating Yesterday's Fashions.** During the Age of Homespun, New York's farmers and workers dressed in a strong, loosely woven clothing of wool or linen. These fabrics came to symbolize their simple way of life. Using history books from your school or public library, find illustrations that show the way New Yorkers dressed in the Age of Homespun. Then make your own illustrations of these styles or your own article of clothing.

THE TRANSPORTATION REVOLUTION IN NEW YORK STATE

In the early 1800s, goods were moved in carts and wagons, and in sleighs in winter. The Appalachian Mountains were a major barrier to trade between the east coast and inland America. It became very important to have a good water route between the Atlantic Ocean and the Great Lakes, because it was much cheaper to ship goods by water. Building a canal to connect the Great Lakes with the Mohawk and Hudson Rivers was expected to greatly increase trade between both areas.

THE ERIE CANAL

> ### As you read, look for answers to the following questions:
>
> 1. Why did some people believe it was important to build a canal connecting the Hudson River and Lake Erie?
>
> 2. In what ways did the canal help to develop New York and the United States?

In 1816, Governor **DeWitt Clinton** of New York proposed that a canal be built between the Hudson River and Lake Erie. Farmers could then ship goods from the Great Lakes to New York City entirely by water. Some New Yorkers thought that the canal would be a waste of money. After long debate, New York State lawmakers voted to build the canal.

▶ Work began in 1817 and continued for seven years. Thousands of workers, many of them Irish immigrants, used hand tools to build the canal. The first section of the **Erie Canal** opened in 1819. The canal was 363 miles long, stretching from Buffalo to Albany.

The canal made huge profits from the tolls it collected. Farmers in the Midwest were able to ship their goods to eastern markets. The cost of shipping a ton of wheat fell from more than $100 to less than $5. Cities along the route, like Buffalo, Rochester, Syracuse, Rome, Utica and Albany, prospered as a result of the canal. The Erie Canal became so successful that lawmakers voted to widen it in 1835. Meanwhile, construction was begun on many smaller canals across New York to connect to the Erie Canal.

TURNPIKES, STEAMBOATS AND RAILROADS

> ### As you read, look for answers to the following questions:
>
> **1.** Describe some of the improvements in transportation that took place during the "Transportation Revolution."
>
> **2.** How did these improvements help the development of New York State?

The completion of the Erie Canal led many people to move to the western part of the state. Besides canals and rivers, people used roads. In the early 1800s, many private companies built special roads in New York called **turnpikes.** Carts, wagons, stagecoaches and riders on horseback paid a special toll to use these roads.

> ### ～   A NOTE ON TURNPIKES   ～
> Where does the name "turnpike" come from? Originally, owners of a section of a road used sharp pointed sticks, called pikes, to stop traffic. This allowed the owner of the road to collect a toll for horses and carriages that traveled along the road. Once the toll was paid, the owner would *turn* the set of *pikes* aside to allow traffic to pass.

PATH OF THE FIRST NEW YORK STATE TURNPIKE: 1815

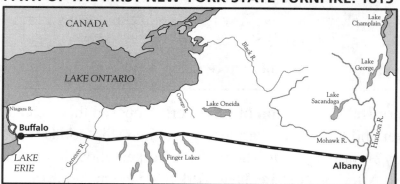

Another important improvement in transportation was the invention of the steamboat. For more than a thousand years, people had used wind to propel their boats or animal power to pull them. In 1807, inventor **Robert Fulton** used the power of steam to move a boat. His steamboat, called the *Clermont,* connected a steam engine to a large wheel with paddles that turned in the water.

Robert Fulton

Steamboats were powerful enough to travel up rivers against the strong current. Fulton began a service up and down the Hudson from Albany to New York City. It took about 32 hours to make the trip. Soon other inventors improved on Fulton's design. By 1830, steamboats were the leading method of water travel throughout the country.

Perhaps even more important than the steamboat was the invention of the railroad. Here, a steam engine was used to power "wagons" on fixed tracks. As early as 1828, the first American railroad started running in Baltimore, Maryland. Three years later, the Mohawk and Hudson Railroad began service in New York State. This line connected Albany and Schenectady. By the 1840s, railroads criss-crossed the state. The New York Central ran through western New York, parallel to the Erie Canal.

The Mohawk and Hudson Railroad in 1831

PATH OF THE ERIE RAILROAD: 1850

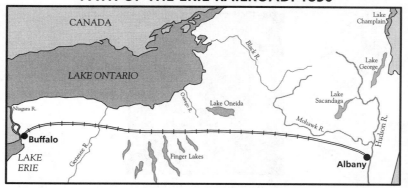

New Yorkers soon had many different ways to travel around their state. Cities along the routes of canals and railroads, like Utica, Syracuse, Rochester and Buffalo, continued to grow. Manufacturers in New York were able to ship their goods by canal and railroad to other parts of the nation.

THE AMATEUR HISTORIAN: RECREATING THE PAST

1. **Pretending to be Governor Clinton.** Look up the Erie Canal in an encyclopedia or history book. Find some of the arguments used by Governor Clinton for building the Erie Canal. Then, write a brief speech that would convince New York State lawmakers to provide money to build the canal.

2. **Completing a Railroad Map.** Copy the map on page 95, showing the route of the Erie Railroad. Using an atlas, write the names of as many cities as you can that are located along its route.

REVIEWING YOUR UNDERSTANDING

Creating Vocabulary Cards

Age of Homespun
What was the "Age of Homespun"?
When was it?

Erie Canal
What is the Erie Canal?
Why was it built?

Creating a Graphic Biography of Alexander Hamilton

Alexander Hamilton was one of New York's most famous people. He was a leader in the move for American independence and helped convince many New Yorkers to approve the new U.S. Constitution.

Alexander Hamilton

What other achievements of Hamilton can you add? Let's create a "visual biography" of his life. For each oval, describe and give the date of one of Hamilton's achievements or of an important event in his life.

HOW WOULD YOU "DIAGRAM" WHAT YOU READ?

3D

In this activity, you will learn about New York at the time of the Civil War. Look for the following important words:

▶ Main Idea   ▶ Reform   ▶ Abolitionists

▶ Supporting Details   ▶ Seneca Falls Convention   ▶ Underground Railroad

Although you have been reading for three or four years, have you ever thought about what a complicated process reading is? Let's look at this process.

> ***Describe what you do when you read something to find its main idea.***

Skill Builder

WHAT DOES IT MEAN TO READ SOMETHING?

When you read, you try to understand the meaning of a group of words. This takes time and practice. To do it easily, you need to develop special skills. This activity will help you improve these skills.

A "reading passage" is usually a series of paragraphs that deal with a common theme. Each paragraph will contain a ▢ **main idea** ▢. The other sentences usually give specific details, supporting or describing the main idea more fully. The following paragraph is an example:

New York has been a leader in educating its people for almost 200 years. During the state's early years, most children were taught at home. Where schools did exist, education was expensive. Children who could afford to go to church-run schools were often taught by untrained teachers. In 1812, the state legislature passed a law providing money for education and encour-

Erasmus Hall Academy in Brooklyn was one of New York State's earliest public schools.

aging towns to establish local school systems. By the 1860s, the state was a leader in the number and quality of its schools. At the same time, working class parents pressured the state into providing free elementary education statewide.

❖ CONTINUED

▶ Notice that the main idea of this paragraph, that New York State has been a leader in educating its people, helps us to understand what the rest of the paragraph is about. The other sentences are supporting details —*specific facts or examples* that explain or illustrate the main idea.

Many people find that a diagram helps them to better understand a reading. Let's see what this reading might look like if it were put into the form of a diagram.

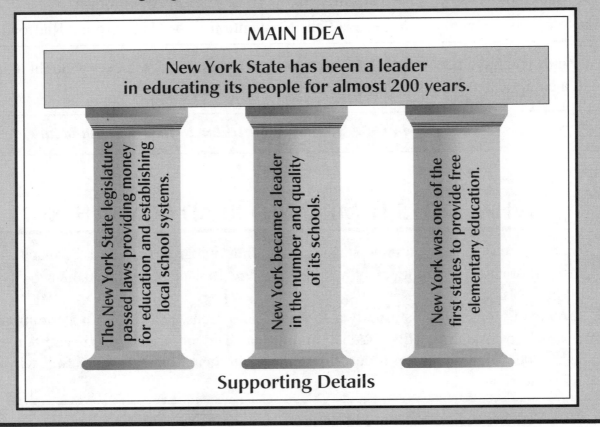

MAIN IDEA

New York State has been a leader
in educating its people for almost 200 years.

The New York State legislature passed laws providing money for education and establishing local school systems.

New York became a leader in the number and quality of its schools.

New York was one of the first states to provide free elementary education.

Supporting Details

Now it is your turn. Read the following passage about New York's struggle for reform. After reading the passage, you will create a diagram showing the main idea and three supporting details for a paragraph in the reading.

THE REFORM MOVEMENT IN NEW YORK

▶ In the early 1800s, several reform movements arose in America. To **reform** something is to change it to make it better. During this period, New York reformers focused on giving more rights to women, improving prison conditions and bettering the treatment of the mentally ill.

❖ CONTINUED

Rights For Women. In the early 1800s, women in New York and other states were treated as second-class citizens. They could not vote, attend college or enter many professions, such as medicine and the law. To protest these conditions, a group of women reformers met in Seneca Falls, New York, in 1848. Their meeting became known as the Seneca Falls Convention . Two of their leaders were **Susan B. Anthony** and **Elizabeth Cady Stanton.**

In July 1848, the delegates at the Seneca Falls Convention adopted a declaration. It stated that women should have equal rights with men. Here is how the declaration began. As you read, try to recall what other document it reminds you of.

Susan B. Anthony was an organizer of the Seneca Falls Convention.

Historic Documents: *A Declaration of Sentiments and Resolutions*

A Declaration of Sentiments and Resolutions

We hold these truths to be self-evident: that all men and women are created equal; that they are endowed [given] by their Creator [God] with certain unalienable [cannot be taken away] rights. The history of mankind is a history of repeated injuries on the part of man toward woman, having as its direct object [purpose] the establishment of an absolute tyranny [total power] over her. To prove this, let the facts be given to the world: He has never permitted her to exercise her unalienable right to vote. He has forced her to submit [give in] to laws she had no voice in forming. He has taken from her all right to property, even the wages she earns.

Prison Reform. Conditions in most of the nation's prisons were horrible. Prisons did nothing to help reform the inmates. Most city and county jails punished criminals by placing alcoholics, thieves and murderers together in one large room. Prisons were often dirty and unhealthy. Some prisons required their inmates to keep a strict silence. Guards often beat the prisoners. Food was of poor quality.

In the 1830s, New York led the world in the effort to reform prisons. **Eliza Farnham** was the warden in charge of a women's prison in New York State. She believed in treating prisoners fairly. She allowed prisoners to talk, ending the rule of strict silence. She opened a prison library and even established a school inside the prison to teach the inmates to read and write.

❖ CONTINUED

Improved Treatment For Mental Illness. In the 1800s, most people lacked the knowledge they needed to care for those with mental illnesses properly. Many mentally ill patients were locked in unheated rooms, chained to their beds and beaten into obedience. Sometimes, mentally ill people were even sent to jail.

Dorothea Dix led the fight for better treatment of the mentally ill. New York became a leader in improving the treatment of these patients. In 1821, a center opened in Manhattan to care for insane patients who were poor. In Utica, mentally ill patients were permitted to work outdoors and to enjoy limited recreation. Some New York counties established separate buildings to care for those with mental illness. However, they had no medical treatment to offer. Major improvements in the treatment of mental illness were not to come for another century.

Your Task

COMPLETING A "MAIN IDEA" DIAGRAM

Let's look at the paragraph dealing with prison reform and convert it into a "main-idea" diagram. Make a copy of the diagram below, and fill in each part that needs to be completed.

MAIN IDEA

Conditions in most of the nation's prisons were horrible

Most city and county jails punished criminals by putting alcoholics, thieves, and murderers together in one large room.

?

?

?

Supporting Details

Sometimes you may want to diagram an entire reading passage, not just one paragraph. In this case, you can create a "reading map." A **reading map** divides the main topic of the reading into smaller and smaller parts. It puts the main idea in the middle and surrounds it with supporting details. Other details are then added to explain these points. Let's see how this is done by reading about New Yorkers and the struggle to end slavery.

NEW YORKERS STRUGGLE AGAINST SLAVERY

People who opposed slavery were known as `abolitionists`. Although slavery ended in New York in 1828, it still continued in the South. Many New Yorkers believed no person had the right to own another and that slavery was wrong. These New Yorkers fought against slavery in many ways.

One way New Yorkers fought against slavery was to try to persuade others to end it. **Frederick Douglass,** who had escaped from slavery himself, was New York's most famous abolitionist. In 1847, Douglass settled in Rochester. He soon started an abolitionist newspaper called the *North Star.* He used his talents as a gifted speaker to travel around the nation, speaking out against slavery.

A minister in Syracuse, **Dr. Samuel May,** led a group that rescued a runaway slave who was waiting in jail for his master to reclaim him. Later he was taken to Canada. **Arthur** and **Lewis Tappan,** brothers from New York City, were abolitionists who formed the American Anti-Slavery Society.

Many individuals took an active part in helping people to escape from slavery. They ran an `Underground Railroad`. This was not an actual railroad, but a way for enslaved African Americans to escape from the South. They traveled from place to place,

Frederick Douglass
What other abolitionists can you name?

A typical slave auction in the South
It was against such inhumanity that the Underground Railroad was established.

◆ CONTINUED

hiding in homes along the way, until they reached a place where slavery was illegal. Many slaves escaped to Canada, so that they could not be returned to the South.

During these years many New Yorkers acted as "conductors" of the Underground Railroad. They operated "stations" along the way where "passengers" could hide, be fed and receive fresh clothes. One such station was operated by **Gerritt Smith,** a wealthy New Yorker. One of the best known "conductors" in the Underground Railroad was **Harriet Tubman.** She escaped from slavery and settled in Auburn, New York. Tubman helped so many people escape through New York State on their way to Canada that she was called the "Moses of her People."

Your Task

COMPLETING A READING MAP

Let's see how this reading might look when put into a "reading map." Make a copy of the map. Then fill in each uncompleted part.

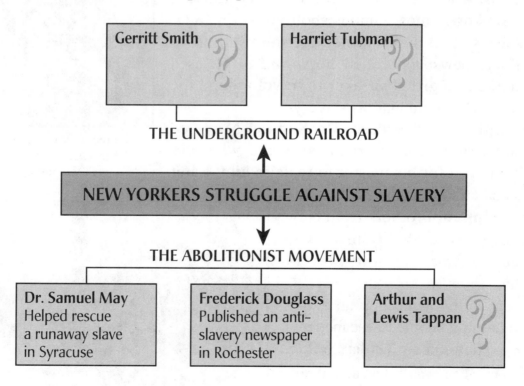

Now let's practice the technique of "mapping" with the final reading in this activity. Read the following passage and create a "reading map" to show how its main ideas are connected to supporting details.

NEW YORK IN THE CIVIL WAR

One of the most difficult periods in New York's history was the Civil War. The Civil War began shortly after Abraham Lincoln was elected President. Many Southerners feared that he would abolish slavery. Southern states broke away from the United States and formed their own country, the **Confederate States of America.** Lincoln refused to allow the nation to be divided in two. Fighting began in 1861.

In 1863, the U.S. government passed a "draft" law requiring men ages 20 and 45 to serve in the army. The law permitted a man to avoid serving if he could find someone to take his place, or if he paid a fee of $300. In July 1863, **draft riots** broke out in New York City protesting the law. Angry mobs attacked abolitionists and African Americans, believing that these groups had made the draft necessary.

However, New Yorkers played an important role in defeating the South. Of all the states, New York sent the most soldiers. Industries in New York helped supply the Northern army. With its larger size and greater resources, the North won the war in 1865. Slavery was abolished and the unity of the country was restored.

CREATING YOUR OWN READING MAP

Now that you have finished reading this passage, create your own "reading map" to show how its main idea and supporting details are connected to each other.

REVIEWING YOUR UNDERSTANDING

Creating Vocabulary Cards

Seneca Falls Convention
What was the Seneca Falls Convention?
Name two leaders at the Convention.

Abolitionists
What was an abolitionist?
Name two abolitionists from New York State.

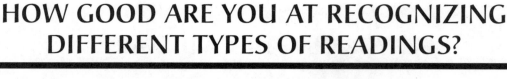

HOW GOOD ARE YOU AT RECOGNIZING DIFFERENT TYPES OF READINGS?

In this activity, you will learn about the Industrial Revolution and its effects on New York. You will also learn new ways to improve your reading skills. Look for the following important words:

▶ Industrial Revolution   ▶ Subway

▶ Urbanization   ▶ Tenements

It would be hard to recognize other people if we didn't know the general pattern of the human face. Knowing this general pattern helps us to detect slight differences in the features that make a person's face unique—the eyes, facial shape, hair color, nose and mouth. It is the same with reading. Although there are many types of readings, we can better understand specific types of reading selections if we recognize their general patterns.

Skill Builder

THREE TYPES OF READINGS: PROBLEM-SOLUTION, SEQUENTIAL AND DESCRIPTIVE

There are three major forms of reading passages: the problem-solution reading, the sequential reading and the descriptive reading. A fourth type, the cause-and-effect reading, will be covered in the next activity.

TYPES OF READING

Problem-Solution	Sequential	Descriptive
This type of reading identifies problems and describes some solutions. Key words in this type include *problem, recommendation, solution* and *result*.	This type of reading presents events in chronological order. Chronological order is the order in which events occurred in time. Key words in this type of reading include *later, before, after, next, following, then* and *preceding*.	This type of reading describes a person, place or event. The main idea sentence often states what is being described. The rest of the selection provides the characteristics of what is being described. Key words will usually focus on the *who, what, when* and *where* of what is being described.

In this activity, you will be presented with three reading passages. For each passage, you will need to identify what kind of reading it is and explain the reason for your choice. As you previously learned, it may help to **first** create a diagram of the reading.

THE INDUSTRIAL REVOLUTION COMES TO NEW YORK STATE

Information

READING SELECTION #1

The Industrial Revolution began in England in the late 1760s. It was called a "revolution" because it changed the way people made goods. Instead of working at home, people began to make goods in workshops and factories. New machines helped people to produce goods more quickly and cheaply.

The Industrial Revolution spread from England to the United States in the early 1800s. The first cotton factory in New York opened in the Mohawk Valley in 1809. In the 1830s and 1840s, the Erie Canal and new railroad lines brought cheap coal from Pennsylvania to New York. This coal provided fuel to run machines in factories throughout New York State. The same railroads and canals also allowed New York manufacturers to sell their goods to consumers throughout the nation.

In the 1860s, the Civil War created a great demand for clothing, uniforms and other supplies from New York. Following the Civil War, New York City became the nation's center for making clothes. Its workshops made coats, dresses, shirts, hats, furs, boots and shoes.

By the late 1880s, New York had emerged as the nation's leading industrial state. There were many reasons for this. The state's rivers, canals and railroads provided excellent transportation links with other parts of the nation. New York had an excellent harbor for shipping goods to Europe. Large numbers of skilled and unskilled workers lived in New York. So did many inventors and businessmen with new ideas. Lastly, New York banks had large amounts of money to lend to growing businesses.

New York City's excellent harbor helped New York State become a center of industry. *What other factors helped New York to become a leading industrial state?*

COMPLETING A DIAGRAM

Your Task

Make a copy of the diagram below. Then complete each part called for in the diagram.

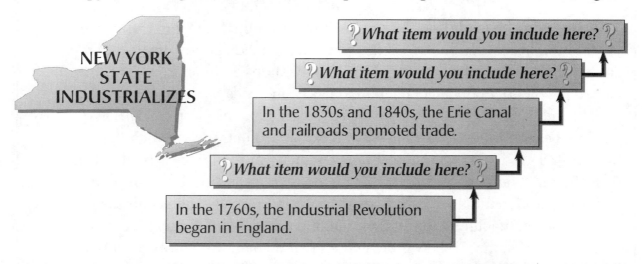

NEW YORK STATE INDUSTRIALIZES

What item would you include here?

What item would you include here?

In the 1830s and 1840s, the Erie Canal and railroads promoted trade.

What item would you include here?

In the 1760s, the Industrial Revolution began in England.

Identify the type of reading: ____?____ Explain your answer.

THE INDUSTRIAL GROWTH OF UPSTATE NEW YORK

Information

READING SELECTION #2

By 1900, the cities and towns of upstate New York were experiencing great industrial growth. To the north, towns along the St. Lawrence River specialized in making lumber and paper. On the Great Lakes Plain, Buffalo became known for its iron products. After the completion of the Erie Canal and the railroads, the people of Syracuse began manufacturing machinery, farm tools, and foods such as candy.

The Burden Iron Works factory in Troy

In the southwestern part of New York, Jamestown became a leading furniture center. Nearby, a successful oil well was drilled at Wellsville in 1879. Binghamton was linked by train to New York City in 1848.

❖ CONTINUED

It became known for its iron products and leather goods. The town of Corning, near Elmira, became home to a famous glass company in 1868.

Cities in the Mohawk Valley benefited from their nearness to the Mohawk River, the Erie Canal and several railway lines. In 1847, a woolen mill was built at Utica. The town of Endicott became known for rubber goods, photographic equipment and books. In 1911, a small adding machine company was formed there named I.B.M.— International Business Machines.

Buffalo's economy was booming in the late 1800s and early 1900s.

Two cities in upstate New York, Rochester and Schenectady, developed very special industries. Rochester, like New York City, was an early center for clothing manufacture. In the 1850s, **John Bausch** and **Henry Lomb** began producing optical goods there, such as lenses for eyeglasses and other uses.

In the 1880s, a Rochester bank clerk named **George Eastman** began a photography company. In 1888, he developed the Kodak Camera. To take a picture, all customers had to do with the Kodak camera was to click its shutter. The customer then returned the camera to Eastman's factory, where the film was taken out and developed. The Kodak camera was an instant success. Eastman became one of the

George Eastman

richest men in America, while Rochester became a national center for photography.

In 1889, **Thomas Edison** formed the Edison General Electricity Company with its headquarters in Schenectady. Edison developed the electric light bulb and many other inventions using electricity. In 1892, Edison's company became General Electric (G.E.), a leading manufacturer of electrical equipment. Today, G.E. is still one of the state's major employers.

COMPLETING A DIAGRAM

Now let's see how this reading can be presented in the form of a diagram.

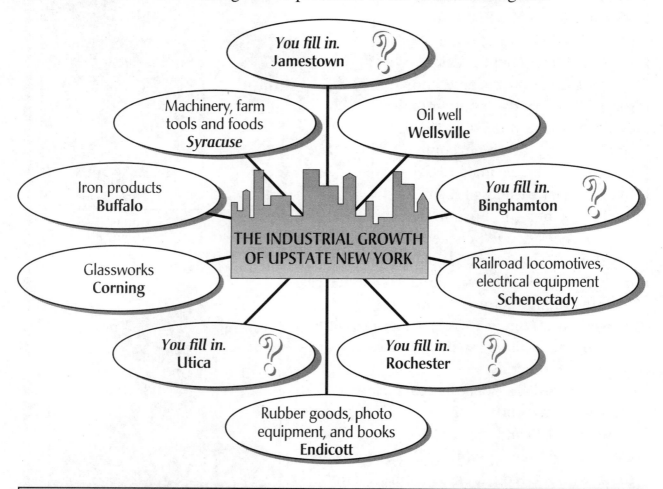

Identify the type of reading: ___?___ *Explain your answer.*

   You have just read how industrialization led to many important changes. New Yorkers were able to enjoy a greater variety of goods and services than ever before. More people began living in cities instead of in the countryside. People could travel by train, buy their clothes in stores, enjoy electric lights at night and speak on the telephone.

   These changes also brought problems. Industrialization created harsh working conditions for many laborers. They worked long hours and were barely paid enough to live on. The workshops and factories in which they worked were often uncomfortable and unsafe. Meanwhile, a few rich industrialists lived in great luxury and splendor.

These contrasts were felt most strongly in cities, where the very rich lived alongside the very poor.

Cities offered exciting opportunities for culture and entertainment. They had their own newspapers, universities, libraries, churches, theaters, and sports teams. Cities were the first places to have telegraphs, telephones, streetcars and electricity. People came to cities in search of work. Foreign immigrants poured into the cities of New York State hoping to find a better way of life. The movement of people into cities is called **urbanization**. The growth of cities is the subject of the next reading.

Broadway in New York City (1886)
What problems did industrialization create for New York's cities?

THE CHALLENGES OF URBANIZATION

READING SELECTION #3

The coming together of large numbers of people in New York's cities created many new problems. Some of these problems were physical ones: how could cities supply fresh water, transportation and housing to so many newcomers? Other problems were the growth of political corruption and the abuse of workers, which became widespread in urban areas.

As the state's largest city, New York City was the first to experience many of these problems. As early as the 1830s, the drinking water of New York was no longer safe. City residents suffered from cholera and other diseases spread by unhealthy water. To solve the problem, the city decided to bring in water from the Croton River to Manhattan. Even this proved insufficient, and the city began building a second aqueduct (*large water pipe*) in 1885. Later, more water had to be carried an even greater distance from the Catskill Mountains. Other cities faced similar difficulties. Rochester taxpayers, for example, had to be persuaded to construct city waterworks. The project was only begun following the Civil War.

A second problem faced by New York and other cities was the need to transport large numbers of workers each day. In the early 1800s, workers had to live close to factories or workshops so that they could walk to work. In 1830, the first coaches on rails were introduced. These coaches were pulled by horses. The horsecar soon became the main method for taking people to work. In the 1880s, **trolleys** (*electric streetcars*) replaced horsecars.

❖ CONTINUED

In New York City, streets were so crowded the city began looking at other ways to travel. The city constructed elevated railway lines, known as "els." However, the overhead tracks, noise and smoke created problems of their own. In 1900, an underground **subway** was begun in Manhattan. By 1930, New York City had the world's largest subway system.

A row of typical New York City tenement buildings

In the late 1800s, a third problem facing city residents was the need for housing. Builders designed special apartment buildings that could squeeze as many families as possible into a tight living space. These five-story brick apartment houses were known as **tenements**. Many lacked daylight, fresh air and adequate plumbing.

In 1890, the writer **Jacob Riis** exposed the miseries of life in the tenements. In his book, *How The Other Half Lives,* Riis discussed what life was like during the hot summer months:

Historic Documents: *From "How the Other Half Lives" by Jacob Riis*

With the first hot nights in June police dispatches record the deaths of men and women who roll off roofs and window-sills while asleep. The time of greatest suffering among the poor is at hand. It is the hot weather, when life indoors is nearly unbearable with cooking, sleeping, and working, all crowded into small rooms in the tenement. In the hot July nights, when the big buildings are like hot furnaces, their very walls giving out heat, men and women lie panting for air and sleep. Then every truck on the street, every crowded fire-escape, becomes a bedroom, preferred to any in the house. Life in the tenements spells death to an army of little ones. Sleepless mothers fan the brow of their sick babies. There is no sadder sight than this.

The growth of cities also gave rise to political corruption. Political "bosses" did favors for city residents to win votes. Then they used their control of city government to make money. In the 1880s, Governor **Grover Cleveland** introduced a civil service law to prevent dishonesty. Under the new law, people had to pass a test to

❖ CONTINUED

work in state government. Governor Cleveland also gave city mayors throughout the state greater power to appoint their own officials.

A final problem that affected cities was the poor treatment of workers. People worked long hours in dangerous conditions for low pay. Many workers were immigrants unable to defend their rights. Other workers were children. To prevent these abuses, the New York State Legislature passed a law in 1886 creating the position of state factory inspector. The state also outlawed some forms of child labor. In these same years, workers started to organize into labor unions.

Your Task

COMPLETING A DIAGRAM

The following diagram maps this reading.

NEW YORK'S GROWING CITIES

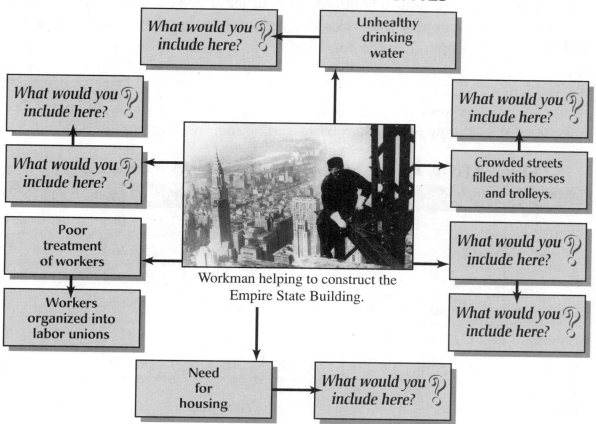

Workman helping to construct the Empire State Building.

What would you include here?

Unhealthy drinking water

What would you include here?

What would you include here?

What would you include here?

Crowded streets filled with horses and trolleys.

What would you include here?

Poor treatment of workers

Workers organized into labor unions

What would you include here?

Need for housing

What would you include here?

Identify the type of reading: ___?___ Explain your answer.

REVIEWING YOUR UNDERSTANDING

Creating Vocabulary Cards

Industrial Revolution

What was the Industrial

Revolution?

How did it change the way goods

were made?

Urbanization

What is urbanization?

Name two problems that came

about as a result of urbanization:

Writing a Letter

Pretend you are Thomas Edison or George Eastman. Write a letter to a member of your family explaining one of your inventions. In your letter be sure to describe what your invention looks like and how it works. Also discuss how you expect this invention to change the lives of people living in America.

Completing a Chart

The following chart shows some cities in New York State where large numbers of people live. Complete a copy of the chart by recording their present populations.

POPULATION OF SELECTED CITIES IN NEW YORK STATE

City	1865	1900	1920	1940	1960	Present Year
N.Y.C.	1,123,682	3,347,202	5,620,048	7,454,995	7,781,984	???
Albany	62,613	94,151	113,344	130,577	129,726	???
Buffalo	94,210	352,387	506,775	575,901	532,759	???
Rochester	50,940	162,608	295,750	324,975	318,611	???
Elmira	13,130	35,672	45,393	45,106	46,517	???
Syracuse	31,784	108,374	171,717	209,326	216,038	???

A. Find and identify each city on a map of New York State.
B. Which city grew the most in population from 1960 to today?
C. What factors do you think caused some cities to grow more rapidly than others?

WHAT EFFECTS HAVE KEY EVENTS HAD ON NEW YORK STATE?

3F

In this activity, you will read about the causes and effects of several key events in the history of New York State from the 1880s to the 1930s. Look for the following important words:

▶ Cause
▶ Effect

▶ Ellis Island
▶ World War I

▶ Depression
▶ New Deal

Have you ever seen the movie *Back To The Future*? In this film, the main character travels back in time. In doing so, he meets his mother while she was still a teenager. His sudden appearance in his mother's teenage life threatens to change events so that he will never be born. Such time travel into the past is fantasy, but part of the excitement of the film is that it reveals an important truth. If we could change even a single past event, we might change the entire course of history. Why is this so?

UNDERSTANDING CAUSE-AND-EFFECT RELATIONSHIPS

Skill Builder

Every event has some effects. Sometimes these effects can influence the entire future of a society. For example, a leader may decide that his or her nation should go to war. This decision can change the country's entire development. Historians often study the events of the past to better understand its cause-and-effect relationships.

❖ The cause of something is what made it happen. For example, turning on a light switch makes electricity flow to the bulb and lights it up. The cause of the light's going on was that someone turned on the switch.

❖ An effect is what happens *because* of a situation, action or event. For example, the light's going on was the *effect* of turning on the switch. Sometimes a single cause can start a whole chain of many effects.

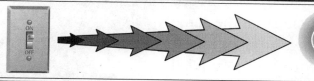

CAUSE
Someone turned on the switch.

EFFECT
The light went on.

In this activity, you will read about three events in New York's history. You will learn how each of them had both **causes** and **effects**.

IMMIGRATION

Between 1861 and 1914, almost 30 million people came from Europe to the United States. About 7 out of every 10 of these immigrants first arrived in New York City and passed through a government inspection station at Ellis Island .

This massive wave of immigration had several causes. Many people were escaping from religious persecution or terrible poverty. Jewish people in Russia, for example, came here to escape attacks on their villages by Russian soldiers and citizens. Italians came because there was not enough good farmland or jobs in parts of Italy.

Immigrants being examined at Ellis Island
What do you think the officials were looking for?

This increase in immigration to the United States had many effects. Until 1880, most immigrants were from Ireland and Germany. After this period, most immigrants came from Southern and Eastern European countries such as Italy, Poland and Russia. These immigrants were often Catholic and Jewish, and most did not speak English. They had little money and different customs.

To overcome these difficulties, the new immigrants often sought the friendship and protection of friends and relatives from the "Old Country"—the country from which they had emigrated. They moved into neighborhoods with names like "Little Italy," "Chinatown" and "Germantown." They went to churches and synagogues where they worshipped with people who came from the same country. Because they were in a new land, they felt comfortable surrounded by those who practiced the same customs and held the same beliefs.

Immigrants often lived with people whom they felt comfortable with.

❖ CONTINUED

Life was difficult for most immigrants. They usually took the hardest jobs at the lowest pay. Because they worked in factories and sweatshops, they crowded into cities to be close to work. The flood of immigrants into cities created a greater demand for city services.

Another effect of immigration was to add to the richness and diversity of American life. Immigrants brought new foods, music forms, arts, literature and ideas to the United States. Some of the immigrants were famous inventors, artists or performers. Others had special skills or a deep knowledge of their own culture.

A final effect of the great wave of immigrants was that it created new prejudices. Many Americans felt hostile to the immigrants. They believed that their own culture and background were superior. The immigrants often faced unfair treatment and discrimination. To stop the flow of immigrants, Congress passed laws in 1921, 1924 and 1929 establishing a **quota system.** This system set quotas or limits on the number of people who could come to America.

COMPLETING A DIAGRAM

If we put the information in this reading passage into a graphic organizer, this cause-and-effect reading would look something like this:

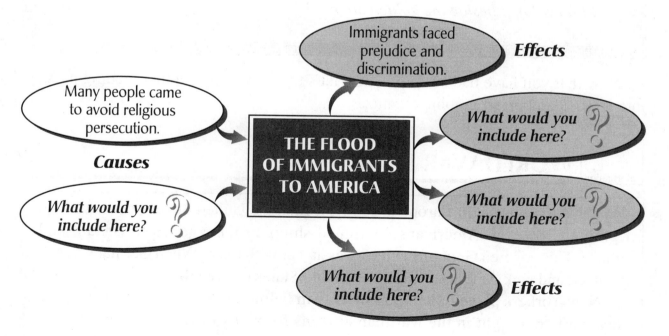

FAMOUS NEW YORKERS

Emma Lazarus (1849–1887) was born in New York City. As a Jew, she felt a close bond with the thousands of Jewish immigrants who fled Russia for the safety of the United States. She worked hard to provide immigrants with food, housing, job training and schools. In 1886, France gave the United States a statue to honor 100 years of American independence. Lazarus was asked to write a poem that could be sold to raise money to build a base for the statue. In 1902, her poem, "The New Colossus" was placed on a plaque at the base of the Statue of Liberty. The statue has stood in New York harbor for over a hundred years as a symbol of freedom and hope. Her poem was addressed to the world, and ended with these words:

The Statue of Liberty

> *Give me your tired, your poor,*
> *Your huddled masses yearning to breathe free,*
> *The wretched refuse of your teeming shore.*
> *Send these, the homeless, tempest-tossed to me:*
> *I lift my lamp beside the golden door ...*

Now that you have had some practice, let's try converting another reading passage into a cause-and-effect graphic organizer.

Information

WORLD WAR I

World War I began in Europe in 1914. At first, the United States kept out of the fighting. However, Americans continued shipping their goods to Britain and France. This angered Germany, which was at war with them. When Germany began to attack and sink American ships, the United States entered the war.

New Yorkers played an important role in helping to win World War I. More New Yorkers fought in the war than citizens from any other state. New York's

❖ CONTINUED

factories made goods for the army and navy. People cut down their use of fuel, despite cold winters. Many African Americans moved from the South to New York seeking to fill the large number of wartime jobs. About 14,000 New Yorkers were killed in the war. The war ended the great wave of European immigration to the United States.

Women demonstrating in front of the White House for the right to vote

The war brought other changes. In New York, voters approved a new law giving women in the state the right to vote. After the war ended in 1918, New Yorkers and other Americans turned away from trying to help foreign nations. In the 1920s, most New Yorkers enjoyed a period of good times known as the "Roaring Twenties." Industries in New York continued to grow. This growth produced new wealth and provided people with leisure time to enjoy music, sports and movies.

Your Task

COMPLETING A DIAGRAM

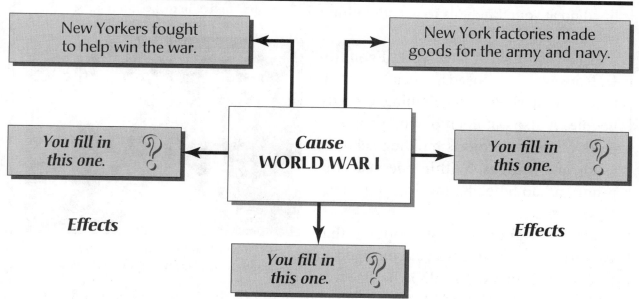

New Yorkers fought to help win the war.

New York factories made goods for the army and navy.

You fill in this one.

Cause
WORLD WAR I

You fill in this one.

Effects

You fill in this one.

Effects

Do you know the saying "practice makes perfect"? Practice converting one last cause-and-effect reading into a graphic organizer to be sure you fully understand it.

THE NEW YORK STOCK MARKET CRASH

In the **New York Stock Exchange** people buy and sell shares (*stocks*) of the nation's large corporations. On October 29, 1929, the price of stocks began to fall as many people started to sell their stocks. Soon people began to panic, afraid that their stocks would lose all their value. By the end of the day, stock prices had dropped tremendously. Hundreds of thousands of Americans had lost all of their savings.

The stock market crash had many effects. Companies could no longer sell stocks to raise money for expansion. People stopped spending except to buy necessities. Businesses were forced to shut down. People were thrown out of work. Soon the nation was in a deep economic **depression**.

In New York State, half a million people lost their jobs between 1929 and 1933. Many people could not afford to buy food. Some New Yorkers resorted to selling apples on street corners in an attempt to raise money to feed their families. Others lined up at soup kitchens to get something to eat.

During the Great Depression many families had to live in makeshift homes.

The Governor of New York, **Franklin D. Roosevelt,** proposed a special program to give food, shelter and clothing to needy people. It also put unemployed people to work on public projects building schools, roads and bridges. Within one year, the program had helped a million and a half New Yorkers.

This program was so popular that Governor Roosevelt was encouraged to run for President. In 1933, he became

President Franklin Roosevelt (*seated*) signs a New Deal program into law.

President of the United States. He adopted many of the ideas he had tried out in New York. Roosevelt called his program the **New Deal**. New government agencies were created that provided work for needy New Yorkers and others.

❖   CONTINUED

Between 1932 and 1937, over a billion dollars were spent on various programs in New York State. By 1938, most people were back at work. The worst of the Great Depression was over. The New Deal had restored self-respect to many Americans. The New Deal increased the size and power of the national government and made it responsible for managing the nation's economy.

COMPLETING A DIAGRAM

Complete the following cause-and-effect diagram based on the reading:

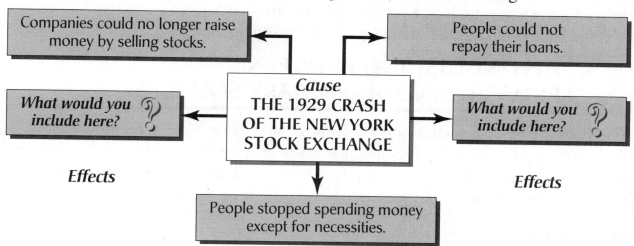

Companies could no longer raise money by selling stocks.

People could not repay their loans.

What would you include here?

Cause
THE 1929 CRASH OF THE NEW YORK STOCK EXCHANGE

What would you include here?

Effects

Effects

People stopped spending money except for necessities.

REVIEWING YOUR UNDERSTANDING

Creating Vocabulary Cards

Cause
What is a cause?
Give an example of a cause:

Effect
What is an effect?
Give an example of an effect:

Finding Causes and Effects in Your Newspaper

The events reported in our daily newspapers also have their own causes and effects. Choose any event described in a recent newspaper article. Create your own cause-and-effect chart showing the event, its causes and effects.

WHAT WAS IT LIKE LIVING THROUGH WORLD WAR II?

3G

In this activity, you will learn about New York State's role in World War II. Look for the following important words:

▶ Primary Source   ▶ World War II   ▶ D-Day
▶ Secondary Source   ▶ Pearl Harbor   ▶ Narrative Essay

A good historian is like a detective. A detective arrives after a crime has taken place. The detective then tries to figure out who committed the crime by looking for clues. He or she may interview witnesses, examine evidence and check facts. From these clues, the detective tries to put together the story of what really happened.

Skill Builder

DISTINGUISHING BETWEEN PRIMARY AND SECONDARY SOURCES

Historians are not involved in solving crimes, but they do try to figure out what took place in the past. Both detectives and historians look through many sources for clues to tell them what really happened. In this section, you will be challenged to act as a historian by looking at several sources. Historians rely on sources of two types:

PRIMARY SOURCES

▶ **Primary sources** are the original records of an event. They include eyewitness reports, records written at the time of the event, letters sent by people involved in the event, speeches, diaries, photographs or audio and video tapes. Most of the facts we know about past events come from primary sources.

> ✔ **CHECKING YOUR UNDERSTANDING** ✔
>
> Can you think of some other examples of a primary source?

SECONDARY SOURCES

▶ **Secondary sources** are the writings and viewpoints of an event presented by historians and other authors who did not experience the event. The author of a secondary source usually does not have firsthand experience of the event. Secondary sources, such as textbooks and magazine articles, provide summaries of the information found in primary sources. Historians often read these writings to learn about other historians' ideas.

✔ CHECKING YOUR UNDERSTANDING ✔

Can you think of some other examples of a secondary source?

Introduction

A TIME CAPSULE IS DISCOVERED

Imagine you and your classmates have been called to the principal's office. She says that La Guardia Elementary School is being torn down to make way for a larger building. Some workers have found a time capsule among the rubble. The principal explains that a **time capsule** is a collection of items buried in a container, to be opened by people living sometime in the future.

The principal knows that your class has been reading about World War II. She suggests that you look at the items in the time capsule. She hopes they will help the class to understand that time period. She proposes that once you finish examining the items you write a **narrative** (*a story relating an event*) about World War II. The principal reaches into the time capsule and pulls out the first item.

A LETTER

It is a note from a group of fourth graders, written over 50 years ago. Here is what it says:

December 20, 1944

Dear Citizens:

We are living at a time of terrible war. We are very concerned about the future. The trouble began when Germany, Italy and Japan came under the control of dictators. Japan attacked China and several other Asian countries. Italy invaded parts of Africa. **Adolf Hitler,** the Nazi dictator of Germany, arrested and murdered Jewish people and other German citizens.

Five years ago, in 1939, World War II started in Europe when Hitler and his armies invaded Poland. Soon, Nazi Germany controlled much of Europe. At first, we Americans kept out of the war. However, in 1941, Japanese planes attacked our ships at Pearl Harbor in Hawaii. This surprise attack brought us into the war. American troops are now fighting in Europe, Asia and the Pacific. The fighting is fierce, but Germany and Japan are slowly pulling back from their earlier victories.

New York's **Franklin D. Roosevelt** is our President. Over 900,000 New Yorkers have fought in this war. Our factories lead all other states in producing tanks, airplanes and other goods for use in the war. Women have been doing factory work and other jobs once held by men. The supply of gasoline, sugar, coffee, shoes and other goods is limited by the U.S. government. These controls ensure there are enough supplies for the army and navy.

This is a very hard period in our lives. We hope that when you read this, the world will again be at peace. As you examine each item in this time capsule, we hope that it will help you to learn what life was like for us growing up during this war.

Sincerely,

4th Grade Students of La Guardia Elementary School

✔ **CHECKING YOUR UNDERSTANDING** ✔

1. Is this letter a primary or a secondary source? How can you tell?

A DIARY

Inside the time capsule is a diary. A **diary** is a daily record of a person's experiences and feelings. This diary contains many interesting entries:

September 14, 1941. Two days ago a German submarine attacked the U.S. destroyer Greer off the coast of Ireland. In a speech to the American people, President Roosevelt compared Hitler to a rattlesnake. He has now ordered U.S. naval ships to escort all merchant ships across the Atlantic Ocean, and ordered U.S. ships to "shoot on sight" any German submarines they find. I fear our nation is moving closer to war with Germany.

December 8, 1941. Japan attacked Pearl Harbor yesterday with hundreds of planes. In less than two hours, 10 warships were sunk or disabled and thousands of U.S. servicemen were killed. President Roosevelt has called a special meeting of the U.S. Congress. It appears he is going to ask Congress to declare war on Japan. This will surely bring the United States into war with Germany too, since Germany and Japan are allies (friends).

May 9, 1942. President Roosevelt has ordered 112,000 Japanese Americans living on the West Coast to move to "internment camps." They must sell their homes, land and all belongings and immediately move to isolated sections in the interior of the United States where these camps are located. The government fears they will try to help Japan win the war. Some Americans believe people of Japanese ancestry are less loyal than other Americans. However, there is no real evidence to show this. In fact, over 71,000 of them were born in the United States like myself.

January 13, 1943. There are stories in the newspapers that Hitler is attempting to murder the entire Jewish population of Europe. The stories tell about concentration camps in German-controlled Europe. It is said that in these camps innocent people are killed with poison gas and their bodies are burned in huge ovens. The article said witnesses are reporting that there are millions of Jews, Gypsies, Poles and others being killed. More and more newspaper stories are calling this attempt to murder an entire group of people a Holocaust.

June 10, 1944. General Dwight Eisenhower, who commands all American troops in Europe, launched an invasion against Hitler several days ago. June 6 is being called D-Day. The radio has said that a fleet of 4,000 warships and almost 3 million soldiers are invading northern France. They plan to attack German positions. I pray that this attempt at liberating (freeing) Europe will be successful and put an end to Hitler's plans to take over all of Europe.

November 4, 1944. President Roosevelt's bid for re-election has been successful. His opponent was Thomas Dewey, the Governor of New York. Election results show that President Roosevelt has been elected to a fourth term as President of the United States. He is the first President to be elected four times.

✔ CHECKING YOUR UNDERSTANDING ✔

1. Is the diary a primary or secondary source? Explain.
2. What does the diary tell you about life during World War II?
3. What does the diary tell you about the writer's concerns and feelings?

PHOTOGRAPHS

Inside the time capsule are three photographs. Each photograph appeared in local newspapers in 1944 and was placed by the students in the time capsule to show something about World War II.

Photo #1

The Mochida family awaits
evacuation to a detention camp
in the center of the nation.

Photo #2

Women are at work in
an aircraft factory.
Factory lights are reflected on
the noses of the bombers.

Photo #3

Jewish slave laborers are
crowded into wooden bunks at a
German concentration camp
somewhere in Europe.

✔ CHECKING YOUR UNDERSTANDING ✔

1. Are these photographs primary or secondary sources? Explain.
2. What do these photographs tell you about life during World War II?

SONGS

Also included in the time capsule is a list of songs that were popular in the 1940s. Each song illustrates a different side of life during World War II.

(In the library, find the words to one of these songs.)

- ❖ Boogie-Woogie Bugle Boy of Company B
- ❖ There's a Star-Spangled Banner Waving Somewhere
- ❖ We Did It Before and We Can Do It Again
- ❖ Rosie the Riveter
- ❖ Cleaning My Rifle (And Dreaming of You)
- ❖ God Bless America
- ❖ He Wears a Pair of Silver Wings
- ❖ Praise the Lord and Pass the Ammunition
- ❖ The Sun Will Soon Be Setting on the Land of the Rising Sun
- ❖ Comin' In on a Wing and a Prayer

✔ CHECKING YOUR UNDERSTANDING ✔

1. Are the songs primary or secondary sources? Explain.
2. What does the song you looked up in the library tell you about life during World War II?

POSTERS

Americans not fighting in the war seldom had a chance to forget the battles going on overseas. No matter where they went, Americans saw posters to remind them. Each poster focused on some message that the government wanted to get across to its citizens. Two of these posters are found in the time capsule:

Poster #1	Poster #2

This poster encourages Americans to use less fuel, rubber, etc.	Americans should watch what they say; since spies could be anywhere.

✔ CHECKING YOUR UNDERSTANDING ✔

1. Are these posters primary or secondary sources? Explain.
2. What do the posters tell you about life during the war?

A CHART

Included in the capsule was a chart listing casualties in World War II up to May 1944.

ESTIMATED CASUALTIES IN WORLD WAR II

	Soldiers Killed	Soldiers Wounded	Civilians Killed
Great Britian	398,000	475,000	65,000
France	211,000	400,000	108,000
Soviet Union	7,500,000	14,102,000	15,000,000
United States	292,131	670,846	very few
Totals	8,401,131	15,647,846	15,173,000
Germany	2,850,000	7,250,000	5,000,000
Italy	77,500	120,000	100,000
Japan	1,576,000	500,000	300,000
Totals	4,503,500	7,870,000	5,400,000

✔ CHECKING YOUR UNDERSTANDING ✔

1. Is the chart a primary or secondary source? Explain.

2. What does the chart tell you about World War II?

WRITING A NARRATIVE ESSAY ABOUT WORLD WAR II

You and your classmates have finished reviewing the items found in the time capsule. It is now time to write a narrative essay about what life might have been like in the United States during World War II. Before you begin your narrative, it will be helpful to read the Skill Builder below.

HOW TO WRITE A NARRATIVE ESSAY

▶ **What is a "narrative"?** Narrative writing is used to *narrate*, or *tell*, about an event or a series of related events. In a narrative, the writer describes each event or detail as it happened in time.

When is narrative writing used? Narrative writing is used to tell a story as events unfold. For example, you might use the narrative form to tell about a historical event like World War II or an interesting day at your school.

Helpful hints. Start at the beginning and move step by step through the story. Stay on the point of the story and try to be specific. You don't need to write every detail that happened. Instead, focus on things that contribute to your theme.

REVIEWING YOUR UNDERSTANDING

Creating Vocabulary Cards

Primary Source
What is a primary source?
Give an example of a primary source:

Secondary Source
What is a secondary source?
Give an example of a secondary source:

HOW WOULD YOU OUTLINE THIS READING?

3H

In this activity, you will learn about some of the key developments in New York State in the past 50 years. You will also learn the skill of outlining. Look for the following important words:

▶ Outline
▶ Roman Numerals

▶ Suburbs
▶ Oral History

An **outline** is a brief plan in which a topic is divided up into different parts. The purpose of an outline is to show how a topic and its parts are related. An outline can also serve as a blueprint to help guide you through a reading.

Skill Builder

HOW OUTLINES ARE ORGANIZED

Outlines begin with general topics and then provide details. The major topics are numbered with **Roman Numerals** (I, II, III). If the topic listed by a Roman numeral needs to be further divided, its sub-topics are identified by **capital letters** (A, B, C). If these sub-topics need to be further divided, each smaller topic is given an **Arabic Numeral** (1, 2, 3).

Let's look at how this process of outlining works. Assume you want to create an outline about your own life. Here is what it might look like:

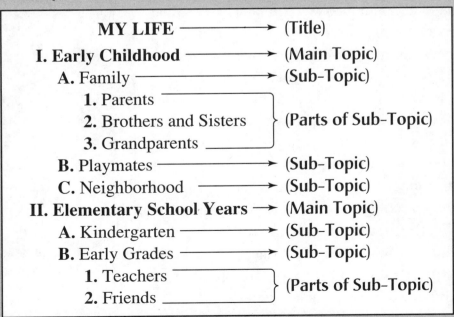

MY LIFE ⟶ (Title)

I. Early Childhood ⟶ (Main Topic)
  A. Family ⟶ (Sub-Topic)
    1. Parents
    2. Brothers and Sisters   ⎬ (Parts of Sub-Topic)
    3. Grandparents
  B. Playmates ⟶ (Sub-Topic)
  C. Neighborhood ⟶ (Sub-Topic)
II. Elementary School Years ⟶ (Main Topic)
  A. Kindergarten ⟶ (Sub-Topic)
  B. Early Grades ⟶ (Sub-Topic)
    1. Teachers
    2. Friends   ⎬ (Parts of Sub-Topic)

Notice that in this example, each smaller part helps us to understand a larger idea. For example, "Teachers" and "Friends" help us to understand the sub-topic "Early Grades." "Kindergarten" and "Early Grades" help us to understand the larger topic "Elementary School Years." This larger topic is one of the two main parts that make up the general theme of "My Life." Now let's look at a reading about the recent history of New York State. After reading the passage, complete the outline that follows.

NEW YORK IN THE LAST FIFTY YEARS

New York has undergone many changes since the end of World War II. Each decade (*10 years*) has seen new and important developments. During the 1950s, many New Yorkers moved out of cities and into suburbs. A **suburb** is a community outside of a city where many people who work in the city live. One of the first of these suburbs was **Levittown** on Long Island. After World War II, families could purchase a house there at a very affordable price—less than $10,000. This helped Long Island's Nassau County become the fastest growing county in the nation.

In the 1950s, New Yorkers became accustomed to new and better ways to travel. New highways were built linking cities around the state. The most important of these highways was the **New York Thruway.** The St. Lawrence River was widened to allow ocean-going ships to sail inland. Airlines introduced jet planes that could fly from New York to Europe in just a few short hours. New York's large airports became some of the busiest in the world. The **State University of New York,** begun in the late 1940s, expanded existing colleges in many cities. The new university system saw colleges grow in Buffalo, Albany, Ithaca, Stony Brook and Binghamton.

The 1950s also saw a new wave of immigrants arriving in New York City. Many of them came from Puerto Rico and Asia. Increasing numbers of African Americans moved from the South to New York. They settled in neighborhoods throughout Manhattan, Queens, Brooklyn and the Bronx. In 1959, Governor Nelson Rockefeller won approval to build the **Empire State Plaza** in the heart of Albany. The plaza consists of a large, central mall with several tall office buildings, an egg-shaped concert hall and reflecting pools.

Manhattan skyline at night. The 1950s saw many changes in New York State.

❖ CONTINUED

The early 1960s were a time of great prosperity for New York. New skyscrapers lined Fifth Avenue in New York City. During 1964 and 1965, New Yorkers celebrated their success by hosting the World's Fair. People visited pavilions representing many countries. The atmosphere changed in the late 1960s, when the nation became involved in a war in Vietnam. Many New Yorkers, and other Americans especially young people, opposed the war. One of the nation's largest rock and roll concerts was held in 1969 at Woodstock. Almost 500,000 young people attended this festival.

The 1970s were a time of economic difficulties for New York. Oil prices rose sharply. Unemployment began to increase. Many taxpayers moved out of the cities to the suburbs or to other states. State and local governments cut services, even though an increasing number of New Yorkers needed public assistance for food, clothing, medical services and housing. For the first time ever, New York State began losing

The "I Love New York" logo appeared throughout the nation.

both population and jobs. Buffalo saw more than twenty percent of its population move elsewhere. In 1977, New York launched its "I love New York" campaign to prevent the loss of more jobs and to restore tourism and a feeling of pride in the state. New York City began promoting itself as the "Big Apple." These campaigns were very successful. Tourism increased, becoming the state's second largest industry.

Nevertheless, the decline in the state's population continued throughout the 1980s. New Yorkers faced other problems as well. The state's forests were threatened by pollution and acid rain. In many large cities, people faced unemployment and inadequate housing. However, some things got better. Lake Placid, one of the two thousand lakes in the Adirondacks, became the site of the 1980 Winter Olympics. Race relations improved so much that Peekskill, once the scene of race riots, elected an African-American mayor in 1987.

In the 1990s, many rebuilding projects were started around the state. Rochester, for example, began reconstructing its downtown area to attract more businesses. Buffalo accomplished a major modernization of its transportation system. The city is now a center for medical, nuclear and aerospace research. Utica built a new business complex of offices and manufacturing plants just outside the city.

❖ CONTINUED

New Yorkers continue to enjoy many advantages that will help them during this new century. New York remains a world leader in finance, commerce, technology and the arts. Important companies like IBM, Kodak and General Electric continue to have their headquarters in New York. The state is rich in many natural resources. Its most valuable resource remains its people. The great diversity of talent that has marked the state since its early beginnings will enable New Yorkers to overcome their present problems and create a better future.

COMPLETING AN OUTLINE

Below is what this reading would look like in outline form. Notice that some items have been omitted. Make a copy of the outline. Then fill in the items that have been omitted.

NEW YORK IN THE LAST FIFTY YEARS

I. New York in the 1950s
  A. Many New Yorkers moved out of cities and into suburbs.
  B. New highways were built around the state.
  C. The St. Lawrence River was widened for use by ocean-going ships.
  D. *What do you think goes here?*
  E. *What do you think goes here?*

II. New York in the 1960s
  A. The early 1960s were a time of prosperity.
  B. *What do you think goes here?*
  C. *What do you think goes here?*
  D. *What do you think goes here?*

III. New York in the 1970s
  A. Oil prices rose.
  B. *What do you think goes here?*
  C. *What do you think goes here?*
  D. *What do you think goes here?*
  E. *What do you think goes here?*
  F. *What do you think goes here?*

IV. What do you think goes here?
  A. New York's population began to decline.
  B. *What do you think goes here?*
  C. *What do you think goes here?*

V. What do you think goes here?
   A. *What do you think goes here?*
   B. *What do you think goes here?*
   C. *What do you think goes here?*
   D. *What do you think goes here?*

REVIEWING YOUR UNDERSTANDING

Creating Vocabulary Cards

Outline
What is an outline?
What is an outline used for?

Suburbs
What are suburbs?
Where did they first develop in
New York?

Creating an Outline about Some of New York's Recent Governors

Let's practice your newly learned skill of outlining. Look over the following reading passage. Then organize it into outline form.

THREE NEW YORK GOVERNORS

The executive branch of the government is headed by the Governor. Since 1777, more than fifty people have held this office. Four of them even went on to become Presidents of the United States. Three of New York's most notable Governors during the last 50 years have been Thomas E. Dewey, Nelson Rockefeller and Mario Cuomo.

Thomas E. Dewey was Governor from 1943 to 1954. He led the state through the final years of World War II. He began the state university system (*known as SUNY*). Dewey began construction of the New York State Thruway and opened Idlewild Airport, now Kennedy International Airport. He ran twice for President of the United States, but lost the election both times.

Thomas Dewey

❖ CONTINUED

Nelson Rockefeller was the grandson of John D. Rockefeller, founder of the Standard Oil Company. He was Governor from 1959 to 1973. Rockefeller increased public services and expanded state facilities. Many of his programs led to greater spending and eventually higher taxes. He turned the state capital into a showcase by building the Empire State Plaza to house state government buildings. In 1973, Rockefeller become Vice President under President Gerald Ford.

Nelson Rockefeller

Mario Cuomo was Governor from 1983 to 1995. Cuomo provided additional social services, increased aid for education, and expanded environmental protection. Despite the demand of many voters to bring back the death penalty, Cuomo continued to oppose it. As New Yorkers struggled with high taxes and other problems, his popularity declined. In 1995, he lost his campaign for re-election to George Pataki.

Mario Cuomo

The outline has been started for you. Copy it into your notebook, and then complete it.

THREE NEW YORK GOVERNORS

I.   **Governor Thomas Dewey (1943–1954)**
    A. He led the state through the final years of World War II.
    B. *What do you think goes here?*
    C. *What do you think goes here?*

II. **What do you think goes here?**
    A. *What do you think goes here?*
    B. *What do you think goes here?*
    C. *What do you think goes here?*
    D. *What do you think goes here?*

III. **What do you think goes here?**
    A. *What do you think goes here?*
    B. *What do you think goes here?*
    C. *What do you think goes here?*
    D. *What do you think goes here?*

PEOPLE IN SOCIETY

**Native Americans:
The First New Yorkers**

A Puerto Rican Day Parade in N.Y.C.

Immigrants Arriving at Ellis Island

Do you like pizza, tacos or egg rolls? Each of these foods was brought to New York by a different ethnic group. An **ethnic group** is a group that shares traditions, customs, beliefs and ancestors. New York's many ethnic groups have created a colorful mix of cultures that makes New York State an exciting place to live. In this unit, you will learn something about the different ethnic groups that live in our state. This will help you to appreciate how each group has contributed something special and unique to New York.

WHY DO PEOPLE HAVE DIFFERENT CULTURES?

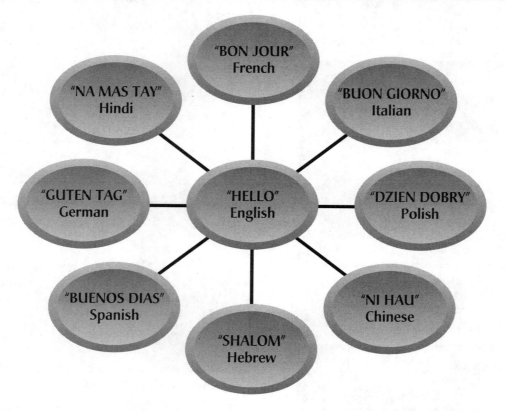

"BON JOUR" French

"NA MAS TAY" Hindi

"BUON GIORNO" Italian

"GUTEN TAG" German

"HELLO" English

"DZIEN DOBRY" Polish

"BUENOS DIAS" Spanish

"SHALOM" Hebrew

"NI HAU" Chinese

o matter how you say it, "hello" still means the same thing. Obviously, there are many ways to say any word. How did these differences in language and culture first come about?

One explanation for cultural differences can be found in a famous Bible story. Once upon a time, all people spoke the same language and followed the same customs. There were not many people, and they moved together from place to place. During their travels, the people of the world came upon a flat plain, where Iraq is now located. They settled there to build a city. First, they made bricks of straw and clay, which they baked to make them as strong as stone. With the bricks, the people built walls and buildings. After the city was built, they

decided to build a very high tower. People hoped the tower would be high enough to reach up to heaven.

According to the Bible story, God looked down from heaven on the people busily building the tower and became angry. God decided to stop them from completing the tower by making them speak different languages. Suddenly, people could no longer understand each other.

Unable to communicate, people stopped their work on the tower. Those who could understand each other joined together. God scattered these people with their different languages to the four corners of the Earth. Since that time, people have had different languages and different ways of life. The abandoned tower became known as the **Tower of Babel.** "Babel" came to mean confusing sounds and voices.

The people of the world speak a variety of languages. *Do you know how these differences in language first developed?*

This story is one attempt to explain how languages and cultural differences developed throughout the world. Other societies have also tried to explain the development of different cultures. The Iroquois, for example, believed that the Great Spirit gave corn to the Mohawks, squash to the Onondagas and beans to the Senecas. They believed these different gifts explained the differences in language and customs among these three tribes. The ancient Greeks thought that different cultures were inspired by different gods and goddesses.

Cultural differences are a fascinating part of human life. At times, cultural differences have led to conflict, while at other times they have brought about cooperation and the spread of new ideas.

How did different cultures come about? What role have cultural differences played in the development of our nation, state and community? The answers to many of these exciting questions await you in the following unit.

HOW WOULD YOU CATEGORIZE YOURSELF?

4A

In this activity, you will see how people often identify themselves with groups based on race, nationality, ethnicity and religion. This activity will help you to understand what each of these terms means. Look for the following important words:

▶ Race   ▶ Nationality   ▶ Ethnicity   ▶ Religion

To help you, the ▶ symbol will appear in the margin where the term first appears.

One of the things that makes the United States very special is its people. Each American is a unique individual, with qualities, talents and abilities that make him or her special. Yet each of us also has some things in common with other Americans. For example, some people share the same customs or religious beliefs. The characteristics that people share sometimes lead them to identify themselves as part of a group.

Introduction

HOW WOULD YOU GROUP YOURSELF?

In this activity, you will learn some of the ways Americans identify themselves. You will look at different racial, national, ethnic and religious groups. Before you start to look at other groups, let's first see how you might "group" yourself:

❖ What is your race?   ❖ What is your ethnic group?
❖ What is your nationality?   ❖ What is your religion?

Did you group yourself correctly? The answer really depends on how you define these words. Each of these words—race, nationality, ethnicity and religion—is a concept. A **concept** gives a name to things that, although different, have something in common. For example, the word "bird" is a concept. It applies to many different creatures: eagles, blue jays, ducks and chickens. However, all these animals share some common characteristics—they have feathers.

Information

HOW PEOPLE ARE OFTEN GROUPED

You have probably heard people use the words **race, nationality, ethnic group** and **religion**. How well can you define them? Let's take a look at each of these terms.

RACE

Over the course of time, human beings in different parts of the world developed slight physical differences. For example, some people have a light skin color; others have a darker skin color. Sometimes these differences are used to identify groups of people.

Most people identify themselves with a racial group. A **race** is a group of people ◄ who are identified by the color of their skin or certain other physical characteristics. The Census Bureau lists six groups in classifying Americans by race:

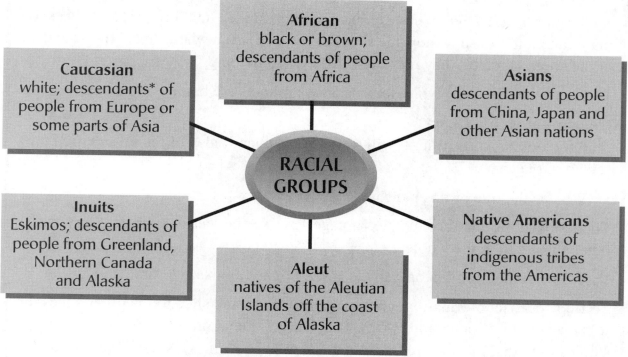

African
black or brown; descendants of people from Africa

Caucasian
white; descendants* of people from Europe or some parts of Asia

Asians
descendants of people from China, Japan and other Asian nations

RACIAL GROUPS

Inuits
Eskimos; descendants of people from Greenland, Northern Canada and Alaska

Native Americans
descendants of indigenous tribes from the Americas

Aleut
natives of the Aleutian Islands off the coast of Alaska

*people's descendants are their children, their children's children, and so on.

People from each of these racial groups have ancestors who came from different places. There are also many people who have mixed racial backgrounds.

> Which racial group (or groups) do you now think you belong to?

The United States is a **multi-racial society,** made up of people of many different races. The pie chart to the right shows the racial makeup of the United States in 1990.

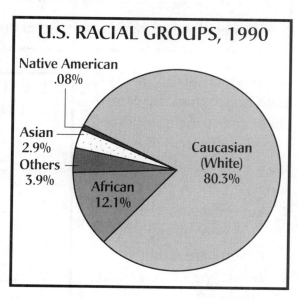

U.S. RACIAL GROUPS, 1990

Native American .08%

Asian 2.9%

Others 3.9%

African 12.1%

Caucasian (White) 80.3%

Having trouble interpreting the information in this pie chart? If so, you should read the following Skill Builder on interpreting pie charts.

Skill Builder

INTERPRETING PIE CHARTS

What Is a Pie Chart?

A pie chart (*or circle graph*) is a circle diagram, divided into different size slices. Its main function is to show how the slices are related to the whole "pie." If you add all of the slices together, they represent 100% of something.

❖ In the pie chart on the previous page, what items are being compared?

Interpreting a Pie Chart

Start by looking at the title. It will give you an overall idea of the information presented in the chart.

❖ What is the title of this pie chart?

Then look at the slices of the pie on page 137. See how each slice is related to the other slices and to the whole pie.

❖ What percentage of people in the United States are Native Americans?

To find specific information, compare the size of each slice to the other slices, or to the whole pie. For example, what is the largest racial group in the United States? You can see that the slice representing Caucasians (*whites*) is the largest—80.3%. Thus, the largest racial group in the United States is Caucasian.

❖ What is the second largest racial group in the United States?

The population of New York State is also made up of people of many different races. The pie chart to the right shows the racial makeup of New Yorkers in 1990.

❖ According to the chart, what percentage of New Yorkers are Asian?

❖ What percentage are Hispanic?

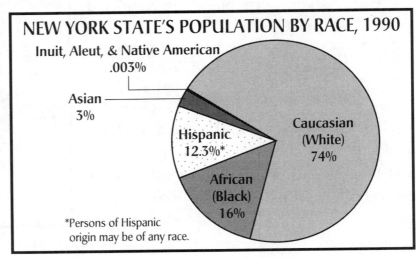

NEW YORK STATE'S POPULATION BY RACE, 1990

Inuit, Aleut, & Native American .003%

Asian 3%

Hispanic 12.3%*

Caucasian (White) 74%

African (Black) 16%

*Persons of Hispanic origin may be of any race.

NATIONALITY AND NATIONAL ORIGIN

The word nationality refers to the country in which a person is a citizen. For example, if ◀ you were born in the United States or became a U.S. citizen, your nationality is American.

National origin sounds similar to nationality, but it means something different. National origin refers to the country where your parents, grandparents or ancestors came from. **Ancestors** are members of your family who lived a long time ago, such as your great-grandparents. For example, the national origin of one of your friends might be German. A German American is an American whose family (*parents, grandparents, or ancestors*) originally came from Germany.

THINK ABOUT IT

When you go home, ask your parents where your family's ancestors came from. What do you think they will say?

ETHNICITY

Ethnic groups are people who have the same national origin, language or race. For example, African Americans are of the same race. Irish Americans have the same national origin. In the United States, people's national origin often forms the basis of their ethnic identity. People who trace their ancestors back to Italy identify themselves as Italian Americans because of their national origin.

People who speak the same language may also be considered members of an ethnic group. **Hispanics,** sometimes known as Latinos, form one of New York's largest ethnic groups based on language. Hispanics may come from or have ancestors from the Caribbean area, Central America or South America. Most Hispanics in New York are from Puerto Rico or the Dominican Republic— two islands in the Caribbean.

✔ CHECKING YOUR UNDERSTANDING ✔

1. What percentage of New Yorkers trace their ancestry back to Italy?
2. From which continent do most New Yorkers trace their ancestry?
3. What ancestry groups might make up the category "other"?

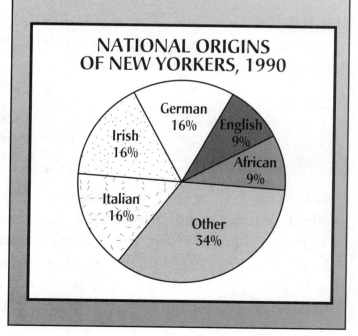

NATIONAL ORIGINS OF NEW YORKERS, 1990

German 16%
English 9%
African 9%
Irish 16%
Italian 16%
Other 34%

Knowing someone's ethnic group may tell us something about that person's way of life. It may tell us what foods the person prefers. We may also be able to guess something about that person's other customs.

However, we also have to avoid the dangers of **stereotyping** (*assuming all people from one ethnic group are the same*). Individual differences are often just as important as ethnic identity.

New York is well-known for its many ethnic groups. We see this ethnic diversity in the wide variety of foods New Yorkers enjoy and the kinds of music they listen to. How many restaurants in your neighborhood serve ethnic foods? Do you also have radio and television stations that broadcast in foreign languages?

A sign in different languages in a New York City neighborhood. *Do you know which ethnic groups live in your community?*

✔ CHECKING YOUR UNDERSTANDING ✔

Name **three** ethnic foods popular with New Yorkers:

Food	This food comes from .....
❖ _____ ?	❖ _____ ?
❖ _____ ?	❖ _____ ?
❖ _____ ?	❖ _____ ?

RELIGION

▶ Another way that people often group themselves is by religion . Most religions usually have the following in common:

a belief in God or several gods	a set of customs and practices	an organization, such as a church, which sets rules for its members

Many people came to America because they were not allowed to practice their religion in their home country. As a result, the United States became a nation with a variety of religious groups. New Yorkers are especially proud of their religious diversity.

Most Hispanics are Roman Catholics. In addition, most New Yorkers of Irish, French, Polish or Italian origin follow the Catholic religion. As a result, Roman Catholics makes up almost 40% of New York's population—the religion with the largest number of members in the state. There are also many Protestant Christians in New York. These include Episcopalians, Methodists, Lutherans and Presbyterians.

About half of all American Jews live in New York State. Jewish New Yorkers make up about 15% of the state's population. Most of them live in New York City and its surrounding suburbs.

Muslims, Hindus and Buddhists are some of the other major religious groups found in New York. Muslims are one of the state's fastest growing groups. Immigrants from Asia, Africa and the Middle East and their descendants are often Muslim. So are many African Americans who have converted to Islam. More than half a million Muslims live in New York today. Hinduism is another religion common among New York's population. Many Hindu families trace their origins to South Asia. New York's Buddhist population tends to come from East and Southeast Asia, especially China, Japan, Korea, Vietnam, Cambodia and Thailand.

A Muslim house of worship.
What houses of worship exist in your community?

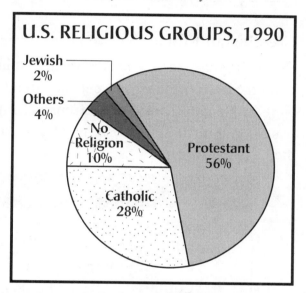

U.S. RELIGIOUS GROUPS, 1990

- Jewish 2%
- Others 4%
- No Religion 10%
- Catholic 28%
- Protestant 56%

✔ **CHECKING YOUR UNDERSTANDING** ✔

Name two major religious groups in New York State.
Name a religious group in your community.

Closing

REVIEWING HOW YOU IDENTIFIED YOURSELF

At the start of this activity you answered questions to "group" yourself. Review what you wrote when you began this activity. How would you now group yourself?

❖ What is your race?   ❖ What is your ethnic group?
❖ What is your nationality?   ❖ What is your religion?

REVIEWING YOUR UNDERSTANDING

Creating Vocabulary Cards

Race
Define the term "race":
Give an example of a racial group:

Ethnicity
Define the term "ethnicity":
Give an example of an ethnic group:

Creating an Ethnic Pie Chart

Every 10 years the Census Bureau conducts a **census**—a count of every person in the United States. In the 1990 census, about 1 out of every 11 persons surveyed said they were of Hispanic origin. The Census Bureau also asked Hispanics to group themselves based on their national origin. The following chart shows what Hispanic people told the Census Bureau:

HISPANICS BY NATIONAL ORIGIN: 1990			
Mexican	60%	South American	5%
Puerto Rican	12%	Dominican	3%
Central American	6%	Spaniard	3%
Cuban	5%	Others	7%

As you can see, about 6 out of every 10 Hispanics (60%) said they were of Mexican origin. This makes Mexican Americans the largest Hispanic group in the United States.

Often, converting information into a pie chart makes it clearer. Let's change this information into a pie chart. Make a copy of the circle to the right. Then take each item from the table and fill in its "pie slice." Use the markings around the circle to help you to divide the "pie." Each space between the marks represents 1% of the whole "pie." The pie chart has already been started for you.

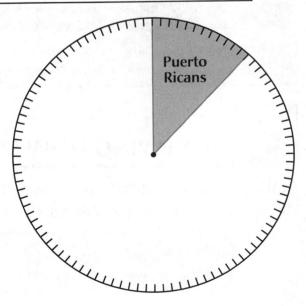

Puerto Ricans

WHAT GENERALIZATIONS CAN YOU MAKE ABOUT NEW YORK'S ETHNIC GROUPS?

4B

In this activity, you will learn about the different ethnic groups that have made New York their home. Look for the following important words:

▶ Generalization

▶ Harlem Renaissance

▶ Anti-Semitism

▶ Barrios

Generalizations are powerful organizing tools. They allow us to summarize large amounts of information in a more manageable form. In this activity, you will examine how generalizations are formed and practice making your own generalizations.

WHAT IS A GENERALIZATION?

Look at the following list:

❖ **New York City** borders the **Atlantic Ocean.**

❖ **Geneva** borders **Seneca Lake.**

❖ **Albany** is located on the **Hudson River.**

❖ **Buffalo** is next to **Lake Erie,** one of the Great Lakes.

It may be hard to remember all of these facts. But if you look at them as a group, you can see a pattern. These four facts about cities in New York have something in common. This pattern may actually be more important than any specific fact.

Rochester is located along the Genesee River.
What other cities are near large bodies of water?

THINK ABOUT IT

What do these four facts about cities in New York have in common?

HOW GENERALIZATIONS ARE FORMED

Skill Builder

The list shows that *major cities are located near large bodies of water*. This general statement describes what all of the specific examples have in common. When a general statement identifies a common pattern, it is called a **generalization**. Let's see how this generalization might be presented in a diagram.

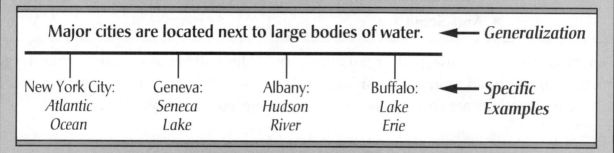

Major cities are located next to large bodies of water. ← *Generalization*

| New York City: | Geneva: | Albany: | Buffalo: | ← *Specific Examples* |
| *Atlantic Ocean* | *Seneca Lake* | *Hudson River* | *Lake Erie* | |

A generalization shows what several facts have in common. A generalization can also help us to make predictions. Each of the previous examples showed a major city next to a large body of water. We might now guess or predict that if we look at any other major city, it will also be located next to a large body of water.

Although generalizations are useful tools, we must be careful in applying them. For example, is our generalization really true for all large cities? Suppose we applied it to Las Vegas. If you look at a map, you will find that Las Vegas is **not** located next to a large body of water. This means we have to change our original generalization. Based on all the facts we now have, we can say that *many,* but not all, major cities are located next to large bodies of water.

When you are asked if a generalization is true, you must find specific examples and facts for support. Remember, generalizations are always subject to change as new information is learned. Now let's see how this modified generalization might look when presented in a diagram:

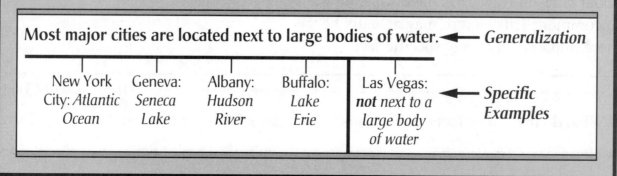

Most major cities are located next to large bodies of water. ← *Generalization*

| New York City: *Atlantic Ocean* | Geneva: *Seneca Lake* | Albany: *Hudson River* | Buffalo: *Lake Erie* | Las Vegas: *not* next to a large body of water | ← *Specific Examples* |

You have just learned how a generalization is formed and changed. How good are you at creating your own generalizations? Let's apply what you just learned to see if you can make generalizations about some ethnic groups in New York.

IMMIGRANTS COMING TO NEW YORK, 1820–1920

THE IRISH AMERICANS

WHY THEY CAME

Irish Americans came from Ireland, an island in Europe off the coast of Great Britain. Hundreds of years ago, the English established control over Ireland. English landowners took over most of the land in Ireland. Ireland only achieved its independence from English rule in 1921.

Some Irish came to New York when New York was still an English colony. After American independence, immigrants from Ireland began arriving in much larger numbers. Most of the Irish immigrants were poor, unskilled workers who followed the Catholic religion. They had few opportunities in Ireland. From 1820 to 1930, about $4\frac{1}{2}$ million Irish immigrants came to the United States, looking for a better way of life.

In 1845, a new disease struck the potato crop in Ireland. Since poor Irish families lived on potatoes, they had no food. During this period, more than a million people starved to death in Ireland. The potato famine in Ireland led to a massive increase in Irish immigration to the United States. Even after the famine, Irish immigrants continued to come to America in large numbers. By 1870, one out of every five people in New York City had been born in Ireland. The same was true of many upstate cities such as Troy.

THE PROBLEMS THEY FACED

Irish immigrants faced a series of hardships that began with their journey across the Atlantic Ocean. On the overcrowded sailing ships, diseases spread quickly among the passengers. As many as one-tenth of the passengers died on the voyage.

Although most Irish immigrants came from farms, they moved into cramped and unsanitary tenements in cities like New York, Yonkers, Rochester and Syracuse. Since most of the Irish immigrants lacked money, education and skills, they often took work as laborers or as house servants. One of the most serious problems that Irish immigrants faced was ethnic prejudice. Many native New Yorkers discriminated against them because of their Catholic religion. Employers often would not hire Irish immigrants. To deal with these problems, Irish Americans formed their own societies, such as the Ancient Order of Hibernians and the United Irish Counties Association, to help each other. They published their own newspapers, started their own community libraries, and found support from the local Catholic Church.

CONTRIBUTIONS OF THE IRISH

Irish Americans made many important contributions to New York. Irish workers helped build the Erie Canal and the railroads that made New York economically successful. Irish Americans built St. Patrick's Cathedral in New York City. Irish-American politicians, like Robert F. Wagner, Robert F. Kennedy and Daniel P. Moynihan, worked to improve the lives of all New Yorkers. Irish folk music and theater enriched New York's entertainment scene. Some Irish New Yorkers, like James Cagney, became famous movie stars.

Young girls participating in a St. Patrick's Day celebration in upstate New York

ST. PATRICK'S DAY

St. Patrick is honored as the saint who brought Christianity to Ireland. Many Irish Americans celebrate March 17—**St. Patrick's Day**—with a parade. In New York it is a time when bands play and politicians march up Fifth Avenue. Students from all over New York head to Manhattan to take part in the parade.

✔ CHECKING YOUR UNDERSTANDING ✔

1. Why did the Irish immigrants come to America?
2. What problems did Irish immigrants face?
3. What contributions have Irish Americans made to American society?

Information

THE ITALIAN AMERICANS

WHY THEY CAME

Italy is a country in Southern Europe. Very few Italians emigrated to the United States until the beginning of the 20th century. Then, between 1899 and 1910, almost two million Italian immigrants came to the United States. They came mainly to escape poverty. Italians were also attracted by transatlantic ships offering fares to America for as little as $10. Steamship companies made it possible for immigrants in America to buy tickets for relatives still in Europe. Many of the Italian immigrants came here to work and save money to buy land back in Italy.

THE PROBLEMS THEY FACED

The voyage across the Atlantic in the early 1900s was difficult, but it was far better than only a few decades earlier. Steamships were larger and faster than before, making the crossing in only six days. Most immigrants still lacked fresh air and natural light while living below deck, but the risks of dying on the voyage were now low.

When they arrived, most Italian immigrants moved into crowded and unhealthy tenements in the major cities of New York State, especially New York City. Most lived in communities with fellow Italians who came from the same village and spoke the same language. Here, the residents could feel comfortable speaking their native language and following their own customs.

Hundreds of immigrants stand on the deck of the S.S. *Patricia* on its Atlantic crossing.

Most Italian newcomers came from rural areas. They lacked money, education and skills. Most of them could not even read and write. In addition, they did not speak English. For these reasons many of them found jobs with Italian-speaking bosses. Italians soon replaced the Irish as the main work force on railroads, streets and other public projects. They also began to develop their own small businesses. Some sold vegetables from pushcarts, while others opened small shops as barbers or tailors.

A major problem that Italian Americans had to face was ethnic prejudice from native-born Americans. Some people disliked the language, unusual clothes and Catholic religion of the Italians. In addition, some American workers disliked Italians because they worked for lower wages. To overcome these problems, Italian Americans formed their own societies, such as the "Sons of Italy."

CONTRIBUTIONS OF THE ITALIANS

Italian Americans made many important contributions to American society. They enriched the arts and music of New York. They introduced many delicious new foods, from spaghetti to pizza. Mario Cuomo, Rudolph Giuliani and Alfonse D'Amato are Italian Americans who became major political leaders. Most important of all, Italians have contributed to a strong work ethic and an emphasis on the importance of the family.

COLUMBUS DAY

Italians enliven the state with their many festivals, such as the **San Gennaro Festival** in New York City's "Little Italy." **Columbus Day** on October 12th celebrates Italian accomplishments. The festival honoring Columbus is observed with parades and parties in many cities in New York State. People wear "Italian Power" buttons, and floats in parades honor a wide variety of Italian groups and accomplishments.

FAMOUS NEW YORKERS

Fiorello LaGuardia (1882–1947) was the son of an Italian father and a Jewish mother. Elected Mayor of New York City in 1933, in the worst year of the Great Depression, he became the first Mayor to serve three straight terms one after the other. He was one of the most colorful and popular Mayors in the city's history. During a newspaper strike he read comic strips over the radio to the city's children. As Mayor, LaGuardia fought corruption, modernized city government, balanced the budget and introduced improvements in health services, housing and recreation. LaGuardia Airport in Queens is named after him.

Fiorello LaGuardia

✔ CHECKING YOUR UNDERSTANDING ✔

1. Why did Italian immigrants come to America?
2. What problems did Italian immigrants face?
3. What contributions have Italian Americans made to American society?

THE JEWISH AMERICANS

WHY THEY CAME

The Jewish people who emigrated to the United States were united by a common religion, culture and history, rather than by coming from a single country. The first Jews arrived in New York as early as 1654. Up until the 1880s, most Jewish immigrants came from Germany. Between 1880 and 1920, over $1\frac{1}{2}$ million Jews left Russia and other Eastern European countries to settle in America.

In Russia, most Jews had lived in the countryside. They were not permitted to own land. Instead, they became craftsmen or traders, working as tailors, shoemakers or barbers. They spoke their own language, Yiddish, and had limited contact with other Russians. Beginning in the 1880s, the Russian government began restricting Jews even further. The government encouraged mobs to attack and sometimes to kill Jewish residents.

Jews fled Russia and other Eastern European countries to escape this harsh treatment and religious prejudice. They were attracted to the United States by news of American prosperity and religious freedom. In many cases, whole families emigrated. German steamship companies offered low fares to New York City, making it possible to emigrate.

THE PROBLEMS THEY FACED

The voyage across the Atlantic Ocean was unpleasant, but not as dangerous as fifty years before. The immigrants were usually crowded into bunks built in large rooms near the bottom of the ship. Many passengers became seasick during the voyage.

Jewish immigrants usually lacked money and did not speak English. But many of them knew how to read and write Yiddish. They often had other skills as well, like the ability to sew clothes. Many times they were recruited soon after they landed, to work making clothes in Jewish-owned workshops.

The lower East Side of New York City early in the twentieth century

A major problem that Jewish immigrants faced was their terrible housing conditions. Most moved into the large Jewish community in the Lower East Side of Manhattan. There they lived in their own world, much as they had in Russia. They spoke Yiddish, read Yiddish newspapers, bought goods from Jewish shops, and rented rooms or tenement housing from Jewish landlords. The tenements were extremely crowded. Hundreds of thousands of people were crowded into a few square blocks. Most tenement dwellings lacked fresh air or natural light.

Besides poor housing and working conditions, Jewish newcomers also faced religious and ethnic prejudice when they tried to leave their own neighborhoods and mix with other Americans. Prejudice against Jews is known as **anti-Semitism** . To ◀ overcome these problems, Jews often formed their own social organizations. They also found support from Jewish Americans already in New York for several generations.

CONTRIBUTIONS OF THE JEWS

Jewish Americans greatly enriched the life of New York. Jewish immigrants and their children became teachers, lawyers, bankers, doctors and artists. Among them were Irving Berlin, George Gershwin and Leonard Bernstein, noted Jewish-American songwriters and composers. Robert Moses, the son of German Jews, reshaped New York by designing Jones Beach and a network of highways and tunnels throughout the state. Two Jewish Americans who were important public leaders in New York were Governor Herbert Lehman and New York City Mayor Ed Koch.

SALUTE TO ISRAEL PARADE

On the first Sunday of each June, New York's Jewish population celebrates Israel's independence with a **Salute to Israel Parade.** New York's Jews use the parade to show their support for fellow Jews around the world.

FAMOUS NEW YORKERS

Irving Berlin (1888–1989) was born in Russia. He moved to New York City in 1893. As a young man, he sang in the streets of New York City and as a waiter in Chinatown. His first hit was *Alexander's Ragtime Band.* Berlin went on to write the words and music to over 1,500 songs. He also wrote songs for Broadway musicals and Hollywood films. Several of his musicals were made into movies. His most popular songs include *God Bless America, White Christmas* and *There's No Business Like Show Business.* He was awarded the Medal of Freedom in 1977 by President Ford.

Irving Berlin

✔ **CHECKING YOUR UNDERSTANDING** ✔

1. Why did Jewish immigrants come to America?
2. What problems did Jewish immigrants face?
3. What contributions did Jewish people make to American society?

Your Task

CREATING A GENERALIZATION

Can you think of a general statement that is true about all three of these immigrant groups? Recall that they all faced ethnic prejudice in America. Such a statement is a generalization.

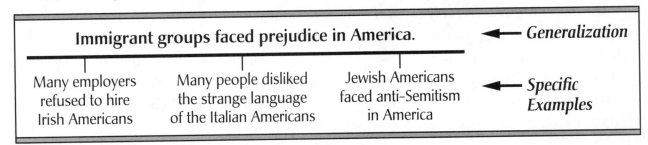

| Immigrant groups faced prejudice in America. | ← *Generalization* |

| Many employers refused to hire Irish Americans | Many people disliked the strange language of the Italian Americans | Jewish Americans faced anti-Semitism in America | ← *Specific Examples* |

✔ CHECKING YOUR UNDERSTANDING ✔

Can you make **one** other generalization about all three immigrant groups? Think about any other similarities between the groups. Write out your generalization using the following guide:

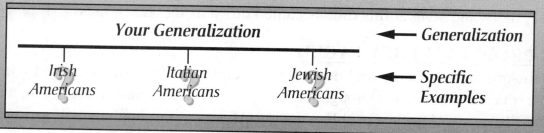

Your Generalization ← *Generalization*

Irish Americans   *Italian Americans*   *Jewish Americans* ← *Specific Examples*

From its earliest days, New York has been a popular destination for immigrant groups. You have just read about three groups that emigrated to New York from Europe in the 1800s and early 1900s. The period following World War I brought several other groups to New York. In the next section, you will learn about three ethnic groups that came to New York State in these years. One group, the African Americans, was already present in New York long before 1900. However, many more African Americans moved to New York after 1910.

MIGRANTS AND IMMIGRANTS TO NEW YORK, 1910–1990

Information

THE AFRICAN AMERICANS

Why They Came. Since colonial days African Americans have lived in New York. Between 1910 and 1930, a large number of African Americans living in the South began moving to New York and other Northern states. In the South, they had received little schooling and were often the target of violence. They also faced public **segregation** (*separate public facilities for people of different races*). Most were poor sharecroppers. A new generation of African Americans, many of them the grandchildren of slaves, sought to make a better life for themselves by moving north. They wanted greater freedom and a opportunity.

Many African Americans moved North in search of better homes and schools. Thousands left the South with only what they could pack in a suitcase or tie to a car.

In these same years, there was a great need for labor in the North. When the United States entered World War I, the supply of European immigrant workers was cut off. After the war, immigration continued to be limited by new laws. For the first time, many African Americans could find jobs in Northern factories. Many settled in Harlem, a neighborhood in Manhattan. A re-awakening of African-American music,
▶ dance, poetry and song at this time became known as the **Harlem Renaissance**.

THE PROBLEMS THEY FACED

African Americans who moved north faced many problems. Most arrived with little money, education or skills. Although their wages were higher than in the South, they still received low pay. Another problem facing African Americans was housing. Most African Americans lived together in separate neighborhoods. Landlords frequently over-charged them. They could not find housing in other parts of the city.

One of the most serious problems they faced was **racial discrimination.** This means prejudice against someone because of race. African Americans were frequently refused jobs and were prevented from buying homes in many areas. As a result, they often experienced greater unemployment and poverty than some other groups in New York.

ADJUSTING TO LIFE IN NEW YORK

To deal with some of these problems, African Americans often formed their own neighborhood churches. As early as 1776, the first black church in New York was started. More recently, African Americans took other steps to fight discrimination. In the late 1930s, Adam Clayton Powell, Jr. organized African Americans to **boycott** stores in New York that would not hire them. This meant they refused to buy from these stores. Eventually, the stores gave in to this economic pressure and hired black workers. Powell was the first African American to be elected to the New York City Council. He later became the first African American to head an important committee in the U.S. Congress. In the 1960s, African Americans organized the Civil Rights Movement to pass laws against racial discrimination.

CONTRIBUTIONS OF AFRICAN AMERICANS

African Americans have made many important contributions to New York. The Harlem Renaissance in the 1920s helped to re-awaken African-American pride in their culture. Langston Hughes wrote poems and plays about the black experience. African Americans have also contributed to the music, food, sports and politics of New York.

Black leadership of the Civil Rights Movement not only ended much of the discrimination against African Americans, but also encouraged new movements to end discrimination against women, Latinos, Asians, Native Americans, senior citizens and people with disabilities. Important African Americans from New York include former Mayor David Dinkins, baseball player Willie Mays, basketball star Kareem Abdul-Jabbar and Malcolm X.

David Dinkins was the first African-American Mayor of New York City.

AFRICAN-AMERICAN DAY

On the first Sunday in September, thousands of African Americans turn out for the **African-American Day Parade.** Hundreds of marchers move up the main boulevard in Harlem. Thousands of spectators line the streets as the parade moves along to the beat of African drums. Many of the marchers wear traditional African clothing such as a *dashiki*—an African-style shirt.

FAMOUS NEW YORKERS

James Baldwin (1924–1987) was born in Harlem. In 1947, he began to write about his experiences involving racism and segregation. In 1953, he published his first novel, *Go Tell It on the Mountain.* The story told of his difficulties growing up as a young child in Harlem. Baldwin also wrote *Notes of a Native Son* (1955), *Nobody Knows My Name* (1961), *Another Country* (1962), and *Blues for Mr. Charlie* (1964). His books helped make him an international celebrity. At his death in 1987, Baldwin was one of America's most popular novelists and an important critic of American society.

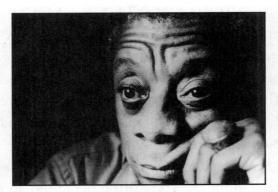

James Baldwin

✔ CHECKING YOUR UNDERSTANDING ✔

1. Why did African Americans come to New York?
2. What problems did African Americans face?
3. What contributions did African Americans make to New York society?

THE PUERTO RICANS

WHY THEY CAME

Puerto Rico is a small island in the Caribbean Sea, southeast of the United States. At one time, it was a colony of Spain. Because of Spain's influence, the main language spoken in Puerto Rico is Spanish. The United States took over the island in 1898. Puerto Ricans are American citizens and can travel freely to the U.S. mainland.

After the United States took over Puerto Rico, health care improved and the island's population grew. This eventually led to overcrowding and increased migration to the mainland United States. New industries opened in Puerto Rico in the 1940s and 1950s, but they did not create enough jobs. When the airlines introduced reduced fares to New York City, Puerto Ricans moved to New York in large numbers hoping to escape poverty and find a better way of life. Many came only for a short time, hoping to save money to take back to Puerto Rico.

THE PROBLEMS THEY FACED

Many Puerto Ricans arrived in New York with a background in farming and were unable to speak English. Men took low-paying jobs as laborers in factories, hotels and restaurants. Women worked as maids or sewed clothes in factories. Puerto Ricans competed with other groups for these jobs. More recently, the move of many manufacturing jobs out of New York City has hurt the Puerto Rican community. Unemployment and poverty remain serious problems.

► Many of the new arrivals lived in **barrios**, neighborhoods where Spanish was the main language. They often occupied some of the worst housing in the city. Landlords failed to repair many of these buildings. In the 1960s, Puerto Rican neighborhoods were often divided up by the construction of new highways and low-cost housing projects. Puerto Ricans also faced prejudice because of their use of the Spanish language and their different customs.

ADJUSTING TO LIFE IN NEW YORK

To deal with these problems, some Puerto Ricans formed neighborhood community groups. They published their own newspapers in Spanish. The Puerto Rican Association for Community Affairs and Puerto Rican Forum worked hard to promote a positive image and deal with problems. Some Puerto Ricans started their own businesses, while others promoted reform. They helped begin day care for working mothers, free health care clinics and free breakfast programs for poor children. Some Puerto Ricans started moving out of New York City to the suburbs and other parts of the state.

CONTRIBUTIONS OF THE PUERTO RICANS

The arrival of Puerto Ricans greatly enriched the culture and diversity of New York State. Puerto Rican cafés opened in different parts of New York City. Puerto Rican music was heard in night clubs and on the streets. The Puerto Rican Traveling Theater and Museo del Barrio encouraged a greater appreciation of Hispanic culture. Puerto Rican reformers like Herman Badillo drew attention to inner city problems and worked to improve conditions for all New Yorkers. Others, like talk-show host Geraldo Rivera and actor Raul Julia, became successful in the entertainment field.

PUERTO RICAN DAY

Puerto Rican Day, held on the first Sunday in June, is celebrated with parades, music and dancing. Puerto Rican politicians, celebrities and ordinary citizens march together up Fifth Avenue. The event has one of the largest turnouts of any ethnic parade held in New York City. Each year the number of participants increases.

The New York City Puerto Rican Day Parade

✔ CHECKING YOUR UNDERSTANDING ✔

1. Why did Puerto Ricans come to New York?
2. What problems did Puerto Ricans face?
3. What contributions have Puerto Ricans made to New York society?

THE KOREAN AMERICANS

WHY THEY CAME

Korea is a peninsula in northeast Asia. It is located in an area where China, Russia and Japan meet. Koreans have a unique culture, with their own language, history and traditions. At the end of World War II, Russian soldiers occupied North Korea, while U.S. troops occupied South Korea. Today, South Korea has a very successful economy and a democratic government. North Korea remains a dictatorship.

The first Korean immigrants to the United States were brought over by American missionaries. In the early 1900s, Japan conquered Korea. This led a handful of refugees to emigrate to the United States. By 1920, new immigration laws prevented Koreans from coming to the United States, except for a few who came to study at American universities. Many of them stayed here and became citizens.

In 1965, the United States passed a new immigration law that gave preferences to immigrants with skilled occupations and professions. This led to an influx of Korean doctors, nurses, accountants, chemists, engineers and technicians. Korean immigrants were often young. They came looking for economic opportunities and a better way of life. In a few years, tens of thousands of Koreans came to the United States. Many settled in New York.

THE PROBLEMS THEY FACED

The Koreans who arrived in the 1970s and 1980s faced fewer problems than earlier immigrants had. Instead of taking ships, they arrived in jet planes. Most were high school or college graduates. Many were professionals or managers. Although they spoke Korean, most had studied English in Korea. However, they did face the problem of starting a new life in New York. In addition, ethnic prejudice was directed against them by some Americans.

ADJUSTING TO LIFE IN NEW YORK

To overcome the problems of making a fresh start, many Korean immigrants moved to communities where other Koreans lived. This was especially true in neighborhoods of Queens like Flushing, Jackson Heights and Elmhurst. They formed religious and social clubs with other Koreans. They published newspapers and started radio and television stations in the Korean language. Many began their own businesses and professional organizations. These organiza-

Korean immigrants formed organizations to keep alive their heritage while in New York.
Wearing ceremonial dress, Korean dancers perform a traditional fan dance.

tions, such as the Korean-American Association, provided support and help to newcomers, enabling them to open shops throughout New York City.

CONTRIBUTIONS OF THE KOREAN AMERICANS

The Korean-American community is relatively new to New York. Despite this, many Koreans have become very successful. The enthusiasm and involvement that Korean American parents show for the education of their children is widely admired. They are well represented in the professions and in universities. Korean Americans continue to make important contributions to all phases of life in New York.

KOREAN HARVEST FESTIVAL

On the third Sunday of September, Korean Americans celebrate the **Korean Harvest Festival** at Flushing Meadow. Participants wear traditional Korean clothing and perform traditional dances with fans and masks. Martial arts experts give exhibitions as spectators browse through arts and crafts displays.

✔ CHECKING YOUR UNDERSTANDING ✔

1. Why did Koreans come to New York?
2. What problems did Koreans face?
3. What contributions did Koreans make to New York society?

CREATING ANOTHER GENERALIZATION

MAKING A GENERALIZATION ABOUT ETHNIC GROUPS

Can you make **one** generalization about the three ethnic groups that you just read about? On a separate sheet of paper, write out your generalization using the following guide:

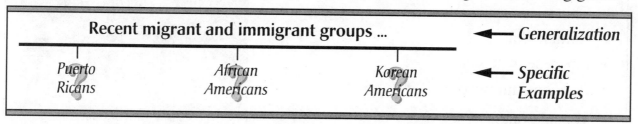

Recent migrant and immigrant groups ...   ⟵ *Generalization*

Puerto Ricans   African Americans   Korean Americans   ⟵ *Specific Examples*

REVIEWING YOUR UNDERSTANDING

Creating Vocabulary Cards

Generalization
What is a generalization?
Give an example of a generalization:

Harlem Renaissance
What was the Harlem Renaissance?
Name a writer of the Harlem Renaissance.

Finding Where Your Foreign-Born Friends Come From

Do you have any friends who are immigrants to the United States?

❖ Which country did they come from?

❖ Find the location of the country in a world atlas.

❖ What things do your friends remember most about their former homeland?

Learning about Immigrants

Would the generalizations in this activity be true of New York's other ethnic groups? Let's find out.

Your class should divide into groups. Each group should research **one** ethnic group from the following list:

❖ Pakistani Americans

❖ Greek Americans

❖ Indian Americans

❖ Chinese Americans

❖ Haitian Americans

❖ Japanese Americans

❖ German Americans

❖ You add one

After the groups complete their research, they should decide on one generalization common to both this new group and the six they have just read about. One representative from each group should then report the generalization to the class. Finally, the class should decide which generalizations would be true for all these ethnic groups as well as the six others you read about in this activity.

Many New Yorkers enjoy eating food from foreign lands.
What generalizations can you make about your ethnic group?

WHICH EVENTS WOULD YOU PLACE ON THE TIMELINE?

4C

In this activity, you will learn about and create a timeline using key events in history. Look for the following important words:

▶ Timeline

▶ Chronological Order

▶ Decade

▶ Century

Reading about history allows your imagination to wander back in time. It is exciting to read about the people and events of the past. Often, while important events are taking place in one part of the world, other important events are happening elsewhere. In order to see these connections, historians use a timeline.

Skill Builder

TIMELINES AND THEIR MAIN PARTS

A timeline is a type of chart. It shows a group of events arranged along a line in chronological order. "Chronological order" means the order in which the events actually happened.

A timeline can cover anything from a very short period to several thousand years. Its main purpose is to show a sequence of events. To understand a timeline, first look at its main parts—the title, events and dates.

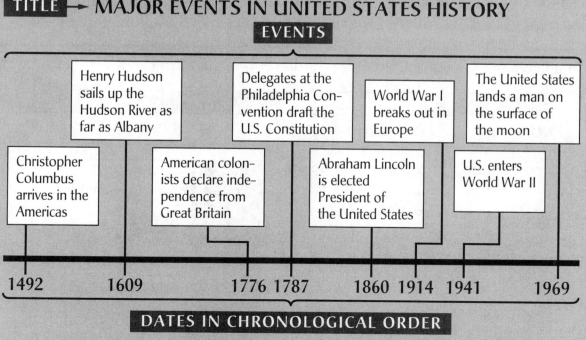

TITLE ➝ **MAJOR EVENTS IN UNITED STATES HISTORY**

EVENTS

Henry Hudson sails up the Hudson River as far as Albany

Delegates at the Philadelphia Convention draft the U.S. Constitution

World War I breaks out in Europe

The United States lands a man on the surface of the moon

Christopher Columbus arrives in the Americas

American colonists declare independence from Great Britain

Abraham Lincoln is elected President of the United States

U.S. enters World War II

1492   1609   1776 1787   1860 1914 1941   1969

DATES IN CHRONOLOGICAL ORDER

TITLE

The title tells you the overall topic of the timeline. In the timeline on page 159, the title indicates that the items listed are major events in the history of the United States.

✔ **CHECKING YOUR UNDERSTANDING** ✔

Selecting a title. A series of events are listed below. What title would you give a timeline that had these events on it?

- In 1777, **George Clinton** was the first person to be elected Governor of New York State.
- In 1817, Governor **DeWitt Clinton** successfully pushed the State Legislature to spend public funds to build the Erie Canal.
- In 1968, former Governor **Averell Harriman** became the chief U.S. negotiator at the Paris peace talks to end the Vietnam War.
- In 1973, **Nelson Rockefeller** stepped down as Governor of New York to become Vice President of the United States.

Governor Nelson Rockefeller

Your Timeline Title: _____?_____

TIMELINE DESIGN

On a timeline, the earliest event appears on the far left. The rest of the events are placed to the right of it, in the order in which they occurred.

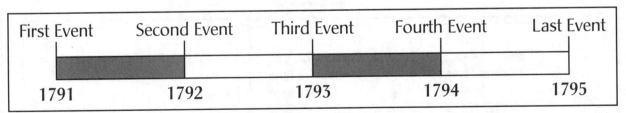

First Event	Second Event	Third Event	Fourth Event	Last Event
1791	1792	1793	1794	1795

Sometimes timelines are drawn up and down (*vertically*) instead of left to right (*horizontally*). In that case, the earliest event is usually placed at the bottom of the timeline. The rest of the events are placed above the first event, in the order in which they occurred.

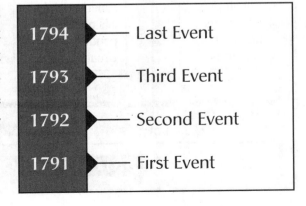

1794	— Last Event
1793	— Third Event
1792	— Second Event
1791	— First Event

PERIODS OF TIME

To fully understand timelines, you must also know about time periods. For short periods of time, you can divide a timeline into one-year intervals. For example:

For longer periods of time, you can divide a timeline into decades. A **decade** is a period ◄ of ten years. For example, the following timeline shows six decades of time:

An even longer period of time is a century. A **century** is a period of 100 years. For ◄ example, the following timeline shows seven centuries of time.

Now you try it. Make a copy of the timeline and put in the years from 1300 to 1800 by centuries:

How we identify centuries may seem confusing at first. The "20th century" means the 100 years from 1901 to 2000. The 1990s, therefore, belong to the 20th century. Let's see why.

1–100	First Century	201–300	Third Century
101–200	Second Century	301–400	Fourth Century

✔ CHECKING YOUR UNDERSTANDING ✔

1. Which century was 701–800?
2. Which century was 1501–1600?
3. What is the present century, 1901–2000?
4. What will the next century be called?

THE DIVISION OF TIME

In most of the world today, dates are based on when it is believed Jesus Christ was born. Although Christians developed this system of dates, many non-Christians also now use it. Dates are divided into two groups: B.C. and A.D. The dividing point is the birth of Christ.

❖ **B.C.** (Before Christ) refers to any time before his birth. Sometimes B.C. is referred to as **B.C.E.**—**B**efore the **C**ommon **E**ra.

❖ **A.D.** refers to the time after the birth of Christ. A.D. stands for the Latin phrase *anno Domini*—"in the year of our Lord." Sometimes A.D appears as **C.E.**—meaning in the **C**ommon **E**ra.

Writers always add B.C. or B.C.E. to a date before the birth of Christ. However, we usually do not bother to write A.D. or C.E. if the date is after the birth of Christ. For example, if the present year is 1997, we generally write 1997—not 1997 A.D.

MEASURING THE PASSAGE OF TIME

To measure the number of years from one date to another, just subtract the smaller date from the larger date. Assume the year is 1997. How long ago was 1500? By subtracting 1500 from 1997, we arrive at 497 years ago.

1997	(1997 years since the birth of Jesus)
− 1500	(1500 years since the birth of Jesus)
497	Years ago

✔ CHECKING YOUR UNDERSTANDING ✔

In 1825, the Erie Canal was completed in New York State. How long ago was that?

EVENTS

Each event on a timeline is related to the topic of the title. For instance, if a timeline has the title "The European Exploration of New York," Henry Hudson's voyage might appear as an event. Christopher Columbus' voyages should **not** appear, since Columbus never explored New York.

SELECTING EVENTS FOR A TIMELINE

Let's practice the skill of selecting appropriate events by choosing events for a timeline titled, "Key Events in the History of New York" **Hint:** Look for events that are related to the title. In the following list of events, you will notice that **not every** event is related to New York State history. Decide which events are related to the title of the timeline. Then, on a separate sheet of paper, make a timeline of these events in chronological order.

KEY EVENTS IN THE HISTORY OF NEW YORK

- ❖ **1989**   David Dinkins becomes N.Y.C.'s first African-American Mayor
- ❖ **1996**   The Summer Olympics are held in Atlanta, Georgia
- ❖ **1959**   The St. Lawrence Seaway opens, allowing ships to travel from Canada to the Great Lakes
- ❖ **1969**   The New York Mets win the World Series
- ❖ **1945**   An atomic bomb is dropped on Japan
- ❖ **1986**   Celebration of the 100th birthday of the Statue of Liberty
- ❖ **1952**   The United Nations building is completed in Manhattan
- ❖ **1992**   Bill Clinton is elected President of the United States
- ❖ **1911**   The Triangle Shirtwaist factory fire in N.Y.C. kills 146 workers

> **HINT:** Often you will have to list a date that falls *between* two dates on a timeline. For example, the year 1903 is between 1900 and 1910. Since 1903 is closer to 1900 (3 years) than it is to 1910 (7 years), you would place it on the timeline closer to 1900 than to 1910.

REVIEWING YOUR UNDERSTANDING

Creating Vocabulary Cards

Timeline
What is a timeline?
What are timelines used for?

Chronological Order
What is chronological order?
Arrange the following dates in chronological order: 1903, 1864, 1987 and 1745.

Making a Timeline about Your Life

A few events that happen during a person's lifetime often stand out. For example, your parents or grandparents may remember what they were doing in July 1969 when **Neil Armstrong** and **Buzz Aldrin** first stepped onto the moon. Think about the important events that happened to you in your lifetime. Choose the five most important events of your life and put them on a timeline. Make the first year the one in which you were born.

WHO WOULD BE YOUR NOMINEE TO THE NEW YORK HALL OF FAME?

4D

In this activity, you will learn about some of the many people who have contributed to the greatness of New York. Look for the following important words:

▶ Biography   ▶ Autobiography

New York Daily

Vol. 1.8 No. 21   First Edition

Geraldine Ferraro Nominated for Vice President

New York Daily

Vol. 1.8 No. 45   First Edition

Martin Van Buren Elected President

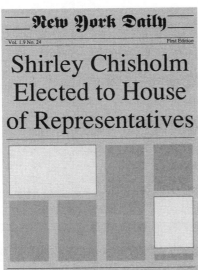

New York Daily

Vol. 1.9 No. 24   First Edition

Shirley Chisholm Elected to House of Representatives

New York Daily

Vol. 1.9 No. 73   First Edition

Walt Whitman Publishes his Book of Poems

THINK ABOUT IT

What do you think all of these newspaper headlines have in common?

WHO ARE THESE PEOPLE?

You may have heard the names of some of these people. Each of them is famous in some special way:

Martin Van Buren

❖ **Geraldine Ferraro** was born in Newburgh, New York. In 1984, she became the first woman ever nominated by a major political party as a candidate for Vice President of the United States. At the Democratic National Convention, Presidential nominee Walter Mondale selected her as his Vice-Presidential running mate.

❖ **Martin Van Buren** was born in Kinderhook, New York. He was elected the 8th President of the United States. He rose to the position of President after serving as a U.S. Senator, Governor of New York and Vice President under Andrew Jackson.

❖ **Shirley Chisholm** was born in Brooklyn. She became the first African-American woman elected to the U.S. House of Representatives. She served in Congress from 1969 to 1983.

Walt Whitman

❖ **Walt Whitman** was born on Long Island in 1819. Whitman's principal work was a book of poetry, *Leaves of Grass*. His poems celebrated nature, democracy and individualism. His freer style helped revolutionize American poetry.

QUALIFICATIONS FOR THE NEW YORK HALL OF FAME

Each of these individuals is unique. They come from different races, religions and ethnic backgrounds. However, they all have **one** thing in common—each one is a New Yorker who has made a lasting contribution to the development of New York State.

Many sports honor their best players in a Hall of Fame. For example, the Baseball Hall of Fame is located in Cooperstown. However, New York State does not have a Hall of Fame to honor its greatest citizens. Can you imagine if it did? Who would you recommend to include? In this activity, you will be asked to nominate a person to an imaginary New York Hall of Fame. Here are the qualifications for admission:

❖ Each nominee must have been born in or lived in New York.

❖ A nominee can come from any field—an athlete, scientist, inventor, politician, corporate executive, artist or writer.

❖ A nominee can still be living or be a figure from the past.

❖ A nominee must have done something that would be considered "great."

WHAT MAKES SOMEONE GREAT?

Notice the last item on the list of qualifications—"great." What does "great" mean? To help you answer this, you should create a list of criteria. **Criteria** are standards we use to evaluate something. For example, you might want to establish that the person must be well-known. If the person is not well-known, he or she would not meet your criteria for "greatness," and would not be admitted into the New York Hall of Fame.

Let's begin by creating some criteria for judging "greatness." Complete the first criterion by pointing out the letter of your choice. Then add two other criteria of your own.

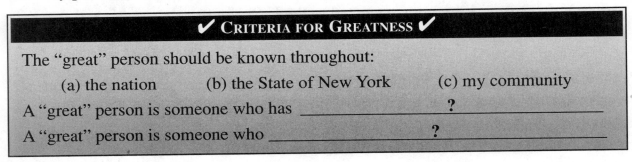

✔ CRITERIA FOR GREATNESS ✔

The "great" person should be known throughout:

    (a) the nation   (b) the State of New York   (c) my community

A "great" person is someone who has _____?_____

A "great" person is someone who _____?_____

RESEARCHING YOUR NOMINEE

Your first task will be to research your nominee. You can find this kind of information in a number of sources.

ENCYCLOPEDIA

Encyclopedias have articles about many well-known people. These articles are arranged in alphabetical order. The encyclopedia has guide words or letters on the spine of each volume. These guide words help you to locate the name of the person you are looking up. In more recent times, many publishers of encyclopedias have made their sets available on computer programs. In fact, many libraries now allow you to search a topic on the library computer.

BIOGRAPHY

A **biography** is a book about a person's life. A biography can be an excellent source ◀ of detailed information about a person. Some well-known people have had several biographies written about them by different authors.

AUTOBIOGRAPHY

Sometimes a person will write a book about his or her own life. This kind of book is called an **autobiography** . When reading an autobiography, you must remember that ◀ the person will usually build up the good things about his or her own life by exaggerating achievements. Likewise, the writer will usually play down any bad things.

Most libraries have entire sections devoted to biographies and autobiographies. They are not found on the library shelf by the name of the author. Biographies and autobiographies are listed in alphabetical order by the **last name of the person the book is about.** For example, a biography of Eleanor Roosevelt by Mary Wade would be under the letter **"R"** for Roosevelt and not under the letter "W" for Wade. You may also try searching the Internet for information about this person.

> ✔ **CHECKING YOUR UNDERSTANDING** ✔
>
> Where Would You Find .....
>
> 1. Under which letter of the alphabet would you look to find information in an encyclopedia about **Governor DeWitt Clinton**?
>
> 2. Under which letter of the alphabet would you look in the library to find a book about the life of **Peter Stuyvesant** by Len Hills?
>
> 3. Under which letter of the alphabet would you look in the library to find an autobiography by **Shirley Chisolm**?

Now you are ready to go to the library to research your nominee. On a separate sheet, complete the following Research Guide:

> ## NAME OF YOUR NOMINEE: _____
>
> ❖ **Source used:** Identify **one** source of information — the title of a book, the name of an article you read or the section of an encyclopedia you consulted.
>
> ❖ **Summary of the person's life.**
>
> ❖ **The person's major accomplishments.**
>
> ❖ **What makes this person great?**
>
> ❖ **Why should this person be in the New York Hall of Fame?**

REVIEWING YOUR UNDERSTANDING

Creating Vocabulary Cards

Biography
What is a biography?
What information is found in a
biography?

Autobiography
What is an autobiography?
How does it differ from an
biography?

Locating Information in a Book

Imagine you want a book about George Eastman. In the library you select the biography, *George Eastman: Inventor.* Suppose you want to find information about his invention of paper-backed film that replaced bulky glass plates. You could search each page of the book, but this would be too time consuming. Information in a book can sometimes be found by scanning the **table of contents.** This is found in the first few pages. It contains a list of headings, broken into chapters, and the pages on which they can be found. In the book about George Eastman, you might find the following section from the table of contents:

In which chapter would you look to find information about

1. how George Eastman invented paper-backed film?
2. the invention of the Kodak camera?
3. the year the company introduced color film for pictures?

ECONOMICS

**Members of the Cloak-makers
Union on strike (1916)**

Wall Street, 1852

**Consumer making a purchase in
Woodstock**

Economics is about how people earn money and what they buy. It is also about banks, factories, stores and farms, and how they work. In this unit, you will learn about the things that are needed to make goods and to provide services—natural resources, labor, and capital goods. You will also learn about starting a new business, conserving natural resources and trading with other countries.

PROFESSOR SMITH VISITS A FACTORY

The year is 1765. Adam Smith, a professor from Scotland, is wearing a handsome light coat, silk stockings, trousers that end at his knees and wide-buckle shoes. He has large eyes and his head shakes slightly when he speaks. He is visiting a factory to find the answers to several questions that confuse him.

"Step right this way, Professor Smith," says a tall, thin man who leads the professor through the doorway. "Thank you kindly, sir," Smith replies. The sound inside the factory is almost deafening. At one end of the room, men are pulling hot iron into long, thin wire. In another corner, a man hammers the wire to straighten it as it cools.

Smith's eyes dance around the workshop. He watches a number of men busily cutting and hammering the red hot iron, and making small circles, each no larger than the head of a pin. "Professor Smith, would you believe that there are 18 separate operations in this workshop for making pins?" says his guide.

"But wouldn't it be much simpler to have each man make the pins from start to finish?" Smith asks, with some excitement in his voice. "In my grandfather's day they would have

Adam Smith

done that," the tall man answers "but we've discovered that it is much faster to divide the work up among all the men. This division of labor allows each man to become more skilled at his own simple task. No time is lost by having the men switch from one job to another."

Smith was greatly impressed by what he saw at the pin factory. The division of labor seemed to him to be the secret that made people more productive than at any other time in history. People were growing more food, making more cloth, and producing more glass and ironware than ever before. And all this from the simple idea of dividing up the work into separate tasks.

Indeed, it seemed to Professor Smith that the division of labor had spread through almost all of British society. Some people were doctors, others were carpenters, farmers or soldiers. Each person did what he or she did best. This seemed to make society more productive.

However, one thing continued to nag him. In the pin factory, each man had a specialty. One man drew iron, while another straightened it into pins. The factory owner hired the workmen and told them what to do. The owner alone decided everything.

But what about society as a whole? What was the guiding force that told each person in society what to do? Who made sure that there were enough farmers to grow wheat for the bakers, and that the bakers baked enough bread for everyone who needed bread to eat? Society was like a huge pin factory, but it miraculously ran without a factory owner telling everyone what to do. How did each person know what job to fill and what to do?

In olden times, people had carried on the same kind of work that their parents had done or obeyed the orders of their king or ruler. It was easy to see how those societies worked—everyone was told what to do. But society in Great Britain and America was quite different now. Each person did what he or she considered to be best for himself or herself, without a single thought about what was good for society. And yet, society was not falling apart. In fact, things were better than ever. Smith wondered, could there be some "invisible hand" guiding everyone?

Adam Smith spent many years pondering this question. In this unit you will learn the answers to some of the questions that had puzzled the old professor, as you study economics.

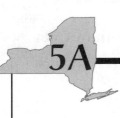

HOW WOULD YOU SPEND YOUR MONEY?

5A

In this activity, you will make decisions about how to spend money. These decisions will introduce you to two key ideas in economics—scarcity and opportunity cost. Look for the following important words:

▶ Economics   ▶ Problem of Scarcity   ▶ Opportunity Cost

To help you, the ▶ will appear in the margin where the **term** first appears.

Today must be your lucky day! You have opened the mail and found a birthday card from your favorite aunt and uncle. Inside the card is a gift of one hundred dollars. Excitedly, you ask your mother, "What should I do with this money?" She says there are many things you could do. She suggests that you make a list of different ways of using the money.

Introduction

WHAT SHOULD YOU DO WITH THE MONEY?

On a separate sheet of paper, list all of the things you would want to do if you had an extra $100:

I Want:	It Would Cost:
1.	$
2.	$
3.	$

What you want to buy will be influenced by your personal tastes and values. You will also be affected by the prices that different things cost. If you are like most people, the things you want probably cost more than $100. So you would have to choose between different things. Whenever you make choices about how to use your money, you are involved in economics.

THE PROBLEM OF SCARCITY

Economics is the study of how individuals, businesses and nations make things, buy ◀ things, spend money and save money. People who study economics are known as **economists.** Economists believe that the basic problem of economics is the problem of scarcity. Something is *scarce* when we do not have enough of it. The **problem of** ◀ **scarcity** involves two basic ideas:

1. People usually have unlimited wants. There are many things you probably want. Once you had them all, you would most likely find new things that you wanted.

2. A society can produce only a limited number of things at any one time. There is only a certain amount of available goods (*video games, cars, clothes*). There is only a certain amount of available services (*car-washing, banking services, restaurants*).

The problem of scarcity exists because (1) most people want an unlimited number of things, and (2) society does not have enough resources to produce an unlimited amount of goods and services. In other words, even with your birthday gift of $100, you would probably want more things than your $100 could buy. Your scarce resources cannot satisfy your unlimited wants.

✔ CHECKING YOUR UNDERSTANDING ✔

Suppose every person were given 5 million dollars a year. Do you think this would end the problem of scarcity? If yes, explain how. If not, explain why not.

Because of the problem of scarcity, economists point out that there is an **opportunity cost** to every economic decision. This "cost" is the opportunity you give ◀ up to do other things. For instance, assume you have saved enough to buy either a radio or a book. You decide to buy the radio. The "opportunity cost" of your radio is the book you **might** have bought instead.

MAKING AN ECONOMIC CHOICE

Now it's time for you to make your decision.

---

1. How would you spend your $100?
2. What would be some of the opportunity costs of your decision?

REVIEWING YOUR UNDERSTANDING

Creating Vocabulary Cards

Economics
What is economics?
How is economics different from
geography?

The Problem of Scarcity
What is the problem of scarcity?
Give an example you experienced
of the problem of scarcity:

Dealing with the Problem of Scarcity

Let's see how the problem of scarcity might affect your school. Imagine that the following is a list of problems facing your school:

Problems	Amount Needed to Fix the Problem
The basketball team needs new uniforms	$3,000
New instruments are needed for the band	$4,000
The school wants to replace certain computers	$6,000
The school needs a new roof	$4,000
The school needs to be painted	$3,000

Your school has only $9,000 in its budget. How would you spend this money? Assume you are writing a letter to your school newspaper. Explain which problems you would attempt to solve by spending the $9,000.

Dealing with Opportunity Costs

Opportunity costs are not just something you read about in a school textbook. In fact, they create economic problems that you face each day of your life. Every action you take when buying something means giving up buying something else. Describe a situation in your life in which you dealt with the problem of scarcity and opportunity costs.

HOW WOULD YOU ILLUSTRATE THE FACTORS OF PRODUCTION?

5B

In this activity, you will learn about the things that go into making a product. These items are called the factors of production. Look for the following important words:

▶ Goods and Services   ▶ Land   ▶ Capital Goods

▶ Factors of Production   ▶ Labor   ▶ Entrepreneurs

Let's take a look at how goods and services are produced.

Definition

WHAT ARE GOODS AND SERVICES?

Goods. Goods are things that people make. For example, foods, toys, clothes, cars and houses are goods. Department stores, shoe stores, bakeries and super-markets all sell goods to consumers.

✔ **CHECKING YOUR UNDERSTANDING** ✔

Name two other "goods" that people make.

Services. Services are things that people do for others. People who provide services include electricians, teachers, plumbers, barbers and auto mechanics.

✔ **CHECKING YOUR UNDERSTANDING** ✔

Name two other "services" that people supply to others.

Information

THE FACTORS OF PRODUCTION

The **factors of production** are all the things needed to produce goods and services. Think of a can of soda: what materials, labor, machinery and management skills came together to produce it?

There are four main factors of production: **l**and (*natural resources*), **l**abor, **c**apital goods and **e**ntrepreneurship. A useful mnemonic device to help you remember the factors of produc-tion might be the word C-E-L-L .

LAND (NATURAL RESOURCES)

▶ Economists use the term "**land**" to mean the resources found in nature. These resources include metals and other minerals, water, plants and soil. For example, steel is needed to make a car. Iron and coal are needed to make steel. These resources— iron and coal—are taken from the Earth. No matter how advanced a society is or how skilled its workers are, it cannot produce new goods without natural resources.

Central New York State
How many natural resources can you identify in this photograph?

✔ CHECKING YOUR UNDERSTANDING ✔

List some of the natural resources that are needed to build a house.

LABOR

▶ **Labor** is the work that people do to make goods or provide services. Labor includes the talents, training, skills and knowledge of the people who make things and provide services. Labor involves many kinds of workers: plumbers, bus drivers, welders, police officers, fire fighters, nurses, teachers, bankers and singers. All goods and services include some human labor. For example, even a completely **automated** (*machine-run*) factory needs workers to design, build, run and repair the machinery.

Old-time illustration of the Buffalo Forge Company
How has the role of labor changed with the use of automation?

✔ CHECKING YOUR UNDERSTANDING ✔

List some of the workers whose labor is needed to build a house.

CAPITAL GOODS

▶ **Capital goods** are things that are used to make other goods and services. For example, machines and tools are capital goods. They are used to make other goods or to help perform other services. Buildings, railroads and trucks may also be capital goods if they are used to produce other goods or services.

✔ CHECKING YOUR UNDERSTANDING ✔

List some of the capital goods you would need to build a house.

ENTREPRENEURSHIP

Land, labor and capital goods must be combined and organized to make something. People who bring these factors of production together are called **entrepreneurs**. They ◀ are the owners of businesses. They combine, coordinate and organize the other three factors of production. An entrepreneur risks his or her money in the hope of making a profit. A **profit** is the money left after the expenses of the business have been paid.

Often a business grows too large and complicated for one person to run. Then the business is run by people called managers. The **managers** work for the entrepreneur.

✔ CHECKING YOUR UNDERSTANDING ✔

What is the person called who acts as the entrepreneur for building a house?

FAMOUS NEW YORKERS

John Jacob Astor (1763–1848). As a young man, he entered the fur trade. He invested his profits by shipping furs to China for silks and spices. By 1800, he was one of the richest New Yorkers. Astor then began investing in real estate. In the early 1800s, lands located just beyond the built-up areas of Manhattan were available at low prices. In 1803, Astor bought 70 acres of land located an hour's ride from the city limits for $25,000. By 1870, the land was worth $20 million. Today this area is known as Times Square. At age 85, Astor was asked if he would have done anything differently in his life. He replied that his only regret was that he didn't buy all of Manhattan. At his death, he was the richest man in America.

John Jacob Astor

"SEEING" THE FACTORS OF PRODUCTION

"Seeing" or "visualizing" is one of the best ways to understand something. By visualizing you connect an idea with a picture. For example, you have just learned about the four factors of production. Now let's tie these factors to a picture. This will make the factors easier to understand and remember. The following photograph shows three of the four factors of production. The fourth factor, entrepreneurship, was responsible for bringing these three factors together.

✔ CHECKING YOUR UNDERSTANDING ✔

Look carefully at the details in the above photograph. Then explain which items in the photograph illustrate each factor of production. Remember, only three of the four factors are shown.

Now it's your turn to find pictures that show the factors of production. Look through some newspapers or magazines. Find a photograph or drawing to show each factor of production. You may use one photograph or drawing to show more than one of the factors.

Generally, all four of the factors of production are needed to produce a good or a service. For instance, to grow a crop a farmer needs soil and water (*land*). In addition, fuel and machinery are necessary (*capital goods*). The farmer must also work hard at plowing, planting, fertilizing and harvesting (*labor*). Finally, the farmer must be able to put these three factors of production together in a reasonable way to get a good harvest (*entrepreneurship*).

REVIEWING YOUR UNDERSTANDING

Creating Vocabulary Cards

Goods and Services
What are goods and services?
Give two examples of each:

Factors of Production
What are the four factors of production?
Give an example of each factor:

Identifying the Factors of Production

Do you wear jeans? Imagine the different factors of production that were brought together to make this product. Jeans are made mostly from cotton. First, farmers must use natural resources like seeds, soil and water to grow the cotton. When it is ready to be harvested, the cotton is picked, cleaned and shipped to factories by workers. The factory uses spinning machines (capital goods) to turn the cotton into thread. The thread is then woven into cloth on other giant machines.

Once the cloth is dyed blue, it is cut into pieces following the patterns for jeans of different sizes. These pieces are then sewn together, a zipper is added and buttons and snaps are sewn on. The jeans are then labeled, packed and shipped to stores. Finally, you enter the store (owned by an entrepreneur) and try on one of the pairs of jeans. They fit! So your parent gives the cashier some money and you take them home.

Now it's your turn. Select any product. What things need to be done to produce it? Describe each process and explain how each of the factors of production are used to make the product. Use the numbered boxes below to help you explain each of the various steps. Add boxes if needed.

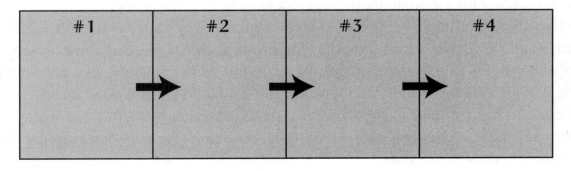

HOW WOULD YOU PROMOTE THE ECONOMY OF NEW YORK STATE?

5C

In this activity, you will look at New York's important resources. Then you will design a campaign to convince foreign businesses to locate in your state. Look for the following important words:

▶ Investments   ▶ Natural Resources   ▶ Minerals

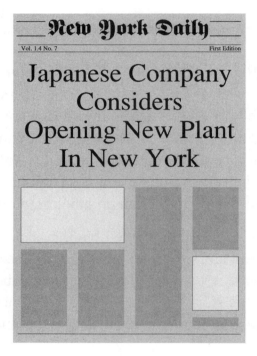

You may have noticed similar headlines in your local newspaper. New York, like other states, tries to attract foreign companies to invest in New York State. These ▶ **investments** (such as building factories or relocating business to New York) can mean more tax dollars for the state treasury and more jobs for state residents.

Many factors attract foreign investors to a state. A key factor is the availability of educated and skilled workers. Another important factor is the existence of valuable ▶ natural resources. **Natural resources** are materials found in nature that are available for human use. They include both the water and land used to grow food and the minerals we use to make products. New York is a state rich in many natural resources.

As you read the following paragraphs, think about how these resources might attract potential investors to our state.

THE NATURAL RESOURCES OF NEW YORK

FORESTS

One of New York's most valuable natural resources is its forested land. More than 18 million acres of forested land cover half of the state. They provide recreation areas in which people can hike, fish, take nature walks and camp out. In addition, a major lumber industry has developed on these lands. New York's trees include sugar maples, red maples, white birches and pine. Some of these trees are cut down and used to make paper, lumber, plywood and other wood products.

MINERALS

A **mineral** is something useful that is found in the ground. New York has many important minerals. During the Ice Age, receding glaciers left large amounts of gravel and sand throughout the state. Zinc is also mined in New York; so is gypsum for use in building materials. Salt is used for animal feed and for melting ice on roads. Iron ore is used to make iron and steel products. Garnets are used for jewelry and sandpaper, while talc is used in the production of paints and talcum powder.

Shipping logs from the Adirondacks (1909)
Are forests still an important resource in New York State?

WATER

New York's 70,000 miles of rivers and streams and 5,300 square miles of lakes provide a key resource. The Great Lakes and the waters off Long Island are centers of fresh and salt water fishing. Commercial fishermen in New York haul in millions of pounds of fish each year. New York is a major supplier of clams, lobsters, oysters, flounder and scallops to the nation. Water is also important in producing electricity. For example, dams at Niagara Falls produce much of the power for New York's homes and businesses.

Rowing on one of New York's many lakes
In addition to recreation, why are New York's waters an important natural resource for the state?

SOIL

Although many people think of New York as a great urban state, it is also important for its agriculture. Its soils are fertile and much of its land is used for farming. New York farmers grow grapes, apples and vegetables. They also raise poultry, hogs, sheep and dairy cattle. Dairy products are an important part of the agricultural scene. Only Wisconsin produces more dairy products than New York.

✔ CHECKING YOUR UNDERSTANDING ✔

1. Describe some of New York State's many important natural resources.
2. How might these resources attract outside investors to New York State?

FAMOUS NEW YORKERS

Alfred E. Smith

Alfred E. Smith (1873–1944). One Governor who was very successful in promoting New York's economy was Alfred E. Smith. Born in New York City in 1918, Smith became the first Roman Catholic to be elected Governor of New York. He later won three more terms in office. Smith was a popular and forceful Governor. He sponsored many important public works around the state—building bridges, office buildings, hospitals, parks and prisons. He increased state money to aid schools. He introduced new laws to help workers injured on the job. Smith brought many new jobs to the state. To pay for these programs, Smith convinced the state legislature to pass New York's first income tax. In 1928, he ran unsuccessfully against Herbert Hoover for President.

Your Task

CREATING AN ECONOMIC PROFILE OF NEW YORK STATE

The Governor of New York State has many responsibilities. One of the most important is to help the state's economy. Imagine that the Governor has asked you to design an advertisement to attract companies to New York State.

Before you can begin this task, you will need to gather information about the economy and resources of our state. Use an almanac or encyclopedia to conduct your research, as well as the material you just read. On a separate sheet of paper, complete as much of the following information as you can find:

I. The Geography and People of New York State

Total Area: _____   Acres of Forest Land: _____

Climate: _____

Major Geographic Features: _____

Population: _____   Rank in Population: _____

Population Density: _____

II. The State's Economy

Major Natural Resources: _____

Major Industries: _____

Chief Agricultural Crops: _____

Major Ports: _____

State Taxes on Business: _____

Average Household Income: _____

Educational System: _____

Unemployment Rate: _____

III. Other Information about the State

Major Tourist Attractions: _____

New York State Motto: _____

Famous People Born in New York State: _____

Other Information about New York State: _____

DESIGNING YOUR ADVERTISEMENT FOR NEW YORK STATE

On a separate sheet of paper, create an advertisement to be read in a foreign country or another state. Which information should you focus on to emphasize New York's many advantages? Remember, as a member of the Governor's committee, your goal is to attract businesses to locate in New York State. In carrying out that goal, keep in mind that:

❖ artistic talent is **not** important for designing the advertisement

❖ creating an interesting advertisement is essential

❖ search magazines and newspapers for pictures to use in your advertisement

❖ you may want to ask your parent for help in taking photographs to use in your advertisement

REVIEWING YOUR UNDERSTANDING

Creating Vocabulary Cards

Investments
What is an investment?
How do investments help the
State of New York?

Natural Resources
What are natural resources?
Name three natural resources
found in New York State:

Examining a Product Map of New York

As you have learned in Unit 2, maps come in different shapes and sizes. They can also provide different kinds of information. The following map is a type of theme map called a **product map.** Examine it and then read the Skill Builder on the following page. It will help you to interpret the map.

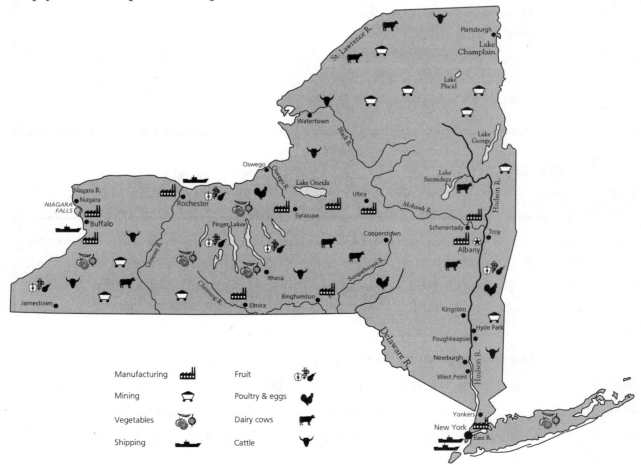

Skill Builder

INTERPRETING A PRODUCT MAP

WHAT IS A PRODUCT MAP?

On a product map, picture symbols are used to stand for various agricultural, mineral and manufactured products. Crops and animals are agricultural products. Valuable resources found in the soil are mineral products.

❖ Name **two** crops grown in New York State.

❖ Name **two** animals raised in New York State.

❖ Name a mineral found in New York State.

THE LEGEND OR KEY

The legend explains what each symbol represents. For example, each area in New York State that grows fruit is shown on the map with a small picture of different types of fruit.

❖ What does the 🛒 symbol stand for?

❖ What does the 🐄 symbol stand for?

❖ What symbol is used for poultry and eggs?

❖ What symbol is used for shipping?

❖ What city is located closest to where poultry is raised?

❖ In what parts of the state does mining take place?

❖ What two cities are located closest to where dairy cows are raised?

✔ CHECKING YOUR UNDERSTANDING ✔

Let's check your understanding of some of New York's natural resources and the products made from these resources. Make a copy of the following list. If the item is:

❖ **a natural resource**, mark **NR**   ❖ **a product**, mark a **P**

1. forests	4. lumber	7. bricks	10. clothing	13. zinc
2. garnets	5. chemicals	8. books	11. plastics	14. talc
3. apples	6. plywood	9. calculators	12. paper	15. steel

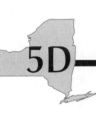

HOW INTERDEPENDENT ARE WE WITH FOREIGN COUNTRIES?

5D

In this activity, you will learn how people in different countries have become economically interdependent (*they rely or depend on each other*). Look for the following important words:

▶ Interdependent   ▶ Exports   ▶ Imports   ▶ Hypothesis

Technologies like the telephone, fax, television, jet planes and computers are said to be "shrinking" our world. Of course, the world isn't actually getting smaller; it just seems that way. Because of these new technologies, people now have more contact with distant places than they had earlier.

THE WORLD'S GROWING INTERDEPENDENCE

This increased contact has made people around the world much more interdependent.
▶ Nations are **interdependent** when they rely on trading with other nations for goods and services. For example, many American
▶ jobs are based on selling **exports**. Exports are goods and services sold from the United States to other countries.

A foreign ship unloads containers in New York.

> New York State accounts for almost 25% of the nation's exports. One out of every eight jobs in New York is related to exports. New York exports food, machinery, instruments, chemicals and transportation equipment.

▶   The United States also relies on imports. **Imports** are products from other countries brought into the United States for sale.

> New York is a leading importer. It has two major areas for goods coming into the United States: New York City and the ports in the Great Lakes District. Like the rest of the nation, New York imports more goods than it exports.

Other countries also depend on importing products from America and exporting products to us.

How many goods in your house do you think come from foreign countries?

❏ less than half   ❏ about half   ❏ more than half

At this point, your answer is only a hypothesis. A **hypothesis** is an educated guess; it may or may not turn out to be right. In this activity, you will find out if you "guessed" correctly. To do this, you will conduct an inventory of items in your house.

MAKING AN INVENTORY IN YOUR HOME

Let's begin by looking at the contents of any two rooms of your home. Examine only small furniture, lamps and other objects that you can easily move.

❖ You will find that many things have the name of the **country of origin** (*country where they came from*) stamped or printed somewhere on them. For example, in the kitchen you might find a can of coffee. Look closely at its label. You will see that it probably came from Brazil or Colombia. If you cannot identify where an item came from, move on to another one.

❖ If an object is made in the United States, include it on your list. You are not just looking for foreign-made items, but also things made in America. If an item has been partly made in two countries, list the names of both countries (Example: USA/Spain).

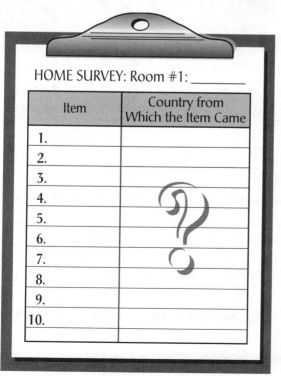

HOME SURVEY: Room #1: _____

Item	Country from Which the Item Came
1.	
2.	
3.	
4.	
5.	
6.	
7.	
8.	
9.	
10.	

HOME SURVEY: Room #2: _____

Item	Country from Which the Item Came
11.	
12.	
13.	
14.	
15.	
16.	
17.	
18.	
19.	
20.	

Your Task

FIGURING THE PERCENTAGE OF IMPORTED PRODUCTS

Make a separate list of all the countries on your chart. Next to each country, write the number of items you found from that country in your two rooms. Convert that number into a fraction by dividing the number of items from each country by the total number of items in your survey. For example, if you found

$$\frac{2 \text{ items from Brazil}}{20 \text{ is the total number of items}} = \frac{2}{20} = \frac{1}{10}$$

In this case, one out of every ten (one-tenth, or 10%) of the items came from Brazil.

You may have studied **percentages** in your mathematics lessons. (*A percentage is a fraction with a denominator of 100.*) Percentages make it easier to compare different fractions. Turn each fraction into a percent by using a calculator. Divide the **numerator** (*top number of the fraction*) by the **denominator** (*bottom number of the fraction*). This method will show you the percentage of products in the two rooms that were made in the United States and that came from other countries. Use the following chart to help you keep track of your calculations.

Country	Number of Products	Fraction	Percent
1.			
2.			
3.			
4.			
5.			
6.			

THINK ABOUT IT

1. Was the percentage of products made in the United States more than half (*over 50%*)?
2. Which country, other than the United States, supplied the most products in your inventory?

MAPPING THE COUNTRIES OF ORIGIN

Get a copy of an atlas from your school or public library. Use the atlas to locate each country on your home inventory chart. Make a copy of the world map below. Then list the items around the outside margin of the map. Finally, draw a line from each item to the location of its country of origin. For example, if one item in your home inventory was coffee, you would write the word "coffee" in the margin surrounding your map. Then you would draw a line from that word to its country of origin—probably Brazil or Colombia.

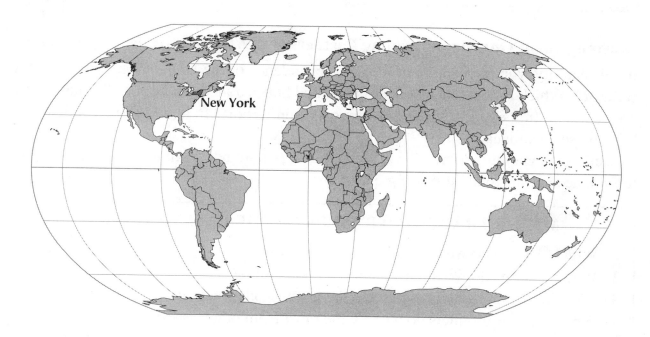

✔ CHECKING YOUR UNDERSTANDING ✔

1. How many items in your inventory came from foreign countries?
2. How accurate was the original hypothesis you made when you began this activity?
3. Were you surprised by the results of your inventory?   ❏ Yes   ❏ No
   If so, how? If not, why not?
4. What conclusions about global interdependence can you draw from the results of your inventory and those of your classmates?

REVIEWING YOUR UNDERSTANDING

Creating Vocabulary Cards

Exports
What is an export?
Name a product that is exported from the United States.

Imports
What is an import?
Name a product that is imported into the United States.

Learning about Our Major Trading Partners and What We Trade with Them —

In this activity, you learned about the interdependence of the United States and foreign countries. Which foreign nations does the United States trade with the most? What goods do we most often export? What do we most often import? In activity 2E, you learned how to use an almanac.

Let's get some further practice in using this important reference tool. Use an almanac to find the answers to the following questions:

MAJOR TRADING PARTNERS OF THE UNITED STATES

1. Which nations do we export the most goods to?
2. Which nations do we import the most goods from?
3. What kinds of products do we sell the most to other nations?
4. What kinds of products do we buy the most from other nations?

GOVERNMENT AND CITIZENSHIP

President Clinton addresses Congress

Governor Pataki signs a bill

New York City's Mayor Giuliani delivers an address to the city

Every society has some kind of government. A government makes laws and has a system to punish people who break the laws. The government also provides a way for people to cooperate. They can work together through the government to make new laws or to change laws they believe are unfair. In this unit, you will find out how governments are organized. You will also learn some of the main features of your local, state and national governments.

A YOUNG AUTHOR STRUGGLES THROUGH THE NIGHT

Thomas Jefferson, a tall, red-haired Virginian, sat alone at his desk. Candles lit up the large, spacious room. It was a hot Philadelphia night in July 1776, and sweat rolled from his brow.

Thomas thought about the exciting events of the past few years. He remembered the taxes that the English Parliament had forced on the American colonists. The Americans had had no voice in deciding whether these taxes were fair. Then Thomas thought about his own role in leading the young representatives in the colonial assembly of Virginia against these policies. The dispute with England over taxes had quickly led to war.

Thomas had been one of Virginia's representatives to the Continental Congress in Philadelphia. George Washington, another Virginian, was appointed to lead the Continental Army. But the English had sent thousands of well-trained troops to fight the colonists. Thomas thought it would be hard for the colonists to win against such a well trained army. Perhaps he and the other members of the Continental Congress would be hanged as traitors if the colonists lost.

The Continental Congress knew that it needed the support of most colonists in order to win the war. A few key members of the Congress had formed a committee to write a public announcement. This announcement would explain to the colonists and to others around the world why the 13 American colonies should declare independence from England. The other members of the committee were older and more experienced than Thomas. But they thought that he would do the best job in writing the declaration. Now it was all up to him.

Thomas Jefferson

Thomas was only 33 years old. He was an experienced writer and lawyer. However, the burden of his task was enormous. Could he write something so powerful that it would inspire his fellow countrymen to support independence? Could he also convince France to enter the war on the side of the Americans, against the English?

Thomas paced back and forth between the fireplace and the open windows of his parlor room. Again and again he wondered: What should he say in the declaration? What could he write that would inspire others to be willing to risk their lives for independence?

Thomas' thoughts went back to his days at college and his favorite teacher, Dr. William Small. Dr. Small had often spoke of the many types of governments. He had also discussed the great variety of views about which type of government was the best.

In recalling these ideas, many new questions entered Thomas's mind. What did the future hold for the American colonies? Would each colony break away and become a separate and independent country? Or would each of the colonists be willing to give up some power in order to unite the other colonies together into a single country? What kind of government should they pick? Should they become a democracy—a government in which the people choose their own government officials? Could such a system of government work in a new and inexperienced nation?

Thomas put down his feather pen on the desk and stared blankly out the window. A cool breeze entered the room. His mind was filled with conflicting emotions. He felt both fear and hope as he thought about the future. What could he write in the declaration that would make things easier for his fellow countrymen in the difficult years ahead?

As you read through this unit, you will learn the answers to these and other questions about the American system of government that raced through the mind of Thomas Jefferson on that warm summer night over two hundred years ago.

WHO REPRESENTS YOU IN THE NATIONAL GOVERNMENT?

6A

In this activity, you will learn who represents you in the national government. Look for the following important words:

▶ Government   ▶ Federalism   ▶ Executive power

▶ Democracy   ▶ Legislative power   ▶ Judicial power

To help you, a ▶ appears in the margin where the term is first explained.

Definition

WHAT IS A GOVERNMENT?

In early times, when large numbers of people began living near each other, cities and nations emerged. A need quickly developed for an organization that would maintain order. The organization people set up to protect their community and to make rules for
▶ themselves is called a **government** . By making and enforcing rules, the government keeps order, protects people's lives and safeguards property.

Information

TYPES OF GOVERNMENT

Throughout history, three main types of governments have existed. They are monarchy, dictatorship and democracy.

MONARCHY
A **monarchy** is a government in which a king or queen has political power. A king or queen is someone who has inherited power. Often, the king or queen claims to rule by "divine right"—being chosen by God to act as ruler. Sometimes the monarch shares power with an elected law-making body. When the king or queen dies, power passes to one of the monarch's children or relatives.

DICTATORSHIP
A **dictatorship** is a system in which all the powers of government are in the hands of one person or a small group. This person or group seizes power because they claim to

King Louis XIV claimed
that God chose him
to rule France.

know what is best for the society. Often, they use force and violence to maintain their rule. The ruler or group decides what everyone must do, and is not concerned about what others want. With power concentrated in the hands of a single person or group, people have no rights.

DEMOCRACY

In a **democracy**, the government's power comes from the permission of the people it governs. The people usually decide on important issues by electing officials, called **representatives.** This type of government, known as a **representative democracy,** exists in the United States as well as in other countries around the world.

Joseph Stalin was a dictator of the former Soviet Union.

> We live in a democracy where people elect their officials. Do you know the names of the people who represent you?

Like many Americans, you may not know the names of all the people who represent you. In this activity you will learn about some of these people. Let's begin by looking at how the government of the United States is organized.

THE DIVISION OF POWERS

In our system of government, power is shared among several levels of government. This division of government powers is called **federalism**. One level is the **national** (*federal*) government. It deals with matters affecting the whole country, such as the defense of the nation. At another level are **state governments.** Each one handles matters occurring

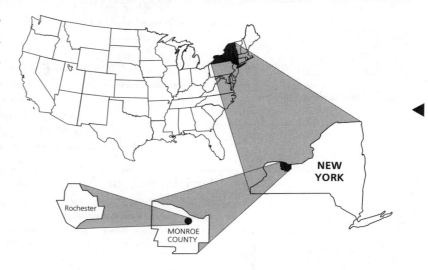

within their state. For example, states make laws about who may drive a car. **Local governments** are a third level. They deal with county, city, town and village matters. For example, local governments maintain and repair neighborhood streets.

THE SEPARATION OF POWERS

All governments—national, state and local—are given three powers to carry out their authority. These powers are:

▶

a legislative power
to make the laws

an executive power
to enforce the laws

a judicial power
to interpret the laws

Each level of our government—national, state and local—has created special institutions or **branches** to help carry out these powers. The following chart describes these different levels of government and their branches.

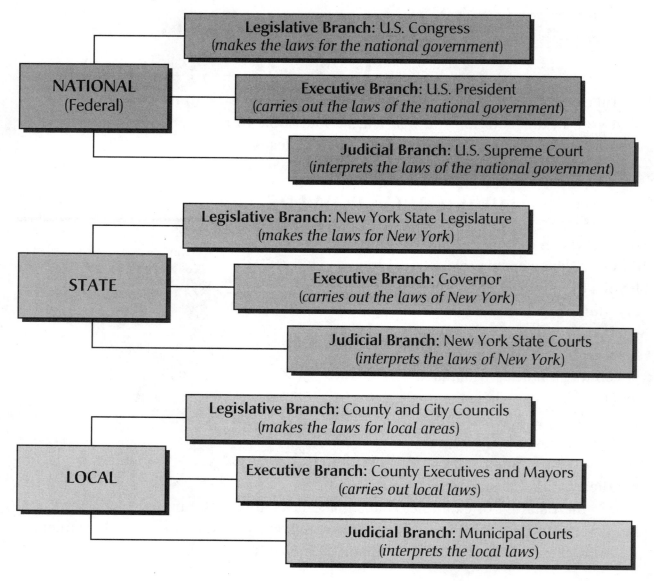

NATIONAL
(Federal)

Legislative Branch: U.S. Congress
(*makes the laws for the national government*)

Executive Branch: U.S. President
(*carries out the laws of the national government*)

Judicial Branch: U.S. Supreme Court
(*interprets the laws of the national government*)

STATE

Legislative Branch: New York State Legislature
(*makes the laws for New York*)

Executive Branch: Governor
(*carries out the laws of New York*)

Judicial Branch: New York State Courts
(*interprets the laws of New York*)

LOCAL

Legislative Branch: County and City Councils
(*makes the laws for local areas*)

Executive Branch: County Executives and Mayors
(*carries out local laws*)

Judicial Branch: Municipal Courts
(*interprets the local laws*)

Now let's take a closer look at our national level of government.

OUR NATIONAL GOVERNMENT

LEGISLATIVE BRANCH

Our national government is located in Washington, D.C. The legislative or law-making branch is called **Congress.** The main job of Congress is to make laws for the nation. Congress has two parts, known as **houses** because they meet and vote separately: the **Senate** and the **House of Representatives.**

Each of the 50 states has **two** members in the U.S. Senate. In the House of Representatives, the more

Members of the House of Representatives pose for a picture. *How many representatives are there?*

people a state has, the more representatives it has. Since 1990, New York State has had 31 representatives. Only California and Texas have more representatives in Congress than New York.

	House of Representatives	Senate
Number of members:	435	100
Length of term:	2 years	6 years
Representation is based on:	The size of the state's population	Two from each state
Elected by:	Voters from a particular Congressional district	Voters from the entire state

✔ CHECKING YOUR UNDERSTANDING ✔

How many people represent New York State in the U.S. Congress?

EXECUTIVE BRANCH

The main job of the **executive branch** is to carry out or enforce laws. Our nation's chief executive is the **President of the United States.** The President runs the agencies of the executive branch. For example, he or she is in charge of the Federal Bureau of Investigation (F.B.I.). The President also represents our country to other nations and serves as Commander-in-Chief of all U.S. armed forces. The President lives in the White House in Washington, D.C.

Bill Clinton being sworn in as President of the United States.
What is the main job of the President?

Length of term:	4 years
Number of terms:	A maximum of two full terms.
Qualifications	At least 35 years old, a resident of the United States for 14 years and a native-born citizen

JUDICIAL BRANCH

The role of a **judicial branch** is to interpret the laws—applying them to individual cases that come before the court. The **U.S. Supreme Court** is the highest court in the nation. There are also other federal courts to enforce our national laws. The Justices of the U.S. Supreme Court base their decisions on our national laws and the U.S. Constitution.

Length of term:	Justices serve for life.
How Justices are selected:	Selected by the President, but must also be approved by the U.S. Senate
Number of Justices on the U.S. Supreme Court:	Nine
Qualifications:	There are no qualifications listed in the U.S. Constitution for being a Supreme Court Justice.

Closing

WHO ARE YOUR REPRESENTATIVES IN THE NATIONAL GOVERNMENT?

Now that you know how the national government is organized, do you know the names and faces of the people who represent you? List the names of the officials who represent you in the national government. Also, try to provide a photograph for each. Use the following sources to help you:

❖ Visit or call your local office of the **League of Women Voters.**

❖ Look in your phone book, under government (often in the *Blue Pages*).

❖ Search local newspapers for pictures of your elected officials.

❖ Search electronic media, such as the **Internet.**

WHO REPRESENTS YOU AT THE NATIONAL LEVEL OF GOVERNMENT

A. President of the United States:
(name) _____   (photo)

B. Vice-President of the United States:
(name) _____   (photo)

C. U.S. Senators from New York State:
1. (name) _____   (photo)
2. (name) _____   (photo)

D. Your Representative in the U.S. House of Representatives:
(name) _____   (photo)

REVIEWING YOUR UNDERSTANDING

Creating Vocabulary Cards

Government
What is a government?
List one reason for having a government:

Democracy
What is a democracy?
List one characteristic of a democracy:

WHO REPRESENTS YOU AT THE STATE AND LOCAL LEVEL?

6B

In this activity, you will learn about our other two levels of government: state and local governments. Look for the following important words:

▶ New York State Legislature   ▶ Governor
▶ State Assembly   ▶ County Government
▶ State Senate   ▶ Town and City Government

The United States is divided into 50 states. Each state has its own government. Each state government has three branches to carry out its powers.

THE GOVERNMENT OF NEW YORK STATE

New York's **state government** handles matters that affect people throughout the state. The state government provides money for schools, builds and maintains state roads, and provides a court system. It also protects the safety and health of its citizens. Like the national government, the state government is divided into legislative, executive and judicial branches. It is located in **Albany,** the state's capital. Let's begin our study of state government with a question:

New York State Capitol Building
Which branch of state government meets in this building?

> What are the names of the people who represent you in state government?

In this activity you will learn about the people who represent you in state government. First let's look at how New York State's government is organized.

LEGISLATIVE BRANCH

▶ The legislative branch of New York State government is called the **New York State Legislature** . It makes the laws of New York. The state legislature consists of two houses

▶ (*parts that meet and vote separately*): the Assembly and the Senate. The **Assembly** has 151 members. Each member of the Assembly is elected for a term of two years.

✔ WHICH ASSEMBLY DISTRICT DO YOU LIVE IN? ✔

The map below shows the 151 districts that make up the New York State Assembly.

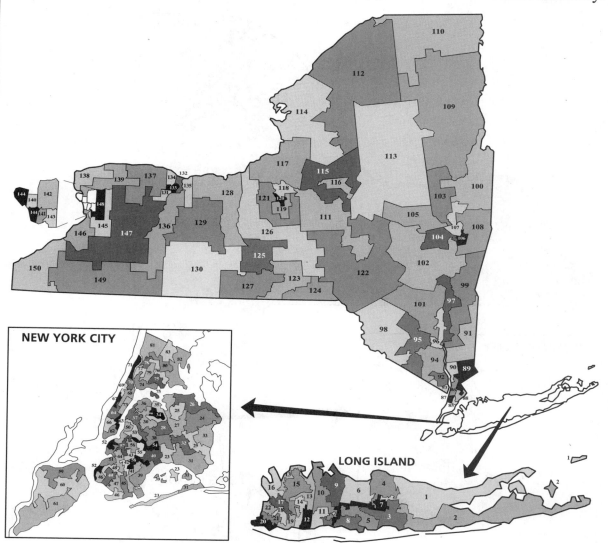

On a separate sheet of paper, answer the following questions:

1. In which assembly district do you live?
2. List the assembly districts that border your district.
3. Why do you think some assembly districts are larger than others?

The second part of the New York State Legislature is the **Senate**. There are ◄ 61 members of the New York State Senate. Senators are elected by voters in 61 separate Senate districts. Members of the Senate also serve a two-year term.

✔ WHICH SENATE DISTRICT DO YOU LIVE IN? ✔

The map below shows the 61 districts that make up the New York State Senate.

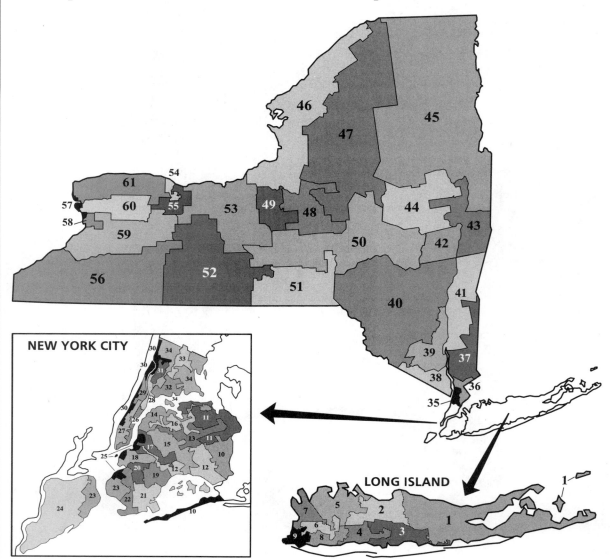

On a separate sheet of paper, answer the following questions:

1. In which Senate district do you live?
2. Name the Senate districts that border your district.

EXECUTIVE BRANCH

▶ The chief executive of New York's state government is called the **Governor** . The Governor's job is to enforce the laws that have been passed by the New York State Legislature. The chief duty of the Governor is to maintain order in the state.

The Governor is in charge of several departments, bureaus and agencies which help run the State government. He or she is also the Commander-in-Chief of the state's National Guard. In the event the Governor is away from the state or becomes ill, the **Lieutenant Governor** takes over some of the Governor's responsibilities. Both are elected for a term of four years.

Many Governors of New York have used their position as a stepping stone to the White House. Martin Van Buren, Grover Cleveland, Theodore Roosevelt and Franklin D. Roosevelt were all New York State Governors before becoming Presidents of the United States.

President Van Buren was once Governor of New York. *Which other New York Governors became President?*

FAMOUS NEW YORKERS

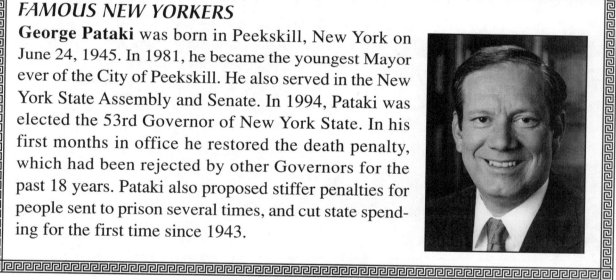

George Pataki was born in Peekskill, New York on June 24, 1945. In 1981, he became the youngest Mayor ever of the City of Peekskill. He also served in the New York State Assembly and Senate. In 1994, Pataki was elected the 53rd Governor of New York State. In his first months in office he restored the death penalty, which had been rejected by other Governors for the past 18 years. Pataki also proposed stiffer penalties for people sent to prison several times, and cut state spending for the first time since 1943.

JUDICIAL BRANCH

The highest court in New York State is the **Court of Appeals**—the state equivalent of the U.S. Supreme Court. It is called the state's "highest court" since there is no further appeal from its decisions except to the U.S. Supreme Court. The Court of Appeals meets in Albany. It has seven members, including a Chief Judge. The judges are elected to fourteen-year terms.

New York State Court of Appeals
What does this court and the U.S. Supreme Court have in common?

Focus on Documents: *New York's Constitution*

A **constitution** is a written plan of government. New York State, like our national government, has its own constitution. In 1776, New York and the 12 other colonies declared their independence from Great Britain. The Continental Congress, the governing body during the American Revolution, asked each colony to write a constitution for itself. A convention of New Yorkers met in White Plains and then in Kingston to write such a constitution. On April 20, 1777, the constitution they developed was adopted.

Under New York's first constitution, only property-owners could vote. It also provided that every 20 years the voters of New York State would have a chance to decide if they wanted to revise their constitution. Since that first constitution, nine conventions have been held to revise the constitution.

The **Constitution of 1821** added a Bill of Rights for the people of New York. Like the U.S. Constitution, it guaranteed citizens freedom of religion, speech and press, the right to a trial by jury and the right to protest peacefully in groups. The Constitution of 1821 also removed some property qualifications for voting. This made New York a more democratic state.

The Constitution was changed again in 1846. The **Constitution of 1846** made our state government even more democratic. It gave the vote to all men over 21, whether they owned property or not.

In the 1890s, dishonesty and corruption in national and state governments became a major problem. New York delegates sought to solve the problem by changing the constitution yet again. The **Constitution of 1894** provided a merit system for choosing government employees. The new system required applicants to pass a test to get their job. This constitution presently governs New York State.

 LOCAL GOVERNMENT

COUNTY GOVERNMENT

Just as the United States is divided into 50 states, New York State is divided into 62 ▶ counties. **County government** dates back to the days when New York was a colony. Counties were first formed because there was a need to build courthouses, jails, poorhouses and orphanages. Today, county governments conduct elections, register voters, collect county taxes, operate courts and provide some health care services.

Some counties are governed by a board of supervisors. Other counties are governed by an elected legislature. In most counties, the chief executive is called the **county executive** or **county manager.**

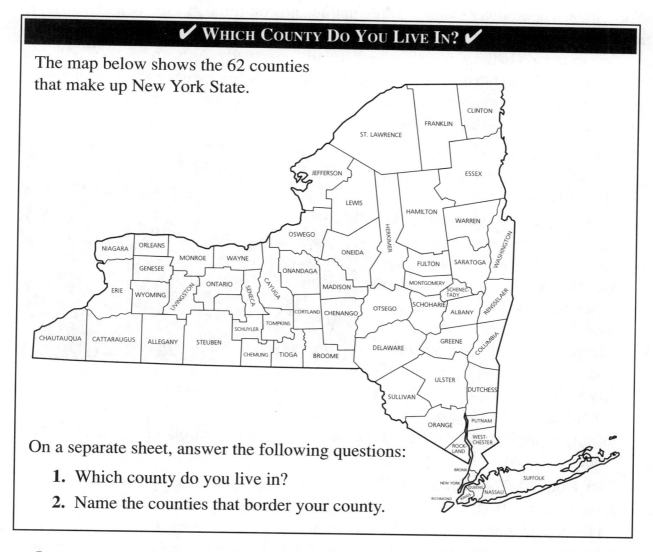

✔ WHICH COUNTY DO YOU LIVE IN? ✔

The map below shows the 62 counties that make up New York State.

On a separate sheet, answer the following questions:

1. Which county do you live in?
2. Name the counties that border your county.

Just as New York State is divided into counties, each county is further divided into cities, towns, villages and special districts.

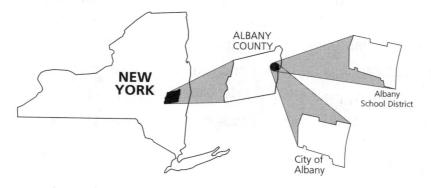

CITY GOVERNMENTS

▶ **City governments** usually control an area with a large population. They date back to the time when New York was a colony. Today, there are 62 city governments in New York State. Their power extends to regulating and controlling property and managing local affairs.

One exception to the way counties are usually governed is New York City. The City's five counties, called **boroughs,** are governed differently from other counties in the state. All five boroughs are governed as part of New York City. Let's take a look at the four main parts of New York City government:

❖ **Mayor.** The **Mayor** is the chief executive of New York City. The Mayor is elected by all the city voters for a four-year term. The Mayor appoints three deputy mayors and the heads of several city agencies. These agencies perform various city-wide services, such as providing police protection, public transportation and garbage collection. The Mayor also prepares the city's budget along with the Comptroller. The **Comptroller** is

Mayor Giuliani at a ceremony opening a
new building in New York City
What other jobs does the city's Mayor perform?

the city's chief financial officer. Like the Mayor, the Comptroller is elected by all the voters of the city.

❖ **City Council.** The **City Council** serves as the city's law-making body. It is has one representative from each of its 51 districts. The **Public Advocate,** also elected by all the voters of the city, presides at meetings of the City Council. The Public Advocate only votes in case of a tie. The Public Advocate also reviews complaints and recommends improvements in city government services.

❖ **The Borough Presidents.** Each borough elects its own **Borough President.** The Borough Presidents appoint members of community school boards, the Board of Education and the Planning Commission.

❖ **City Courts.** The city has both civil and criminal courts to apply city laws.

In addition, local communities have their own community planning boards and community school districts. These give communities some local control.

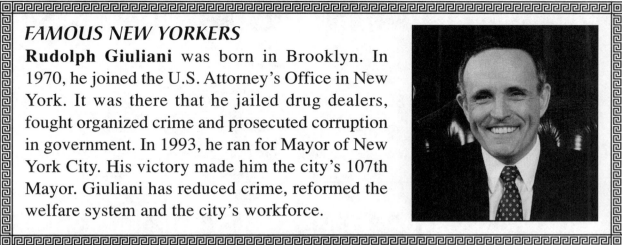

FAMOUS NEW YORKERS

Rudolph Giuliani was born in Brooklyn. In 1970, he joined the U.S. Attorney's Office in New York. It was there that he jailed drug dealers, fought organized crime and prosecuted corruption in government. In 1993, he ran for Mayor of New York City. His victory made him the city's 107th Mayor. Giuliani has reduced crime, reformed the welfare system and the city's workforce.

TOWN GOVERNMENT

In New York State, a "town" is a local area under a specific form of government—a township. There are over 930 towns in New York. The number of towns differs from one county to another. For example, there are three towns in Nassau County and 32 towns in Steuben County. **Town governments** usually handle such matters as water, sewage and ◄ drainage systems and local roads.

VILLAGE GOVERNMENT

Towns themselves are often further divided into **villages** or smaller units called **hamlets.** These first developed when people in an area wanted a specific service, such as fire protection or street lights. The almost 600 villages in New York vary in size from a few dozen people to more than 40,000 residents. Village governments handle law enforcement, operate water systems, sewers, parks and cemeteries.

DISTRICT GOVERNMENT

Sometimes a need arises for a service that is not provided by a city, town or village. In such cases, a **special district** is created to provide that service. Special districts often provide water, garbage disposal and snow removal. The largest number of special districts are school districts and fire districts.

WHO REPRESENTS YOU IN STATE AND LOCAL GOVERNMENT?

Earlier you identified the elected officials representing you on the national level. Can you also identify the officials who represent you in state and local government? Let's find out. Using the same sources of information from the previous activity, identify and provide a photograph of each of the following elected officials:

WHO REPRESENTS YOU AT THE STATE LEVEL OF GOVERNMENT

A. Governor of New York:
(name) _____   (photo)

B. Senator from your State Senate District:
(name) _____   (photo)

C. Representative from your State Assembly District:
(name) _____   (photo)

WHO REPRESENTS YOU AT THE LOCAL LEVEL OF GOVERNMENT

A. Mayor, City Manager or other local executive:
(name) _____   (photo)

B. County Supervisor or other local legislator:
(name) _____   (photo)

C. County, City or Town Judge:
(name) _____   (photo)

THINK ABOUT IT

Which government officials were the most difficult to find information about? Explain.

REVIEWING YOUR UNDERSTANDING

Creating Vocabulary Cards

New York State Legislature
What is the job of the New York State Legislature?
Which two houses make up the New York State Legislature?

County Government
Define county government.
What types of jobs are county governments responsible for?

Interpreting a Bar Graph: The Governments of New York State ———

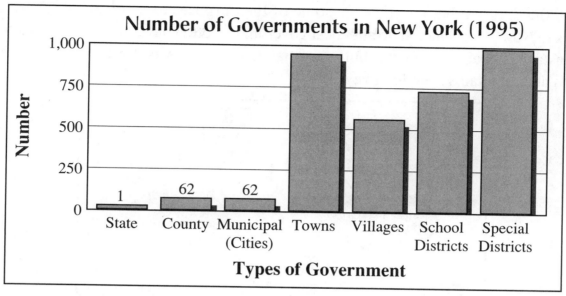

To better understand this graph, read the following Skill Builder:

INTERPRETING BAR GRAPHS

What Is a Bar Graph?

A ⟨bar graph⟩ is a chart that shows parallel bars of different lengths. It is used to compare several items.

❖ Do you know what items are compared in this bar graph?

Keys to Understanding a Bar Graph

Bar graphs have a vertical axis, which runs from top to bottom, and a horizontal axis, which runs from left to right.

❖ In this graph, what do the vertical and horizontal axes show?

Interpreting a Bar Graph

Start by reading the title. It gives you an idea of the information presented by the graph. To find specific information, look at each bar in the graph. For example, how many school districts were there in New York State in 1995? Slide your finger along the horizontal axis until you reach the bar marked "School Districts." Next, run your finger up to the top of the school district bar. If you look at the number scale along the vertical axis, you will see where the bar ends.

❖ About how many village governments were there in New York in 1995?

❖ What type of government in New York State has the most number of governments?

Interpreting a Diagram

Study the diagram below. It shows some of the purposes of state and local governments in New York State. State and local governments often have overlapping functions. For instance, local governments build and maintain local streets, while state government builds and maintains state highways.

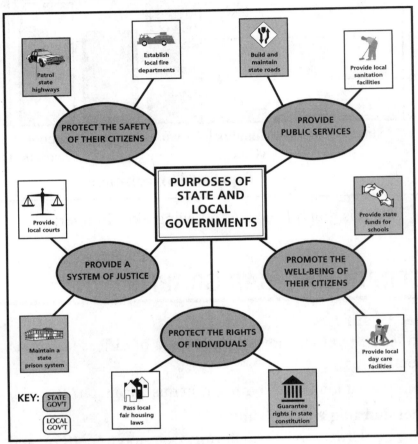

Make a copy of the following chart. Then list the jobs that state and local governments have. Use the diagram above for this information.

Some of the Things That State and Local Governments Do	
State	Local

HOW WOULD YOU DEFINE A "GOOD" CITIZEN?

6C

We begin this activity by examining what citizenship is. Then you will conduct a survey of two adults to find out what they think makes a "good" citizen. Look for these important words:

▶ Citizenship   ▶ Survey   ▶ Duties

▶ Naturalized Citizen   ▶ Rights   ▶ Responsibilities

Definition

WHAT IS A CITIZEN?

In some ways, **citizenship** is like a membership card. Citizenship means a person is a member of a particular nation. The idea of citizenship goes back to ancient Greece and Rome. In modern times, every nation has developed its own rules to define citizenship. ◀

In the United States, you are an American citizen if you were born here or if your parents are American citizens. People who were not born here and whose parents are not American citizens can also become citizens. To do this, such a person has to live in the United States for a period of years and pass a citizenship test and take an oath. These people are called **naturalized citizens**. ◀

Skill Builder

CONDUCTING A SURVEY

Now that you know what a citizen is, what makes someone a "good" citizen? How do you think adults in your community might answer this question? In this activity, you will have the chance to find out. You will need to interview **two** adults to find out how they define a "good" citizen.

WHAT MAKES SOMEONE A GOOD CITIZEN?

In the interviews you are about to conduct, there are no right or wrong answers. The purpose of the **survey** is to find out how adults in your community define a "good" citizen. ◀
To carry out your survey, follow these steps:

❖ Ask your parent to suggest **two** adults who would be willing to participate in your project. One volunteer might even be your parent or guardian.

❖ Begin your survey by reading the following statement to each adult:

> As part of a school project, I am surveying two adults to find their answers to the question:
>
> ### *How would you define a good citizen?*

❖ After you have received a response to your question, thank your volunteer for his or her help in the survey.

COLLECTING DATA AND COMPARING ANSWERS

Make a copy of the following tally sheet to record the answers of your volunteers:

How would you define a good citizen?
❖ What did your first volunteer say?
❖ What did your second volunteer say?

After your survey is completed, share your answers with your classmates. The class should then choose the answers they feel best define what a "good" citizen is.

A good citizen is someone who is ...

HOW EXPERTS DEFINE A GOOD CITIZEN

How does your class definition of a good citizen compare with those of the experts? Following are qualities that some experts think a good citizen should have.

A good citizen is someone who is ...

❖ **Respectful.** Good citizens treat others with respect, even when they disagree with other people's opinions.

❖ **Responsible.** Good citizens are responsible for their actions. They use self-control and follow the rules. They keep their promises and are willing to pay the penalty if they do something wrong.

❖ **Civic-Minded.** Good citizens sometimes donate their time and money to help improve the community.

❖ **Open-Minded.** Good citizens listen to others' opinions and sometimes change their minds. Good citizens will compromise in order to solve problems. They accept others with different traditions, customs and ways of living.

Now that you have read the views of the experts, would you change your definition of a good citizen? If so, how would you now define a good citizen?

> *A good citizen is someone who ...*

REVIEWING YOUR UNDERSTANDING

Creating Vocabulary Cards

Citizenship
What is citizenship?
What are some of the qualities of a citizen?

Naturalized Citizen
What is a naturalized citizen?
How is a naturalized citizen different from a native-born citizen?

Creating a "Good Citizen" Scrapbook ————————————

Have you ever read a newspaper story about a person who rushed into a burning building and saved a family? That person was not only performing an act of bravery, but was also being a good citizen.

Your daily newspaper will often have stories of people who are outstanding citizens. In order to focus on these deeds of good citizenship, let's create a scrapbook of good citizenship stories appearing in your daily newspaper. Over the next 10 days:

❖ cut out **two** articles dealing with acts of "good citizenship"

❖ paste each of these articles in a scrapbook

❖ write a brief summary about each article for your scrapbook

❖ Finally, briefly explain why you think each article represents an example of good citizenship.

YOU BE THE JUDGE!

6D

In this activity, you will examine some of the rights that citizens in a democracy have. Look for the following important words:

▶ Bill of Rights   ▶ U.S. Supreme Court

In the United States, we enjoy the benefits of a government dedicated to protecting the rights of its citizens. The Declaration of Independence stated that the main goal of any government should be to protect the people's rights to "life, liberty and the pursuit of happiness."

The Declaration of Independence did not spell out what **specific** rights Americans should have. The U.S. Constitution originally listed only a few rights. When the Constitution was sent to the states for approval, many Americans believed it should be rejected. They felt it created a government so powerful it was feared the national government might abuse the rights of citizens.

The Declaration of Independence being read to a Philadelphia crowd

THE BILL OF RIGHTS AND OTHER PROTECTIONS

Definition

The new U.S. Constitution was finally approved after its supporters promised that a "Bill of Rights" would be added. The first ten amendments were adopted in 1791. These
▶ amendments are known as the **Bill of Rights**. Many later amendments also focused on defining and protecting the rights of citizens.

The Bill of Rights guarantees each individual special rights that cannot be denied or taken away by the government. These special rights generally fall into two categories:

❖ **rights that protect our freedom of expression.** For example, the First Amendment guarantees individuals freedom of speech.

❖ **rights of people accused of a crime.** For example, the Sixth Amendment guarantees individuals the right to a fair and impartial jury trial.

Some of the amendments written after the Bill of Rights go even further in protecting our rights than the Bill of Rights itself. These amendments guarantee such rights as the right to vote and the right to the "equal protection" of the laws.

Often, disputes have developed over how the language of a particular constitutional right is to be interpreted. This is because no general rule can ever be so exact that it can tell in advance all of the situations that might arise. For this reason, we need courts to apply our laws to specific situations. The courts determine if a particular situation falls within the rule. For example, look at the sign to the right:

NO VEHICLES
IN THE PARK

THINK ABOUT IT

We are fairly certain that the sign means no cars or trucks in the park. But what about bicycles, baby strollers and wheelchairs? Are they "vehicles" in the sense intended by the sign? Explain.

A court must interpret the words of a law to decide just what the law means. A court might say that the purpose of the rule prohibiting vehicles in the park is to avoid danger to pedestrians. Since wheelchairs and baby strollers are no danger to pedestrians, they are not "vehicles" in the sense intended by the rule.

Because we live under the "rule of law," we want each person to be treated fairly. In every court, each party has certain rights. These rights include the right to have a lawyer, the right to hear opposing evidence and the right to present one's case. In criminal cases, the defendant also has the right to have the case tried by a panel of unbiased citizens known as a **jury.**

After a trial, the losing side will often ask a special court, known as a court of appeals, to reconsider the decision. The court of appeals will only change the decision if there has been an error in interpreting or applying a law. The **U.S. Supreme Court** is ◄ the nation's highest court of appeals. The Supreme Court often hears appeals in which it must interpret what is written in the U.S. Constitution.

THE EXERCISE OF JUSTICE

What would it be like to be a Justice on the U.S. Supreme Court? In this activity, you will have a chance to act as a Supreme Court Justice. You will review a famous case that once appeared before the Supreme Court. Like a real judge, you will weigh the evidence presented by both sides. Then, you will make a decision based on your understanding of the law. Good luck on your first case—your Honor!!!

SCHENCK V. UNITED STATES (1919)

THE FACTS OF THE CASE

Schenck was a member of a political party that opposed U.S. participation in World War I. When the government called up men to serve in the military, Schenck mailed leaflets telling these men that the war was both immoral and against the law. However, the pamphlet never directly told the men to refuse to serve, since such advice would have been against the law.

Schenck was accused of preventing the government from calling up men for the army. He was also accused of encouraging soldiers to disobey their officers. He was found guilty at his trial, but appealed his decision to the U.S. Supreme Court. Schenck claimed that his conviction violated his right to free speech.

ARGUMENTS USED BY SCHENCK

Schenck's lawyers argued that Schenck's right to free speech had been violated. The purpose of free speech is to allow people to criticize their government. Schenck's leaflet was clearly within this right. His lawyer admitted that it would be wrong to use free speech to call for an armed uprising against the government. But Schenck had done nothing of the kind. He had merely given his readers a different viewpoint about the war, and asked them to act for themselves.

The lawyer concluded that the government should not be allowed to imprison Schenck merely for questioning its decision to go to war. What other things might the government then attempt to do without allowing citizens to engage in free debate? Schenck was clearly not guilty and should be freed from prison.

ARGUMENTS USED BY THE U.S. GOVERNMENT

The lawyers for the United States argued that Schenck's pamphlet had only one purpose: to encourage men to disobey the law by refusing to serve in the armed forces. Failure to serve when called upon is against the law. People have a right to discuss whether or not to go to war, but they do not have a right to refuse to serve when called on. Urging people not to serve is disobeying the law.

The government's lawyers recognized that the First Amendment guarantees the right to free speech. But this freedom does not mean we can encourage people to break the law. There are some limits to free speech. For example, a person cannot shout "fire" in a crowded theater as a joke and then claim he or she was exercising free speech. A person has the right to free speech, but not the right to create a dangerous situation. No one has a right to use words that would create an *obvious* and *immediate* danger.

◆ CONTINUED

> Schenck's pamphlet clearly created an immediate danger, and should not be protected as free speech. If people had listened to Schenck, they would have refused to serve in the armed forces or even disobeyed their officers by refusing to fight. This would have caused chaos in the military. Schenck deserved to be in prison.

HOW WOULD YOU DECIDE THIS CASE?

You have now heard all of the evidence. It is time for you to decide the case. Before doing so, let's review what you learned in this case:

1. Summarize **two** arguments used by Schenck's lawyers.
2. Summarize **two** arguments used by the lawyers for the United States.
3. Based on the facts and your understanding of the law, how would **you** decide the case? Explain your decision.

REVIEWING YOUR UNDERSTANDING

Creating Vocabulary Cards

Bill of Rights
What is the Bill of Rights?
List some of the rights mentioned in the Bill of Rights.

U.S. Supreme Court
What is the U.S. Supreme Court?
Why is the U.S. Supreme Court such an important voice in interpreting our laws?

Classifying Constitutional Rights

The rights that Americans enjoy can be classified based on whether they protect a person's political, social, economic or religious rights. Here is what each of these rights is concerned with:

❖ **Political rights** allow a citizen to participate in government.

❖ **Social rights** deal with our ability to live in a community.

❖ **Economic rights** concern our ability to function in the economy.

❖ **Religious rights** protect our freedom of worship.

Listed below are several rights guaranteed to citizens of the United States. Try to classify these rights to see if they are political, social, economic or religious rights. You might first want to review the information about classifying found on page 217.

❖ The government cannot set up an official religion or limit people's freedom of religion.

❖ Citizens have a right to assemble peacefully and to send their complaints to government officials.

❖ The government cannot send soldiers to live in a citizen's home in times of peace without first getting the citizen's permission.

❖ Police and other government officials cannot arrest people without good reason.

❖ The police cannot search a person's home, business or body without a search warrant (*special permission from a judge*). A judge will only issue the warrant if the search seems reasonable.

❖ No citizen can have his or her life, liberty or property taken away without proper legal procedures being carried out, such as a fair trial.

❖ An accused person has the right to be informed of the charges against him or her.

❖ A state government must give its citizens all of the privileges and liberties that citizens of the United States are entitled to.

❖ The right to vote cannot be denied to a person because of his or her race, or the color of his or her skin.

❖ All persons 18 years or older can vote.

A synagogue is used by Jews to pray.
How might you classify the right to worship enjoyed by Jewish Americans?

Make a copy of the following chart. Then classify the rights above by putting a check mark (✔) in the appropriate column. (*The first one has already been done for you.*)

Description of the Right	Political Right	Social Right	Economic Right	Religious Right
Government cannot set up an official religion or limit people's freedom of religion				✔

HOW DO PEOPLE PARTICIPATE IN A DEMOCRACY?

6E

In this activity, you will learn about the differences between "direct" and "representative" democracy. You will also explore the ways in which citizens participate in a democracy. Look for the following important words:

▶ Democracy ▶ Direct Democracy ▶ Representative Democracy

Imagine that each year your school library sponsors a poster contest on a topic students are studying in school. This year, the library is sponsoring a poster contest about democracy. A section of the library has been set aside for the winning posters.

Introduction

CITIZEN PARTICIPATION IN A DEMOCRACY

You want to enter this poster contest, so you ask the librarian for the details. The librarian hands you a packet that describes the contest. Here is what it contains:

CONTEST PACKET

History of Democracy

In ancient times, most societies were governed by one ruler or a small group of rulers. About 2,500 years ago, the people of Athens, Greece, made a change from this system. They organized their government into a democracy. A **democracy** is a form of government in which the citizens rule themselves. In a such a government, the people hold the power. ◀

In Athens, citizens took part directly in important government decisions. Of course, not everyone was a citizen. This system of **direct democracy** worked well because Athens was a small city-state. However, sometimes there are too many people in a society for everyone to decide and vote on every issue. As a result, another form of democracy developed. In an indirect or **representative democracy**, such as the United States, citizens elect people known as **representatives** to serve in their place and to make important government decisions for them. ◀

Characteristics of Democracy

Democracy is an extraordinary form of government. It is admired by people all over the world for some of its unique characteristics:

❖ Democracy recognizes the worth and dignity of each person. For example, each person, no matter how rich or poor, is a valued and important member of society and is treated equally before the law.

❖ CONTINUED

❖ Democracy stands for **majority rule,** but it also protects the rights of those not in the majority. In a democracy, decisions are made by a majority of the people. A **majority** is more than half the voters. Members on the side with less than half, called the **minority,** have the right to disagree. People in the minority are allowed to object and to criticize. One day they may even convince enough people that they are right, and their opinions will become the majority opinion.

❖ Democracy allows more individual freedom than any other form of government. For example, people are free to express their opinions. The right to vote would have no meaning if people did not have the right to communicate and exchange ideas.

Ways to Participate in a Democracy

A citizen in a democracy should actively participate in his or her community. Here are some of the many ways in which citizens participate actively in our democracy.

Participation in your Community

❖ Participate in a school service project

❖ Pay taxes

❖ Serve on a jury

❖ Join a school club or organization, such as the P.T.A.

❖ Run for office in a school club or community organization

❖ Act directly to solve some local community problem

❖ Write letters to a local newspaper about community issues

❖ Help people in the community who are in trouble

❖ Contribute time or money to a local charity

❖ Speak at community meetings on public issues

❖ Serve as a hospital volunteer

Participation in your State and National Government

❖ Discuss issues of statewide and national importance with other people

❖ Help in an election campaign

❖ Serve in the armed forces of the United States

❖ Vote in statewide and national elections

❖ Join a political party

❖ Send letters to a representative, the President, or other policy-makers

❖ Publish articles on issues of state or national importance

❖ Run for election to public office

❖ Attend public meetings or demonstrations

❖ CONTINUED

Closing

CONTEST RULES

Students who enter the contest should create a poster about democracy. Your poster should:

- illustrate some of the actions that people do when they participate in a democracy.
- contain at least **three** illustrations. These illustrations can be drawings or pictures from newspapers or magazines, or your own drawings.

The person who makes the most creative poster will be declared the winner. May the best contestant win!

Now that you have read the contest rules, design a poster and compare your design with those of your classmates.

REVIEWING YOUR UNDERSTANDING

Creating Vocabulary Cards

Direct Democracy
What is direct democracy?
In what kind of society does direct democracy work best?

Representative Democracy
What is representative democracy?
In what kind of society does it usually work best?

Defining Democracy

A dictionary defines "democracy" as a government in which power is in the hands of the people. However, democracy means different things to each of us. Ask **two** adults how they define "democracy" and what they think is its most important characteristic.

DEMOCRACY

Person #1	Person #2
Definition: _____?_____	Definition: _____?_____
Main Characteristic: ____?____	Main Characteristic: ____?____

Interpreting a Line Graph: Voting Patterns of Americans

Most observers agree that for a democracy to work, its citizens must vote. But how often do Americans come out to vote on election day? Are Americans taking their voting responsibility seriously? The following line graph provides some answers:

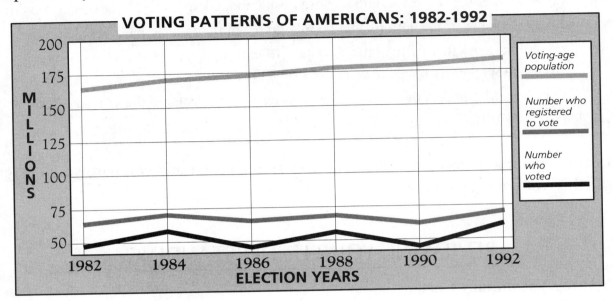

Are you having trouble understanding this line graph? If so, it will help if you first read the Skill Builder that follows.

INTERPRETING LINE GRAPHS

What Is a Line Graph?
A **line graph** is a chart made up of a series of points connected by a line. It is used to show how something has increased, decreased or remained the same.

❖ What three items are shown in this line graph?

Keys to Understanding a Line Graph
Line graphs have a vertical axis, which runs from top to bottom. They also have a horizontal axis, which runs from left to right.

❖ In this graph, what does the vertical axis show?

❖ What does the horizontal axis show?

Interpreting a Line Graph
Start by reading the title. It will give you an idea of the information presented.

 ❖ CONTINUED

❖ What is the title of this line graph?

If the graph has more than one line, a "legend" is usually needed. Like the legend of a map, the legend of a line graph shows what each line represents. In this graph, the top line shows the size of the voting age population—the number of Americans who were of voting age. The middle line shows the number of Americans who were registered to vote.

❖ What does the bottom line show?

What was the total number of voting-age Americans in 1984? To find this answer, first go to the horizontal axis and find the line marked "1984." Next, run your finger up the "1984" line until you reach the point where the "Voting Age Population" line crosses the "1984" line. If you look at the number scale to the left (*along the vertical axis*), you will see the number at this point is about 170 million voters.

❖ What was the total number of voting-age Americans in 1986?

❖ What was the total number of registered voters in 1990?

❖ What was the total number of people who actually voted in 1988?

Looking for Trends in a Line Graph

Sometimes a line graph can be used to identify a trend. A **trend** is the general direction in which things are moving. You can find a trend by following the direction of the points on the line graph. For example, one trend in the graph is that the voting-age population has continued to increase from 1982 through 1992.

❖ What has been the trend for the number of people who registered to vote?

❖ Do you see a trend for the number of people who actually voted?

❖ How might you explain any one of these trends?

Finding Your County Vote in Presidential Elections ———————————

Many people consider the U.S. President to be the most important elected official in the world. Every four years voters determine who will be the next President. In 1996, **President Bill Clinton,** a member of the Democratic party, ran against **Bob Dole,** a member of the Republican party.

Which candidate do you think voters in your county supported in that election? One way to find the answer is to look in an almanac. Check the index under the heading "Elections." Under this heading you will find the category "Presidential." Turn to the page listed. When you have located the information, complete the following chart:

NUMBER OF VOTES	1996 PRESIDENTAL ELECTION: CANDIDATES' NAMES
?	(D) Bill Clinton
	(R) Robert Dole

In the 2000 Presidential race, Democrat Al Gore ran against George W. Bush, a member of the Republican Party. Which Presidential candidate do you think the voters in your county supported in that election? Check your answers in an almanac.

NUMBER OF VOTES	2000 PRESIDENTAL ELECTION: CANDIDATES' NAMES
?	(D) Al Gore
	(R) George W. Bush

FAMOUS NEW YORKERS

Franklin Delano Roosevelt (1882–1945) In 1928, Roosevelt was elected Governor of New York. Four years later, he was elected the 32nd U.S. President. Once in office, he was faced with the Great Depression. During the Depression, the American economy almost collapsed and millions of people were thrown out of work. Roosevelt restored the nation's spirit and remolded American life with his "New Deal" programs. His policies made the national government responsible for restoring the nation's economic well-being. His programs provided work for the unemployed, food for the hungry and protection for the

Franklin D. Roosevelt

nation's resources. Roosevelt also led the country during World War II and was re-elected to a second, third and fourth term. He died in April 1945. You can visit where he once lived at Hyde Park, close to Poughkeepsie, New York.

SHOULD WE LIMIT THE AMOUNT OF VIOLENCE SHOWN ON TELEVISION?

6F

In this activity, we will look more closely at the citizen's task of decision-making. You will be asked to take a stand on a public issue by reading several different sources. Then you will form your own conclusions and write a letter explaining your views. Look for the following important words:

▶ Issues   ▶ Informed Decision   ▶ Editorials

Should the President send soldiers to other countries to protect U.S. citizens there?	Should your state lower the age for driving a car?	Should your county raise taxes to build a homeless shelter?

These are the kinds of public issues that citizens often think about and discuss. When you are 18 years old you will be able to take a stand on these and other important issues by voting. To be an informed voter, you must learn to make wise decisions on public issues. In this activity, you will have a chance to practice this important skill.

∼ WHAT ARE ISSUES? ∼

Issues are different from problems. An **issue** is something that people disagree about. It often concerns whether or not the government should do something, such as pass a law. There must be at least two different viewpoints for it to be an issue.   ◀

Skill Builder

STEPS TO MAKING AN INFORMED DECISION

In making **informed decisions** on public issues, you will need to: ◀

Identify the issue **1**	For example, you might be concerned that watching violence on television leads people to become violent in real life. Others may say that people are not affected by what they watch.
Get information from several sources **2**	The more sources you look at, the more information you will find to help you learn about the issue. You will also get the benefits of understanding different points of view.

❖ CONTINUED

Evaluate the information 3	You should compare what each of your sources of information has to say about the issue. When you evaluate information, be sure to separate facts from opinions.
Compare different viewpoints 4	You should think of all the possible ways of dealing with the issue. Then you should compare these different viewpoints.
Make your decision 5	Finally, you should choose the view you think is best. You may come up with a view of your own. This could be a compromise of several views. A **compromise** is a solution in which each side gives up something, but also gets something in return.

When you need to make an informed decision, try to think of the illustration below. Recall that each step is part of the process of reaching a decision on a public issue. Now that you understand this, let's look at a real-life example in which you are asked for your opinion about a public issue. This example will help you to better understand these five steps and how they can help you to make an informed decision.

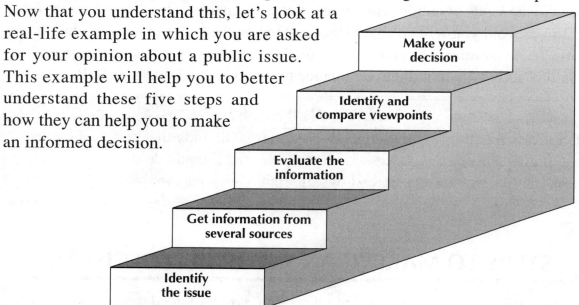

 WOULD YOU SIGN A PETITION TO LIMIT VIOLENCE ON TELEVISION?

One evening at dinner, you are telling your parent what you learned in school about making informed decisions. Just then, the doorbell rings. It is one of your neighbors. He is holding some pamphlets and a **petition** (*a request or demand for action, sent to someone in authority such as a government official*).

STEP 1: IDENTIFYING THE ISSUE

Your neighbor reads the petition to both of you. It is addressed to your representative in Congress. The petition states that violence shown on television is one of the major reasons for rising crime throughout the nation. The petition states:

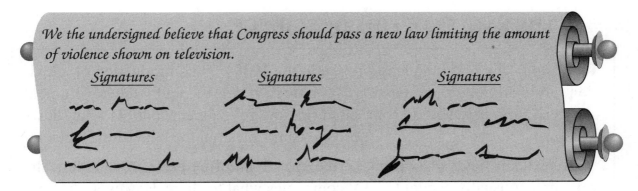

We the undersigned believe that Congress should pass a new law limiting the amount of violence shown on television.

Signatures   *Signatures*   *Signatures*

Your neighbor asks your parent to sign the petition. Signing the petition would mean that your parent agrees that this law is needed. Your parent says, " I would like more time to think about it."

After your neighbor leaves, your parent turns to you and says: "This is an important public issue. I don't know enough about it yet to make up my mind. Why don't we use the method you learned in school today to help me make an informed decision?"

✔ CHECKING YOUR UNDERSTANDING ✔

The first step towards making an informed decision is to identify the issue. What issue has your neighbor raised?

STEP 2: OBTAINING INFORMATION FROM SEVERAL SOURCES

In order to make an informed decision, you should gather information about the issue from different sources. Using special reference sources is a good place to begin. They give you basic information about the issue. Also, they can tell you where to find other information, such as articles written by experts.

Encyclopedias and almanacs are good starting points for any investigation. As you learned earlier, you must be careful to separate **facts** from **opinions.** Your parent suggests visiting the library together to find material.

✔ CHECKING YOUR UNDERSTANDING ✔

More information about the issue can be found in a variety of other sources. Name **three** other sources you might look at to find more information about the issue.

STEP 3: EVALUATING THE INFORMATION

Bringing together different sources of information is only the first step in making an informed decision. Next, you have to read and compare the different sources. Let's take a look at the first of several sources you might find in the library.

Source: THE ENCYCLOPEDIA OF SCIENCE

Television. The first broadcasts began in the 1930s. The introduction of television raised an important question: Should television be run by the government or by private companies? In some countries, the government controls what shows will appear. In the United States, private companies run the television channels.

Americans have a tradition of free speech and free press. As a result, the government usually cannot tell TV companies what to show. However, the government does not let private television stations do just anything they want. The government still has the power to refuse to allow some shows to be aired. It rarely uses this right, but it always can.

Many critics believe the government should exercise this right more often, such as to limit violence on television. They propose that government rate all television shows for violence, just like the film industry rates the movies. Others say America would have much better programs if the government simply took over running the television stations.

✔ CHECKING YOUR UNDERSTANDING ✔

1. What question did the introduction of television raise?
2. How was this question answered in the United States?
3. What powers does the government have in the United States when it comes to television?

Now that you have some knowledge about the background of television, let's look at a second source of information you might use: a newspaper article.

Source: THE NEW YORK DAILY

The New York Daily

First Edition   Friday

TWO TEENS DIE IN HIGHWAY "DARE"

It all began as a joke. On Thursday night, Channel 3 was showing the latest action-adventure picture. In the movie, several teenagers lie down on the center divider line of a highway to show their friends they are not afraid.

After watching the movie, teenagers living near Albany began daring each other to lie down on the center line of the highway, just as the teenagers in the movie had done. Two teenagers took the dare, and now they are dead—run over by a driver who could not see them in the dark.

This is part of a growing number of violent, senseless deaths in America. Movies and television shows often influence us. Sometimes, we imitate what we see, as these teenagers did. Other times, we are influenced without even knowing it.

Parents, teachers and doctors across the nation are becoming alarmed at the growing amount of violence shown on television. Children watching television see thousands of acts of violence before they are old enough to go to school. Even cartoons often show violence between the cartoon characters. Some experts believe television violence may be partly responsible for the increasing violence in America. They are calling for Congress to pass new laws to ban all violence shown on television before 10 o'clock at night.

✔ CHECKING YOUR UNDERSTANDING ✔

1. What did this newspaper story have to say about violence on television?
2. Why are some people alarmed about the growing amount of violence on television?

Next, let's look at the third source of information you might use: a newspaper editorial.

NEWSPAPER EDITORIAL

Editorials are opinions written in newspapers and magazines. They are not news articles, which report facts. They usually represent the opinions of the editors. This allows them to speak out about a topic that concerns them. When trying to make an informed decision, it is a good idea to read editorials in several different newspapers and magazines. This allows you to learn about the opinions that different people have on the topic.

Source: EDITORIAL IN THE NEW YORK WORLD REPORT

WHERE WE STAND ON TELEVISION VIOLENCE

A growing number of people are seeking a new law to limit the violence shown on television. They think that violence on television is the main cause of violence in America. They are wrong. Poverty and the large number of guns are the main causes of violence.

Have the people in favor of this new law thought about the dangers of government control? Who in the government will decide which television programs are violent and which are not? Will the government also prevent stations from reporting violent stories on the news? Once the government controls some subjects on television, it may try to control others. Soon, the government will control everything we see. This violates our rights of free speech and a free press.

We believe it is better to let television stations show what they want. Parents should decide what their children can watch. If parents don't want their children to watch a show because it is too violent, there is a simple remedy: change the channel or turn off the set. If we allow the government to control what we watch, who can say where government controls will end?

✔ CHECKING YOUR UNDERSTANDING ✔

What does this editorial tell you about allowing the government to control what private television stations can show?

A final source of information you might locate is a book about raising children.

Source: "HOW TO RAISE CHILDREN: ADVICE FOR PARENTS"

Page 231

Nightmares. As we all know, nightmares are terrifying dreams in which the dreamer feels helpless, afraid or sad. Tests show that children are the ones most likely to suffer from nightmares. Children may seem to enjoy television programs that show violence. However, once they are asleep, they often suffer from nightmares caused by these programs. For this reason, many parents and educators support the use of a special computer chip in televisions to prevent children from watching violent programs.

Educational Television. Since the 1960s, there have been many attempts to create interesting television programs. There are many shows that are both educational and fun to watch. The most successful of these has been "Sesame Street." Tests show that three-year olds watching Sesame Street regularly do better in learning some skills than those who do not watch the program. For this reason, many parents are asking the government to sponsor more educational programs.

✔ CHECKING YOUR UNDERSTANDING ✔

1. What does the book say about nightmares?
2. What does the book say about how television can shape our behavior?

STEP 4: COMPARE DIFFERENT VIEWPOINTS

You have just completed reading several sources. Now go back to the original issue:

Should the government limit the amount of violence shown on television?

Think of all the different opinions you have read for dealing with this issue. They range from having the government do nothing to banning all the violence shown on television. After reading all of these different viewpoints, you may also have developed a solution of your own.

The following is a list of possible recommendations based on your reading. Make a copy of the chart. For each proposal, write down its advantages and disadvantages.

Views You Have Found— The government should:	Advantages	Disadvantages
❖ make no changes	?	?
❖ rate television shows like movies based on the violence they show	?	?
❖ place microchips in television sets to block violent programs	?	?
❖ ban all violent television shows before 10:00 at night	?	?
❖ (you provide a possible solution)	?	?

STEP 5: MAKING YOUR DECISION

Now that you have listed the advantages and disadvantages of each proposal, it's time to make an informed decision. Compare the disadvantages and advantages of each proposal. Decide which advantages and disadvantages are most important to you. There is usually no "correct" answer. All views have some advantages and disadvantages. Use a copy of the chart on page 232 to rank the possible actions, from the best (#1) to the worst (#5).

Possible Actions — The Government Should:	Number
❖ make no changes	?
❖ rate television shows like movies based on the violence they show	?
❖ insert microchips in television sets	?
❖ ban violent television shows before 10:00 at night	?
❖ (your solution)	?

Remember where we first began when your neighbor asked your parent to sign a petition? Now that you have made an informed decision, would you recommend that your parent sign it? ☐ Yes ☐ No   Explain.

Did you make the right decision? If you think so, maybe you should try to persuade others to adopt your point of view. Write a letter to a newspaper, television station or your elected representative.

Skill Builder

WRITING A PERSUASIVE LETTER OR ESSAY

A letter or essay that seeks to win someone over to your point of view is called a **persuasive essay.**

WHEN IS A PERSUASIVE ESSAY USED?

You use a persuasive essay to get a person to change his or her mind on a particular issue. For example, let's assume you wanted others to adopt the view that it is necessary to limit the amount of violence shown on television. You would use a persuasive essay to win them over to your point of view.

HINTS WHEN WRITING A PERSUASIVE ESSAY

You should clearly state your viewpoint. Then present logical reasons why the reader should adopt your view or suggested course of action. Avoid appeals to emotion. Instead, focus on presenting logical arguments and conclusions through the use of examples and comparisons.

❖ CONTINUED

WRITING A PERSUASIVE LETTER

In writing your letter, follow the "cheeseburger" format you learned about on pages 8 and 9. Let's review some of the steps you might take to write such a letter.

❖ **Introductory Paragraph.** Your introductory paragraph should state the purpose of your letter. In this case, your purpose is to convince the reader that the government should limit the amount of violence shown on television.

❖ **Body of the letter.** Present as many reasons as you can to convince the person to support your viewpoint. Follow a clear and logical order. Each reason, for example, might be in a separate paragraph. Mention specific facts whenever you can to support your point of view. For example, you might mention that some young people are known to have acted in a "copycat" way after they saw violence on television or in the movies.

❖ **Closing the letter.** End with a summary of your main points. Try to impress your reader by concluding with some key fact or a memorable quote by someone about the subject. For example, point out how many people in our nation die each year from senseless violence. Conclude that this tragic situation cries out for immediate action.

MAILING YOUR LETTER

If you think you have written a strong persuasive letter, consider actually mailing it to your Congressperson in Washington, D.C. To do so, put your letter in an envelope addressed to your representative.

Your Name
Address
City, New York Zip Code

The Honorable (*name of representative*)
C/o The United States House of Representatives
House Office Building
Washington, D.C. 20515

REVIEWING YOUR UNDERSTANDING

Creating Vocabulary Cards

Issue
What is an issue?
Name two issues facing
Americans today:

Editorial
What is an editorial?
How are editorials helpful in
making an informed decision?

Finding Information in an Almanac

The following is part of an index from an almanac. Review the topics in this index. Then answer the questions that follow.

ALMANAC

New York

1. The almanac gives information about New York State. List two pieces of information you could learn about New York in this almanac.

2. On which page of the almanac might you look to find:
   A. the name of the Governor of New York State?
   B. some minerals found in New York State?
   C. the highest and lowest points in New York State?

3. This almanac provides information about New York's schools. Name what type of information you might find about New York's schools.

THE IMAGE
I NOW HAVE OF NEW YORK IS … ?

CLOSING ACTIVITY

At the beginning of this book, you were invited to take a journey through New York—its land and its people. When you started out, you wrote what New York meant to you. Your trip through New York has covered its geography, history, people, economy and government. We hope you have learned a great deal about New York and your community.

Closing

WHAT DOES "NEW YORK" MEAN TO YOU NOW?

Your journey is about to come to an end. You should think once again about what New York means to you. One way to do this is to create an "ABC" book about New York:

❖ Each page should have one letter of the alphabet at the top.

❖ Each page should describe something different that you have learned about New York's geography, history, people, economy or government. What you describe should start with the same letter that is written on the top of the page.

❖ Each page should have a different illustration. These illustrations can be drawings you make yourself, pictures you cut out or photocopy from a newspaper, magazine or book. Each illustration should have a description or explanation.

Here is a sample of how one page dealing with the letter "A" might look:

Aa
Albany

Albany skyline

Albany is located near where the Hudson and Mohawk Rivers meet. Originally called Fort Orange, its first settlers were Dutch. It soon developed into a city because of the fur trade. Its population grew after the Erie Canal was built. Although the city is small in area, it is the capital of New York State.

To help you to organize your ABC book about New York, copy the following chart:

LETTER	WORD OR NAME	DESCRIPTION	ILLUSTRATION
A			
B			
C			
D			
E			
F			
G			
H			
I			
J			
K			
L			
M			
N			
O			
P			
Q			
R			
S			
T			
U			
V			
W			
X			
Y			
Z			

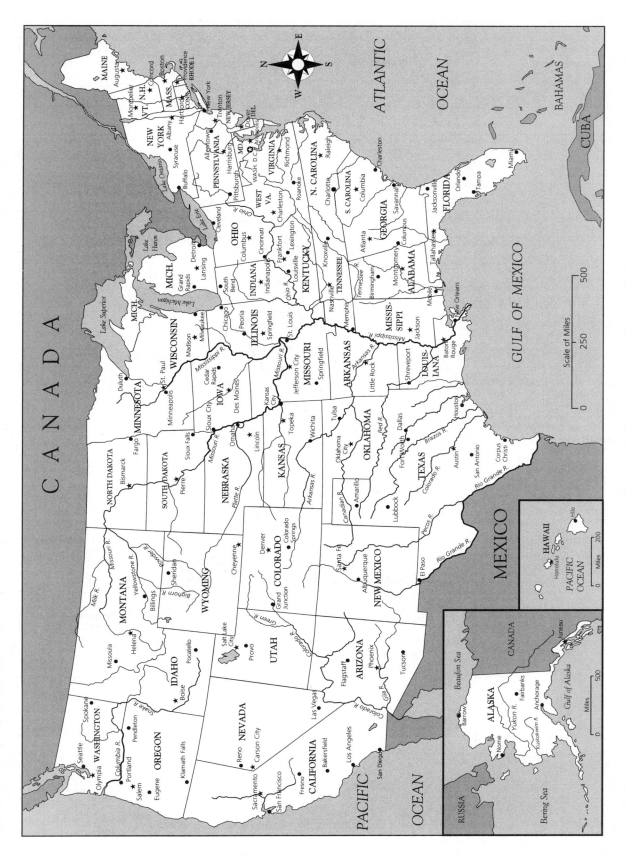

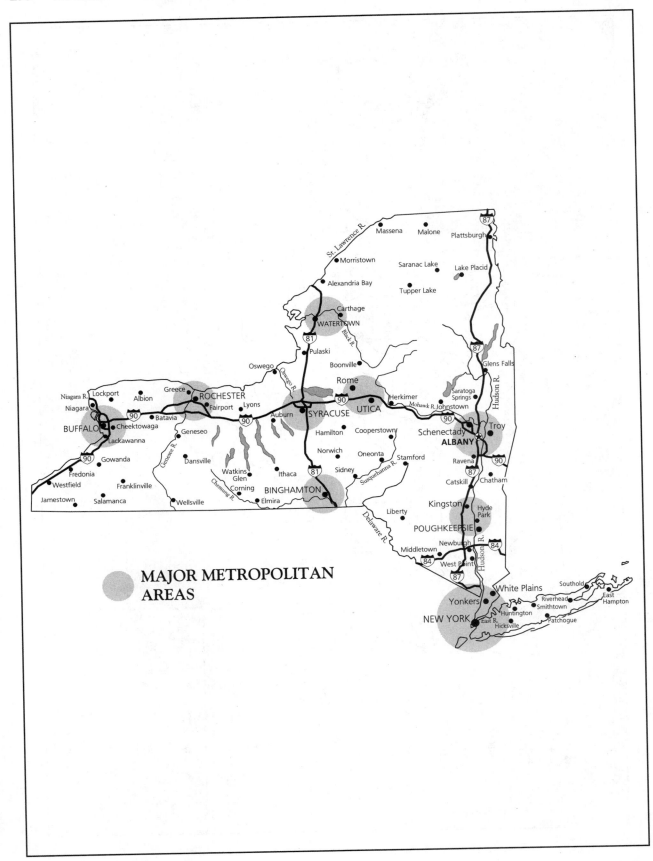

MAJOR METROPOLITAN
AREAS

INDEX